THE 99 DAY DIVERSITY CHALLENGE

Saundarya Rajesh, founder and president of the AVTAR Group, is one of India's most respected thought leaders on diversity and inclusion (D&I). She has influenced and guided the D&I journey of over a hundred organizations, resulting in measurable positive impact.

Celebrating 35 Years of
Penguin Random House India

PRAISE FOR THE BOOK

'Our embracing of D&I principles truly determines how we live and work meaningfully. In this delightful collection of stories, anecdotes and life situations, Dr Rajesh drives home this message emphatically'—Anil Chaudhry, Zone President and Managing Director, International Operations, Schneider Electric

'Diversity is a business imperative; inclusion, a behaviour, an attitude. This distinction is brought through beautifully in *The 99 Day Diversity Challenge* by Dr Saundarya Rajesh. A must-read for all D&I enthusiasts'—Chaitanya N. Sreenivas, VP HR and HR Head India South Asia, IBM

'Organizations that practise the concept of diversity and inclusion are more creative and adaptable. They usually live longer and beat others in terms of growth and profitability. I also feel that companies having diversity and inclusion provide the right platform to foster happy, involved and closely knit teams. Having pioneered the concept of diversity and inclusion along with spearheading the work for providing second careers for women, Saundarya is the best person to write *The 99 Day Diversity Challenge*. Having walked the talk, there is no better person to elucidate and throw more light on diversity and inclusion'—C.K. Ranganathan, Chairman and Managing Director, CavinKare Private Limited

I find great value in both the concepts around inclusive leadership and the stories that reflect these concepts in *The 99 Day Diversity Challenge*. Very innovative and engaging! Dr Rajesh has chosen a unique format that appeals both to the head and to the heart'—Deepak Iyer, Managing Director, Mondelez International, India

'We live in a strange, shrinking world, where distances between people are getting minimized but identities are either fading or growing sharper. Organizations being a reflection of society, diversity and inclusion become a wonderful lever to support employees play to their strengths and expand human possibilities. With her pioneering and path-breaking work in the area of diversity and inclusion, the publishers could have found no better person than Saundarya to write this book. Her experiences and insights are sure to be enlightening and inspiring for readers, and with her compelling style of writing, she will be engaging and thought-provoking too'—Gangapriya Chakraverti, Director HR, GBS, Ford India

'Inclusion and diversity are integral to attracting and retaining the best talent in the market as well as providing exceptional service to clients in a fast-paced and ever-changing business environment. I have worked closely with Saundarya in the inclusion space for many years, and her subject-matter expertise in the field is unmatched'—Jaya Virwani, VP, Diversity and Inclusion, EY Global Delivery Services

'In this day and age of multicultural workplaces, no topic assumes more importance than diversity and inclusion. A lot of workplace issues can be resolved, and a happier workplace can be created by understanding these two concepts well. As they say, getting from "0" to "1" is the most difficult part in any transformational journey. They also say a job well begun is half done. Dr Rajesh, through her work in this area for several years, is best placed to author a book on this topic. She explains the basics and weaves in stories and exercises to make this book an engaging read. Ninety-nine days is all it will take for you to be well on your way to making your workplace an inclusive one' —Mohan Narayanaswamy, Chief Operating Officer and Managing Director, BNY Mellon Technology

'Diversity and inclusion are driving Intel's transformation and growth as a company. Diversity invites different perspectives, experiences and ideas to our company and to the many innovative solutions we deliver to markets around the world. We believe that diverse teams, thinking and leadership styles create more opportunities for innovation, creativity and strategic thinking'—Nivruti Rai, Country Head, Intel India, VP, Data Center Group

'The cultural and cognitive diversity of our workforce enables us to make path-breaking content, "think big" and explore new avenues of growth, including those that fall outside traditional industry norms. Being an inclusive organization is not a choice; it is a necessity for business success. Dr Saundarya Rajesh's book *The 99 Day Diversity Challenge* uses the unique and unexplored style of storytelling to illustrate this emphatically'—N.P. Singh, CEO, Multi Screen Media Pvt. Ltd (Sony Entertainment)

'Dr Rajesh's book cleverly weaves D&I theory with masterful storytelling—a must-read for any professional looking to broaden one's understanding on this pressing corporate need'—Dr P.V. Ramana Murthy, Executive VP and Global Head HR, The Indian Hotels Company Limited (Taj Hotels)

'I haven't come across a book on diversity and inclusion that is so compelling with personal anecdotes, yet outcome-driven and organization-focused. Dr Rajesh has taken a very non-linear approach in delivering her product with substance and character that has her signature all over it'—Raj Raghavan, Senior VP, HR, IndiGo (InterGlobe Aviation Limited)

'Business case for diversity and inclusion has been well researched, established and unequivocally proven. And yet, progress has not been adequate whether in public or private enterprises due to multiple reasons—cultural, historical, conscious and unconscious biases. That's why D&I has to be championed by the CEO/head of the organization with passion, conviction and commitment. Dr Rajesh has researched and championed women's workforce participation at multiple levels for two decades. She is internationally recognized and respected for her deep insights into the theory and practice of D&I. I invariably came away with new perspectives on the subject after interacting with her and attending her sessions and workshops. I cannot think of a better person to write a book on D&I than Saundarya, and I am convinced that the book will exude her passion and in-depth understanding of the topic'—Dr Raman Ramachandran, Head South Asia, Chairman and Managing Director, BASF India Ltd

'Organizations with diverse and inclusive leadership at the top create a better world where individuals and organizations not only grow, but they also thrive, get more out of their talent and, therefore, deliver better performance. Dr Saundarya Rajesh's passion for creating inclusive cultures and helping women with potential achieve their career goals is unshakable'—Ramesh Iyer, CEO, Mahindra & Mahindra Financial Services Limited

'By engaging the reader in a combination of riveting storytelling, role plays, quizzes and practical tools, Dr Rajesh invites us into a CEO's world and his/her journey to becoming an advocate for diversity and inclusion. *The 99 Day Diversity Challenge* is filled with real-life, practical examples of strategies and techniques that can be used to shift mindsets and drive meaningful change'—Rohini Anand, Senior VP Corporate Responsibility and Global Chief Diversity Officer, Sodexo

'Dr Saundarya Rajesh is uniquely positioned to write this book because she has lived this journey personally and has been a teacher and collaborator to both individual women and their companies for a couple of decades. This book synthesizes her best thinking and experiences. The ability to have a handy resource as reference when you are on your company's inclusion journey is critical. This is the book you want in your arsenal. Be sure to get your copy'—Subha Barry, VP and General Manager, Working Mother Media

'I think Dr Saundarya Rajesh is most qualified to write on the topic of D&I, as she has great passion for the subject combined with the gravitas of research over many years. I also think that she has moved beyond qualifications and made a change in the society with Project Puthri. She has also created a huge influence in the way subliminal gender bias has been addressed in the Indian workplace, and that is showing the way for organizations to put this on the top of their agenda—something that was never spoken about'—S.V. Nathan, CHRO, Deloitte India

'A simple, practical and engaging read on diversity and inclusion presented innovatively. The stories shared are profound and relatable. Saundarya's *The 99 Day Diversity Challenge* has something to offer to all who wish to be part of or create a diverse and inclusive ecosystem'—Uma Ratnam Krishnan, Co-CEO, Barclays Global Service Centres, and Head of Finance, India, Barclays Global Service Centres

THE 99 DAY

DIVERSITY
CHALLENGE

Creating an Inclusive Workplace

SAUNDARYA RAJESH

BUSINESS

An imprint of Penguin Random House

PENGUIN BUSINESS

USA | Canada | UK | Ireland | Australia
New Zealand | India | South Africa | China

Penguin Business is part of the Penguin Random House group of companies
whose addresses can be found at global.penguinrandomhouse.com

Published by Penguin Random House India Pvt. Ltd
4th Floor, Capital Tower 1, MG Road,
Gurugram 122 002, Haryana, India

Penguin
Random House
India

First published by Sage Publications India Pvt. Ltd 2019
Published in Penguin Business by Penguin Random House India 2023

10 9 8 7 6 5 4 3 2

The views and opinions expressed in this book are the author's own and the
facts are as reported by her which have been verified to the extent possible,
and the publishers are not in any way liable for the same.

ISBN 9780143461579

Typeset in 11/14 pt Arno Pro and 9/13 pt Aleo by Fidus Design Pvt. Ltd., Chandigarh
Printed at Replika Press Pvt. Ltd, India

www.penguin.co.in

Dedicated at the lotus feet of my Divine
Mother, Goddess Abhirami of Thirukkadaiyur.
You chose me, in this lifetime, to protect and
guide. Ever grateful, Amma.

CONTENTS

PREFACE

Let me say this straight. It's a hyper-connected world filled with so much diversity that if you did not know how to be inclusive, that's one less skill in your repertoire.

And that, dear reader, is practically the long and short of this book.

I fervently believe that the ability to survive in a world of diversity and espousing inclusion will be among the most sought-after skills in this world, right after the 3 R's (the proverbial Reading, wRiting and aRithmetic). Managing people of different generations, leading a gender-diverse team, working out deals with a client at the other end of the globe, sending your kid off to a country you have only seen on Travel & Living—all of these and more are what we call 'the business case for Diversity & Inclusion (D&I)'. D&I is here to stay, especially in a world where 'human-izing behaviour' (a topic for another book) will be the key competitive differentiator when mundane tasks are overtaken by machines.

So, what comes first? Is it (a) diversity—the bringing together of different people in a workplace or a community or (b) inclusion—the willing acceptance of the importance and value of each of these different people? This typical chicken-and-egg conundrum is one that I have often been asked.

Diversity is that manifestation of all aspects of your identity that make you so very uniquely 'you'. It's your gender, the generation that you belong to, your race, the culture that you proudly wear on your sleeve, the cuisine you prefer, the education you have had or are having, the city you grew up in and the team that you support in the Indian Premier League (IPL). Diversity also means that the person sitting right next to you at work and in whose hands the successful delivery of your project lies might not even know what IPL is.

And inclusion? Ah! inclusion is that beautiful state of seeing the common thread of universalism that connects all these differences. It is a celebration of all diversity to create an environment of collaboration, of synergy. Diversity is a real-time situation and inclusion is a call for action. It is a positive embracing of the fact that people will be different, that there will be multiplicity of truths and that all truths are equally important.

In a world where the shape and type of your next customer is unimaginably different from what you are used to, it is inclusion that comes to your rescue. Being inclusive is the most effective resource to work and fit seamlessly in a diverse world, where, increasingly, there is greater acceptance of the fact that it's okay to be different. The world needs all types of talents to solve interestingly different problems that emerge with new intelligence-gaining ground. In a volatile, uncertain, complex and ambiguous (VUCA) world, the philosophy of accepting diversity and assimilating inclusion is an antidote.

But wait, I haven't yet answered the question: What comes first—diversity or inclusion?

This book, *The 99 Day Diversity Challenge*, is my version of the answer. It is the natural consequence of a career of the past couple of decades in corporate India, where I have been witness to a blitzkrieg of change. This book is a narration of the concepts of D&I, which has its roots in my own journey as an advisor to many prominent organizations that were absolutely, genuinely keen on creating an inclusive workplace. Through their experiences, through the many conversations that I have had with managers, chief executives, managing directors, CXOs, entry-level professionals and the likes—bringing their own differing perspectives about D&I and its importance in today's context—I have learnt what it is to masterfully unravel this very practical concept.

Spoiler alert! I believe that inclusion precedes diversity. Inclusion is where you bring your skill to bear—it is the intentionality of constantly building a frame of reference that allows you to respect and appreciate

The 99 Day Diversity Challenge

all humans, all points of view, all truths as equally important. It is that preparation of our minds to allow diversity to take root. Ultimately, while diversity is the 'what' of the equation, inclusion is the 'how'. And in my experience, the leaders, individuals and organizations who have mastered the 'how' have gone on to create outstanding futures and amazing outcomes for the world at large.

HOW TO GET THE BEST OUT OF *THE 99 DAY DIVERSITY CHALLENGE*

The fact that you are holding this book in your hands means that you are an inclusion enthusiast! Let me share what I have planned for you.

I am essentially a storyteller. I learned the art at the knees of my father and my grandmother, and have passed it on to my own children and mentees. I have found it immensely beneficial to depict a learning by framing it as a story. I have found it to be cognitively light, triggering imagination and excitement. It is, in my humble opinion, the best form of learning.

The 99 Day Diversity Challenge has been designed to be a set of stories, right from the anchor story of Bharat Manush, the chief executive officer (CEO) of AcceLever, to each of the stories in the 10 sections. In order to make it even more interesting for you, I have added crosswords, wordfinders, self-assessment tools and activities—all in the space of D&I.

An effective way to use this book is to proceed in the order in which it is written. Starting from the story of Bharat Manush and then traversing each chapter sequentially is a way to advance with a logical acceleration of the intensity of the topics. However, the beauty of storytelling is that you can just pick up the book and begin reading from whichever chapter you fancy today. This is a book about inclusion, and how will it be inclusive if I restricted you from choosing your own style!

The 99 Day Diversity Challenge is a journey. Your appetite to devour the concepts of inclusion and diversity determines how long you take to complete the proverbial 99 days. It could be just a question of hours or a matter of months. The one thing that I promise you, though, is that once you are smitten by this amazing, powerful, all-encompassing concept of inclusion, there's no looking back! You are in it for life.

Enjoy your
own personal
99 Day Diversity
Challenge!

ACKNOWLEDGEMENTS

A book and that too a first book is a miracle produced by the direct and indirect efforts of many people. I have tried to express my gratitude to all of you here. In case I have missed out any of you, my sincere apologies. I thank you, named and unnamed allies.

To Appa, my hero, my role model, my most cherished mentor, whose life and actions I have lived and relived repeatedly through my own life and actions. You are not with me in your physical presence, but wherever I see energy, I see you. Wherever I see charisma, I see you. Wherever I see never-say-die attitude, I see you. Thanks Appa, just for being 'you'.

To Amma (Smt. Shantha Chandrasekar) and Amma (Smt. Uma Venkatram)—you each are so different yet so similar in your love for me. I could not have asked for greater support systems than you both. Together, you have lifted my life in unimaginable ways.

To Rajesh, retail expert, guru, friend, tough taskmaster, co-adventurer, four-times author, all-time inspirer, life partner and the sole motivation for me to write this book. Even when we are on the opposite sides of a point, you inspire respect in me for you. And that's why you are my forever and ever. Here's to a book that we will co-author some day!

Akshey, my first-born, the unintended reason for my exploring the seas of D&I and a huge torch-bearer for his mom; Rajshree, my daughter-in-law, very generous in her encouragement and love; and Shivangi, my youngest one—soulmate, co-conspirer and unlimited source of verve—thank you my darlings. Each one of you is magnificent and unique. I admire you all and am proud to be your Amma.

Umasanker, cofounder of AVTAR, firebrand of dynamism, inimitable colleague and friend—I could go on—you are about the most positive guy I have ever seen. Thanks for being a great co-passenger in our wonderful expedition of AVTAR and also for the unlimited supply of trust that you have in me.

Karthik—such a wise counsel at all times! Your sensible assistance and robust professionalism, right since the time of inception of FLEXI Careers India, has always been tremendously useful. Thanks for the painstaking effort behind the scenes in making the D&I advisory that emerges from AVTAR, and therefore this book, so practical, authentic and experiential.

Anju—your incredible thinking and attention to detail has shaped and reshaped the 99 Day Diversity Challenge, Nisha—the passionate impactor, Divya—the dedicated researcher and Lakshmi—the assiduous contributor—you are my amazing girl gang! What would I have done without you! Thanks for the diligent effort on the 99 Day Diversity Challenge the past few months. Your work will pay off when we see our vision of a '50-50 gender balance in the workplaces of India' come alive!

To my extended family—both at work and outside of it—my sister Priya and her family, my colleagues (also siblings from another mother!) Priya, Roy, Eswar, Richard, Rashmi, Sada, Guru and the entire team at AVTAR Career Creators, FLEXI Careers India and AVTAR Human Capital Trust— you are my constants! Thanks for being part of my life.

To all authors of D&I, not just of that topic but also of everything spiritual, everything inclusive, everything universal, who have fashioned my thinking, given me clarity and chased my fears—thank you Masters!

All those living the principles of D&I—my amazing role models of the corporate world—all those leaders who have worked with me, allowed me to guide their thinking, helped me make my own focus razor-sharp and given me opportunity after opportunity to deliver sessions and break new ground every day in the space of D&I—my thanks to you will not be in words, it will be in the actions that we together take to ensure that each of our organizations is inclusive to its very DNA!

PRELUDE: THE CEO'S TOWNHALL

Bharat Manush, MD and CEO of AcceLever, looked at himself once again in the beautiful Chettinad-framed mirror in his 26th-floor corner office. He was satisfied. The image that greeted him was successful without being overbearing, tastefully dressed without being pretentious and confident without being brash. He liked the generous swaths of white in his boyish mop that Evita, his wife, was constantly asking him to colour (in the interest of still being a 'young' dad to their two little girls!) but he felt it only added to his mystique. He would turn 47 that year and he was AcceLever's most successful CEO till date, not to mention its youngest one ever. After having been groomed for the top job by his mentor and predecessor, Bharat knew that he had not let his guru down. After the rocky start of the previous year, he had managed to bridle the downward graph of the organization. The past two quarters were proof—the results were brilliant and AcceLever's share prices were going north to the delight of his board. And this quarter would be no different. The process changes, the new marketing plan and the aggressive promotions were paying off.

At this morning's townhall, he was going to do something that he knew would firmly procure for him the undivided loyalty of his supporters and even the grudging admiration of his detractors. He was going to announce a 50 per cent spot bonus for everyone at AcceLever! He had thought about the huge packet that would cost but had still managed to convince the board.

He walked towards the bonsai banyan tree that adorned a special spot in his office. Gently turning the tray to give the tree a little more of the streaming sunlight, he let his fingers run through its perfect tiny reddish leaves and long external roots. It held a singular significance to him. It was gifted to Bharat by his mentor on the day he had become MD and was a daily reminder that business was to be conducted with the highest of ethics, even if the purpose of business was profit. Early Portuguese travellers to India had witnessed the shade of the tree being frequented by Baniyas (a community of Indian grocers or merchants) who chose the spot because they believed that the ancient tree was sacred and allowed people to only conduct fair and just business under its auspices. The name struck and the banyan tree, known to botanists as *Ficus benghalensis* (The Indian Banyan), obtained the distinction of being the National Tree of India.

… … … … …

The townhall, as expected, had ended with joyous cries and deafening applause. The entire organization was on a high and as Bharat crossed the long vestibule that led to his office, he passed happy faces and energetic conversations. It was a huge win and he knew he was securing the performance surety of AcceLever via the motivation of his employees. He was riding a tidal wave of success, and while it would have its ebbs and flows, he wanted to savour the thrill of the moment fully today. He paused near his secretary's cabin, as was his wont, to check if he had any visitors.

Mrs Abel, his secretary, a true relic of times past, with impeccable efficiency and an aura of power that Bharat sometimes felt even surpassed his own, stood up to brief him about the visitor. 'Congratulations, Mr Manush, a great speech. Everyone is delighted'. Mrs Abel's voice had uncharacteristic happiness. 'And thanks for the bonus!' she added. 'Very helpful when I have a grandkid coming my way'.

Bharat did a little bow by way of acknowledgement and smiled deeply. These were the people who formed the backbone of AcceLever—its very DNA. 'Any visitors, Mrs Abel?'

'You remember the email exchange you had last month with the young management trainee (MT) Advaita Gyan? She had written to you about organizational culture and you had wanted to meet her. We gave her a slot today. She is waiting in the board room'. Bharat always encouraged the company's fresh recruits—his MT set—to be in touch with him. During the induction, he gave them his email id and mobile number, urging them to reach out to him if they had any concerns, feedback or even ideas to share. He recalled an interesting email he had received from Advaita. It had intrigued him enough to ask Mrs Abel to set up a meeting. 'This should be fun', he thought to himself as he walked into the board room.

Advaita Gyan, 23, tall and gangly, with a prominent nose on which a pair of Potteresque specs perched, stood up abruptly, the carefully arranged papers in front of her scattering to the floor. It seemed that the CEO's quiet entry into the room had interrupted a reverie in her mind.

'I am so sorry, Sir, one minute!' she apologized artlessly and gathered the papers.

Bharat waited for her to regain composure and began on what he felt would put her most at ease. 'So, congratulations! You would have got the spot bonus, right?' he said.

'Yes, Sir, thank you, Sir', she replied with no expression changing on her visage. She seemed vaguely familiar and Bharat thought about when he had last met her—must have been at the MT's induction party.

'So, are you happy about it?'

'Yes, Sir, but I feel I don't deserve it, Sir. I have been in the organization for just seven months, Sir, how could I have contributed to this success, Sir?'

Bharat knew he had a mentoring opportunity right there. 'That's the thing, Advaita', he said, leaning back more comfortably in his chair and stretching his long legs out at an angle.

'It's about teamwork. When the team wins, everyone enjoys the fruits of success. You are part of the Logistics and Distribution vertical, right? This time, you are a young learner, so you have enjoyed the benefit of the team's success. As you grow deeper into your role, you will earn more successes for your team'.

'But, Sir, I am not sure if my team will be successful', Advaita's quiet statement seemed full of foreboding.

Bharat straightened up a little and prepared himself for a conversation around work stress or office politics or interpersonal issues. 'Maybe I should involve Saahitya (the HR Director) in this chat?' he thought to himself.

Out loud he said, 'All teams have challenges in the beginning. As you get to know them better, you will learn how to work with them. But why do you feel they will not be successful?'

'Simple, Sir—because this team is not inclusive'.

'What do you mean they are not inclusive? Of course they are. There are policies and guidelines which govern every team and set boundaries for performance. Everyone's capability is taken into account. Of course it is inclusive!'

'No, Sir. Not only this team, but none of the teams at AcceLever are inclusive, Sir'.

'That is a very bold statement, Advaita', Bharat was smiling, but a trace of irritation tinged his voice. This young girl surely didn't know what she was speaking about. Bharat prided himself on running a successful company. 'D&I is part of the values of the company. It is driven from our New York head office and we at AcceLever India follow it. At AcceLever, we are very inclusive of everybody's ideas'.

'No, Sir. Forgive my saying this, but even though I have been in the system for just seven months, I have had ample opportunity to interact with various teams as part of the MT induction programme. In some teams, there is no diversity, Sir, but in almost all teams, there is no inclusion, Sir'.

'Now, here is the confusion', said Bharat—this time, the impatience in his tone evident.

'Diversity and inclusion are one and the same thing. And AcceLever has it. A young girl like you, I think, should spend more time with your manager, understanding how things work here. This is a very successful organization and we won't be so successful if we didn't know what we were doing'.

'Sir, in fact, I will even predict that unless AcceLever becomes truly inclusive, your next quarter results will not be as successful, Sir. And I have data to prove this', Advaita handed over the sheaf of papers that she had been carrying in her hand.

Astounded by her audacity, Bharat quickly took the stick file from Advaita. 'I am glad you are backing up your claim with data', he said shortly, the morning's positive energy having been replaced fully with a deep rumble of restlessness. 'Let me go through this. But I have to tell you that I don't appreciate predictions that are baseless'.

'Sir, in case you find even one of my points not founded on data, I am ready to resign, Sir'. The girl had stood up and the resolute expression on her face revealed that she had thought this through.

Bharat too stood up to signify that the exchange was at an end.

'I am asking Mrs Abel to set up a meeting tomorrow morning with you. I will review this data tonight. But if I do find anything that is the product of a hyper-imaginative mind, I won't ask for your resignation, Advaita, I shall terminate you on the spot'.

…… ……… …

The evening meant to be one of celebration turned into one of discovery. A very preoccupied Bharat called the dinner party short under the pretext of an early-morning run the next day, and his guests were very understanding. Evita, his wife, expressed concern, but then there was something on Bharat's mind and she quietly served him dinner in his den as he pored over the report. The long night turned longer as Bharat read and re-read the report that Advaita had prepared. With a sense of discomfort, he went through the minutes of meetings of the various department heads he was copied on. They too reflected the truth that Advaita referred to. Not satisfied with his search, Bharat messaged Saahitya, his HR Director, at the ungodly hour of 11.00 p.m. to ask her for the Employee Engagement Survey results. As expected, Saahitya responded within 10 minutes and the study too confirmed Bharat's suspicion.

The next morning, Evita found Bharat curled up on the sofa, reading glasses still in place, sleeping tiredly, the lights of the den still switched on. It had indeed been a long night.

… … … … …

This time, Advaita was ushered into Bharat's office by Mrs Abel.

'Good morning, Sir', said Advaita, appearing even taller and thinner than before, the glasses on her nose seeming to cover most of her face. Again, Bharat had the fleeting thought that he had met her before—somewhere.

Bharat nodded and waved to a chair and waited till Advaita settled herself in it with a lot of noise and clattering, arranging her papers and bag and phone in front of her with nervous energy.

'I must say I am very impressed with you, Advaita. Your report fully supports everything you said yesterday. But, frankly, I am more distressed than impressed', Bharat stated with his characteristic candour.

'What you mentioned yesterday is true'. His voice revealed the unhappiness and disappointment he felt. 'If AcceLever continues this way, then it is very likely that performance will again dip and good people will soon start leaving. Performance bonuses will have only a short-term effect. D&I seem to be the lowest priority', Bharat seemed to be speaking more to himself than to Advaita.

'Sir, sorry to have been the bringer of bad news', replied Advaita, her round rimmed glasses reflecting off the light that streamed in from the windows.

'Bad news yes. But what is worse is that I have not seen this till now. As the CEO, my job is to anticipate. It is to strategize and lead, but more than that, it is to see what is coming. And I didn't. I didn't have even the slightest shred of doubt that my organization could be so weak on D&I. I didn't know that meetings were so non-inclusive. I didn't realize the many microaggressions that people knowingly and unknowingly practised'.

'Sir, one only sees what one knows. If you don't know, how can you see?' Advaita's words seemed too profound for a young person.

'Evidently, AcceLever needs help. I need help. But I don't know why I am sharing this with you. I should be talking to organizational experts. I should be discussing this with culture Gurus. You made a statement and have given me evidence to prove that you are right. But what can you give me by way of a solution?'

'Sir, I can help'. Advaita sat up in the chair even taller and peered quietly at Bharat. Was it just his imagination or did her eyes appear even larger? 'Sir, please take the 99 Day Diversity Challenge!'

'99 Day Diversity Challenge?? Never heard of it', said Bharat. 'What is this? Some quick fix? Sounds suspiciously like one of those weight-loss challenges, where right after the programme, you just put back all the kilos you lost!'

'Sir, one minute', Advaita stood up and rummaged through the large bag that sat in front of her. After what seemed like a long time, a slightly ragged and immensely dog-eared book emerged. It seemed like a manuscript with blue canvas binding. Placing it flat on the table, Advaita smoothened it, apparently trying to remove the folded edges.

Holding it out to him with both hands, Advaita announced, 'Sir, this is the one—the 99 Day Diversity Challenge! 99 days of immersing yourself in what D&I is. Just three months. Take it'. She sounded as fervent as a life insurance salesman.

Bharat seemed to be truly seeing Advaita for the first time. She was clad in a long white kurta and blue jeans that gave her the appearance of a modern-age spiritual teacher. Her hair was pulled back in a tight ponytail and her eyes seemed to be blazing with an intensity that he had not seen in any of his MTs before.

'I am quite amazed', he said wonderingly. 'You are an MBA from one of the B-Schools and here you are, mentoring me on what D&I is….'

'Sir, take it', she nodded at the book holding it out even closer to Bharat's face. Taking it from her, Bharat looked at the cover—'The 99 Day Diversity Challenge—a Guide to Workplace Inclusion'.

'Who wrote this book?' Bharat turned it over in his hands and flipping through, noticed that it had several comments written along the columns. 'And who wrote these notations?'

'Sir, it does not matter who wrote it, please just read it. If you don't mind, can I ask Mrs Abel for your appointment in four weeks' time?'

Bharat was not used to people not answering his questions. What did this little chit of a girl mean by saying it did not matter who wrote the book?? It did, to him.

Yet, he did not feel like pressing the question. 'Yes, talk to Mrs Abel', he said, looking at the index of the book. 'And if I feel this is a waste of time, I shall not hesitate to junk it. Do you want it back?'

Bharat looked up to see that he was alone. Advaita had left.

The **99 Day Diversity** Challenge

SECTION 1

THE BASICS OF DIVERSITY

DIVERSITY AND INCLUSION LEXICON

S. No.	Words	Definition
1.	**Achievement gap**	Widespread disparities that exist in the achievements between the majority and the minority groups
2.	**Compressed work hours**	A kind of work arrangement in which employees work the same number of hours, over fewer days in a given period of time
3.	**Diversity index**	A quantitative measure of workforce diversity in an organization
4.	**IMP**	Indian male professional
5.	**IWP**	Indian woman professional
6.	**Professional ecosystem**	Refers to the collective conditions in which a professional works
7.	**Career intentionality**	The extent to which a professional deploys intentions to chart his/her career trajectory; the concept of intentionality, being a critical determinant of career success, especially in the context of women's careers, was pioneered by Dr Saundarya Rajesh. She has also developed a psychometric instrument called 'C-InQ' (career intentionality quotient) to help professionals measure their levels of career intentionality.
8.	**Career-primary orientation**	A kind of career orientation wherein the individual is ambitious and focused with respect to his/her career and gives greater priority to his/her career over home

S. No.	Words	Definition
9.	Career returners/ returnees	The professionals who make successful career comebacks after a break
10.	Career span	The span in years of a professional's successful career
11.	Cognitive diversity	Diversity in an organizational workforce in terms of the differences amongst individuals on the basis of their thought processes and cognitive capabilities
12.	Cultural diversity	Diversity among individuals based on cultural/ethnic backgrounds and the consequent cultural exposure and upbringing
13.	Discrimination	In an organizational context, this refers to differential treatments meted out to different groups of employees in an organization
14.	Diversity champion	An individual who exemplifies an unyielding commitment to D&I throughout his/her campus communities, across academic programmes and at the highest administrative levels
15.	Diversity consciousness	An attitude of welcoming and integrating diverse employees in an organization
16.	Diversity maturity	Organization's level of commitment towards diversity, also indicative of its progression in the diversity journey
17.	Diversity of physical capabilities	Diversity in an organizational workforce in terms of the differences among individuals based on their physical capabilities
18.	Diversity readiness	An organization's capacity and preparedness to foster diverse viewpoints, support employees and partner organizations through inclusive and equitable practices and culture

S. No.	Words	Definition
19.	**Diversity recruitment**	An organization's recruitment process that focuses on hiring people from currently underrepresented diversity groups, to improve innovation at work
20.	**Diversity sensitization**	The awareness programmes that an organization conducts in order to sensitize its employees of the need for workplace diversity
21.	**Double burden**	The term used to describe the workload of women (and men) who work to earn money, but also shoulder the responsibility of unpaid, domestic labour
22.	**Ethnicity**	The shared sense of a common heritage, ancestry or historical past among an ethnic group
23.	**Female LFPR**	The labour force participation rate of women in the workforce
24.	**Inclusion**	The process of putting the concepts and practice of diversity into action by creating an environment of involvement, respect and connection wherein the underlying workforce diversity is harnessed to create business value
25.	**Inclusive workplace**	A workplace that has been able to successfully implement practices for greater employee inclusion and development
26.	**Labour force**	All individuals who are of legally employable age in a community and are employed or looking for work
27.	**Labour force participation rate (LFPR)**	The rate of participation of a certain group of professionals in the active labour force
28.	**Labour market**	A group within the labour force whose members are eligible for a particular job

S. No.	Words	Definition
29.	Male LFPR	The LFPR of men in the workforce
30.	Multiculturalism	A work culture that acknowledges and promotes the acceptance and understanding of different cultures working in an organization
31.	Race	Personal characteristics associated with race (such as hair texture, skin colour or certain facial features)
32.	Rural LFPR	The LFPR of rural workers in the workforce
33.	Tolerance	Recognition and respect of values, beliefs and behaviours that differ from one's own
34.	Underrepresented	Groups who have been denied access and/or suffered past institutional discrimination
35.	Urban LFPR	The LFPR of urban workers in the workforce
36.	Workforce	People engaged in or available for work, either in a country or area or in a particular organization or industry
37.	Workforce diversity	Differences amongst individuals in an organization's workforce in terms of age, gender, cultural background, physical abilities, race, religion, sexual orientation, education, experience, etc.
38.	Workforce profile	An organizational 'snap shot' illustrating the dispersion of race, ethnicity, gender and/or disability groups for the total workforce or within specified employment, pay, award and other categories

WHAT DOES A DIVERSE WORKPLACE REALLY MEAN?

Interviewer: Good afternoon, Ms D'Souza! At the outset, hearty congratulations on receiving the 'Women Professional of the Year' (WPOTY) award! It is quite remarkable that only a few months back you were seriously considering quitting the workplace. Ms D'Souza, could you tell our readers what made you change your decision? You were originally planning to leave your job after the birth of your child. Yet, you did not and now, you have gone on to win the WPOTY award!

Susan D'Souza: Thanks! There are many answers to this question. But let me begin with what engages me at my workplace. It is diversity! One of the things that I most enjoy about my job is the workforce diversity. At my workplace, I can safely say that no two colleagues are alike. Our culture encourages us to interact and build relationships with a wide range of people. I have built friendships with both older and younger colleagues, married and single and those from India and outside. During our offsites or team lunches, I am always surrounded by very interesting, different people and the conversation is so energizing and refreshing. My lesbian friend would share about her life with her partner and my staunchly conservative colleague in the next cubicle would speak about the religious rituals he practices. Yes, it is true that I considered quitting my job after the birth of my child, but the fact is that I am always surrounded by people who are all so unique and whose life experiences make my day so much more interesting. Needless to mention, the diversity helps us approach problems in a very out-of-the-box manner and also ensures that we find solutions that are creative and different. The diversity not only makes our day-to-day work interesting, but also ensures that our productivity increases. I have only my workplace to thank for enabling me to win the WPOTY award!

Diversity is a field of culture and behaviour that has been prevalent in the corporate world for about 6–7 decades now. In India, D&I as a field has been practised for about 3 decades, ever since the liberalization, privatization and globalization (LPG) revolution ushered in a war for talent and manpower scouts began to see the value in including different pipelines.

Broadly, diversity at the workplace has come to mean the presence of people from a wide range of backgrounds and possessing different traits. Differences in gender, age, generations, ability, race, ethnicity, culture, religion and sexual orientation are some of the possible 'strands' of diversity. The benefits of having a heterogeneous workplace rather than a homogeneous one have been researched extensively and have led to the espousing of the practice of diversity by vanguard organizations and their leaders. While accepted as a hugely constructive and valuable practice, diversity does pose significant challenges, especially in the form of biases and stereotypes which are difficult to eliminate. In order to obtain the full benefit of D&I practices, companies offer diversity training and sensitization skilling to promote tolerance and develop inclusion and acceptance of differences. Cultural awareness and sensitivity training are the two common general components in a diversity training programme.

PRIMARY, SECONDARY AND TERTIARY DIMENSIONS OF DIVERSITY

Alice was lying on the bank of the river with her head resting comfortably on her sister's lap. Her sister was reading her a story and Alice felt warm and cool at the same time as the breeze from the river bank blew gently. Her sister's voice was musical and low and Alice snuggled her head even more cosily into her sister's flouncy, soft, paisley-patterned skirt. She wondered when she would get to wear a dress like that, so thick and rich, with pretty trims and a beautiful bow at the back. Her eyes began to slowly close, when all of a sudden a White Rabbit appeared, very distinguished, peering into a pocket watch.

He seemed to be in a great hurry and was just about to jump into a nearby rabbit hole, when he noticed Alice spying on him. A bit peeved at the unwanted audience, the White Rabbit stopped and said rather curtly, 'What are you staring at, young lady?'

'Who are you?' asked Alice, quite simply, fascinated by the sight of the White Rabbit. He wore a checked brown jacket with a red bow tie and a spotless white shirt and had a slim umbrella tucked under one arm. His large long ears twitched furiously as he looked worriedly at the watch. It appeared that he was decidedly late for something important.

'Who am I? What do you mean who am I?' said the Rabbit rather vexed. 'I am a rabbit, of course.'

'What kind of rabbit?'

'Well, for your information, I happen to be a Flemish Giant Rabbit. We are among the oldest breeds in existence.'

'I mean, what kind of rabbit speaks?!' asked Alice, mystified.

'If you must know, I have descended from the Great Stone Rabbit on my mother's side and the Fearless Patagonian on my father's. And we do speak,' said the Rabbit, sounding hurt. As he proceeded to hop into the burrow, Alice called out quickly.

'Wait! But if you are Flemish—which means you must be from Belgium—how do you speak flawless English?' she asked.

'You are inquisitive, aren't you?' exclaimed the Rabbit, frowning. 'My parents lived in Ireland where my father was an Army officer. I picked up English from the Army cantonment where we lived. Goodness, I am late,' he added, looking hurriedly at the time on his watch, which for its size, had a disproportionately loud tick-tock.

'One more question!' interjected Alice. 'The jacket you are wearing seems like a sports jacket. Are you an athlete?'

'Oh my goodness, so many questions! Yes, I am a sprinter and one of the rising stars of the BS Sports League, although we don't get paid all that much,' said the Rabbit.

'For someone who isn't paid much, your watch sure is fancy,' said Alice looking pointedly at his shiny pocket watch which hung on a polished gold chain attached to a button on his coat.

'You, young lady, are the nosiest person I have ever come across,' said the Rabbit, obviously irritated at the barrage of questions. 'I happen to be a horologist.'

'A what?' asked Alice, baffled.

'A horologist, or in simpler words for someone like you, a watch collector,' said the Rabbit rather pompously. 'This watch was made in 1908, and it is an 18-size 17-jewel Grade 85 watch. It has a thick brass core surrounded by two thin layers of gold. It was gifted to me by a great author whose name is inscribed on the reverse.'

'Oh!' began Alice happily, counting off on her fingers.

'So then, you are a rabbit, a rabbit who speaks, a speaking rabbit who is Flemish, a Flemish Rabbit who speaks English, an English-speaking Flemish Rabbit who is an underpaid sprinter, and finally, an English-speaking, Flemish Rabbit who is a professional under-paid sprinter and who has a passion for watch collection. Wow! So many identities.'

'You missed something. I am also a very angry rabbit who has been delayed for a meeting by a meddlesome young girl!'

The answer to the simple question, 'Who are you?' can be given in a variety of ways, from the simplistic to the philosophical. The identity of an individual can be described in numerous ways. These identity factors translate into diversity strands from an organizational perspective. Lee Gardenswartz and Anita Rowe were among the earliest researchers who spoke about the different dimensions of identity. In 2003, they came up with the four-layer model of identity which consisted of personality, internal dimensions, external dimensions and organizational dimensions. This is among the most popular models that is prevalent today.

While advising an organization on their diversity agenda, I find it easier to look at the three-dimensional model comprising primary, secondary and tertiary layers of identity or diversity. The primary layer consists of facets such as gender, generation, race, ethnicity, sexual orientation and ability. This is the 'individual' layer that remains largely static and is probably what you are born with. When an organization chooses dimensions to focus its diversity agenda on, it usually chooses aspects from this primary layer.

The secondary layer or 'demographic' layer has items such as geographic location, income, education, marital status, parental status, religion, languages known, value systems, personality, work experience, spiritual beliefs, political affiliations, appearance, entertainment behaviour and media habits. The individual exercises a higher level of control over these characteristics than he/she does in the next (tertiary) dimension. This layer is subject to change over a period and largely decides how time is spent by an individual. It is generally dependent on the stage of life, the type of work, income level, etc.

The tertiary or organizational dimension represents the most transitory layer and consists of features such as functional level, management status, seniority, work location, department and industry body affiliation. These would have limited control with the individual and would mostly be influenced by the organization.

RECOGNIZING DIFFERENCES

DAY
4/99

It was a long, hot tiring day at the new state-of-the-art pencil manufacturing plant of Orange Writing Instruments, and Sanjoy, the Plant HR Head, was sensing the beginning of a headache as his forehead creased into a worrying furrow. This was the third time that Raghu, the 50-year-old Manufacturing Manager with over 20 years of service at Orange, had raised a complaint about Prem, the young MT posted at the plant as part of his induction. This time, the complaint was more vehement.

'Sirji, I am not aware of Facebook or whatever that is. Is that a crime? I have more number of years of experience in this department than even his age, yet he behaves as if I am totally useless. He replies to my emails with single word answers and if I point out that there is something called culture, he just laughs it off. Have we built this organization without respecting elders? I agree he is very smart and does his work promptly and all that, but are not respect and seniority also important?'

Your organization is an amalgam of differences—old and young, men and women, senior and junior, IT-savvy and not. And the potential for leveraging these differences to build a culturally strong, diverse and inclusive organization is just phenomenal. You ask why? Just imagine if everyone in your organization had the same linear, analytical, planned approach to everything, or if every single individual in your workplace was impulsive, creative and off-beat. Homogeneity, even of great things, is an overkill. Heterogeneity is what pushes us out of our comfort zones and gets us to thinking about new approaches. Most leaders that I have worked with are able to recognize that the best teams leverage diversity to achieve long-term success.

While differences ought to be leveraged and managed for greater productivity and problem-solving, the same differences also have the danger

11

of creating fissures within your teams. Definition of what constitutes respect, felicity of leveraging technology, the advantage of experience— all are differentiators in your organization which a leader/manager must be cognizant of. These create ripples of discomfort and are possible avenues of cracks within teams. What serves as a competitive edge for one individual could be another's Achilles heel. It is the leader's imperative to ensure that everyone's voice is heard. If the same people are talking in every meeting and are the only ones being listened to and getting attention, clearly your inclusion focus is not working.

People are different and each individual prefers to work a certain way. By observing the work style differences in our colleagues, a leader can leverage the strengths of each of those work styles. Understanding the values of each style and recognizing how to work together as a team can create a more productive and happier work environment. By ensuring that different work styles are represented on every project, you position your team and your company for innovation, growth and sustainability.

DAY 5/99

D&I GAME: EXPERIENCING DIVERSITY AND INCLUSION

This is an individual-cum-group activity. Do this activity with a mix of people from your team and other teams. Ideally, one team should have 6–8 members. You can do this activity with multiple teams.

THE SCENARIO

Your company is organizing a trip to the Everest Base Camp. You have been entrusted with the task of selecting 10 employees who will make this trip. The number of passengers has been restricted to 10 because the aircraft from Kathmandu to Lukla (a small airport in Nepal) can carry only 12 people including the pilot and a staff member.

Initially, each person in your group has to select the list of passengers on their own. They can decide the list of people who they think are the most deserving to make this trip. After that, the entire group has to come together, and as a team, the final list of passengers has to be prepared. Please note that while preparing the final list of 10 passengers, everyone in the group should agree on the selection of each passenger in the list. The agreement has to be 100 per cent. If someone disagrees on any passenger, you cannot opt to take a vote of majority to check how many people in the team agree while making the decision. All the names in the passenger list have to be 100 per cent agreed upon by every team member.

HERE IS THE PASSENGER LIST:

1. Naina—The female marketing professional in her 20s who is a national level swimming champion and is prone to mood swings.

2. Salim—Highly competent and self-reliant male recruitment professional in his 30s with a hearing disability.

3. Mohammed—The sporty male finance professional in his early 30s who met with a motorcycle accident 6 months back, but is fine now.

4. Sharon—The well-travelled sales professional in her late 20s who is a mother of two toddlers and is known to be emotional at times.

5. Alex—The male talent acquisition head in his 40s who used to be an avid trekker and adventure junkie, but had a knee surgery one year back.

6. Rekha—The highly spirited, health conscious female business development manager in her 40s who is a diabetic and is the mother of two teenage children.

7. Kumar—The athletic male training head in his 30s who is unmarried and is rumoured to be a gay.

8. Tina—The admin head in her 50s who runs marathons, but recently lost her husband.

9. William—The energetic male CEO in his late 40s who is going through a messy divorce.

10. Nita—The female research associate in her early 20s who is a recent victim of sexual harassment.

11. Anne—The spirited female marketing head in her late 30s who is undergoing infertility treatment and is battling weight issues.

12. Leena—The determined female office support staff in her late 20s who is separated from her husband and is the mother of a young child.

13. Tony—The ex-army security chief in his 50s who has conservative views about women.

14. Adya—The receptionist in her early 40s who is an avid cycling enthusiast and often complaints about trivial things in life.

15. Kabir—The talented 22-year-old male HR trainee who plays gully cricket is an MS Dhoni fan from a humble background and is the single breadwinner of the family.

16. Zayn—The male accountant who was a football player and has an occasional binge drinking problem.

17. Neil—The go-getting male sales VP in his late 40s who is accused of sexual harassment and is currently undergoing internal investigation.

18. Lisa—The tomboyish female IT head in her late 30s who is unmarried and is taking care of her ailing parents.

DAY
6/99

UNDERSTANDING YOUR DIVERSITY BIODATA

It was Shveta's first day at Creative Rains—a contemporary ad agency in Mumbai. As Content Director for corporate social responsibility (CSR) projects, this was a huge, experimental leap for Shveta who had 20+ years of experience in conventional journalism, the last as Chief Editor of a local daily. After the routine first-day formalities, she checked her mailbox to be greeted by the welcome mail from her on-boarding buddy Varun. He had attached a form—a visually appealing four-page bunch titled 'D&I biodata'.

This was nothing like the forms she had ever filled before—beyond the basic demographic details about her, it asked her about her likes and dislikes, about the places she had travelled to, about the kind of music she liked listening to, about her favourite hang-outs in the city and about her exciting life experiences and even if she was right-handed or left-handed! With child-like enthusiasm, she called up her on-boarding buddy Varun and asked him if she could take a couple of days to fill and return the form. Having seen such reactions many times over, Varun replied in the affirmative. Throughout the meetings she had scheduled for the day, the form kept coming back to her. Shveta couldn't wait any longer to discover her identity.

Have you wondered about your identity? Is it what appears on the outside or what is on the inside? Or is it a combination of the two? Your diversity biodata is a tool to help you understand who 'you' really are—that summation of experiences, influences and life moments. As a diversity enthusiast, it is your first step in this beautiful journey to understand who you are and what motivates you. This understanding then helps build the path to greater awareness of people around you. The old adage of 'know thyself' is never truer than in the context of the inclusion principle. How well do you know yourself before you begin understanding others? When you have a true demonstration of diverse cultures and ideas at your workplace, you create a stronger organization. This organization is capable of managing uncertainties and problem-solving in a way that a homogenous team never ever can.

THE DIFFERENCE BETWEEN DIVERSITY AND INCLUSION

Guru Dronacharya, the teacher of the Kuru princes, an expert in all forms of warfare, stood under the shade of the wide neem tree, waiting for his favourite student, Arjuna. He had sent Arjuna on a task. He waited with eager anticipation to see if his student would exceed his expectations.

As time went by, the Guru's patience began to wear thin. Pacing irritably under the tree, Guru Dronacharya was about to give up and leave when he saw Arjuna emerge from the forest, breathless and apologetic.

'Arjuna, what took you so long? I had asked you to bring the archery manuscript from our new library which you only are in charge of. It should have been a very easy and simple task,' began the Guru, not losing time.

'My apologies, oh Guru. I was trying to get the new students to sort out the manuscripts and they seem to have not done a good job at all,' said Arjuna.

'If I remember correctly, Arjuna, you have put together a very diverse group on the job, am I right?'

'Yes, Guruji. It is indeed a diverse group as per your instructions. We have the tall warrior, the princess from the hills, the Sanskrit scholar who is here to learn mace fighting, the poet, the lady warrior who practises kalari, the painter and tribe lord from the village by the sea.' 'Excellent!' exclaimed Guru Drona. 'That is indeed a very diverse group with everybody being different. So, you have got together a team which demonstrates diversity. Now, what did you say was the problem? Why did it take you so long to obtain the manuscript?'

'Forgive my saying so Guruji,' began Arjuna with temerity.

'That diversity itself appears to be the problem. Nobody seems to get along. And as their leader, I am at a loss as to what to do. I keep asking the tribe lord and the Sanskrit scholar what we should do, as they are the oldest, but none of their ideas seem to work.'

'Arjuna, listen well. Diverse teams do not work, when they lack inclusion,' said Drona, his voice calm and sonorous.

'But I thought diversity and inclusion went hand in hand, Guruji,' asked Arjuna, puzzled.

'Oh, then I am sorry I gave you that impression, Arjuna. Diversity is focusing on the differences, on getting the mix right. Inclusion is when you create an environment that welcomes and celebrates the diversity and helps it succeed. When everyone on your team, not just the tribe lord and the Sanskrit scholar, feels included and wants to contribute ideas to make the team do its duties well, then your diversity has inclusion in it.'

With the powerful advent of D&I into workplace practices, there is a need to define and understand what each of these terms really mean. In most corporates, these two terms, 'diversity' and 'inclusion', are very often used, with an inference that they are interchangeable. However, even though the words and the theories associated with them are similar and related, they are not the same.

According to the *Oxford English Dictionary*, diversity is defined as 'a range of many people or things that are very different from each other'. In this sense, diversity is a synonym of 'variety'. It is used to denote the many differences such as religious diversity, age diversity, ability diversity, gender diversity or ethnic and cultural diversity that describe the people in the workplace. As such, diversity is used as a term to denote the many differences among people who work together.

'Inclusion', on the other hand, is defined as 'the act of including somebody/ something, the fact of being included.' It is also further explained as 'to make somebody/something part of something.' It is easier to comprehend the meaning of inclusion by understanding the opposite of it. Exclusion is the act of not allowing someone or something to take part in an activity

The Difference between Diversity and Inclusion

17

or to enter a place. Thus, inclusion in the workplace is about adding people to the workplace and also making sure that they feel respected and valued.

Diversity, therefore, is a characteristic—it points to the differences in people within the workplace. Inclusion is a value—it is the 'how' of the culture practised in the workplace. If you are invited to a meeting because of a certain identity characteristic that you possess (woman, single mother, millennial, programmer, salesperson), that is diversity. But if your opinion is solicited and added to the conversation, then that is inclusion. Diversity is all about quantity, inclusion is all about quality. A large organization which has people from various backgrounds and experiences is a diverse organization. If it consists of different people working together, feeling respected, solving problems as a team, then that constitutes inclusion.

There are many workplaces which are diverse without being inclusive. This means that even with the addition of people who are very different from each other, only a few people take all the decisions, get all the credit and voice their views all the time. If inclusion is absent, then there is no central value or cultural assimilation that binds them together. Diversity is the first step towards inclusion. When inclusion follows diversity, then the true power of the differences emerges and is used to facilitate the progress of all individuals and therefore the advantage of the organization.

DAY
8/99

HOW IS DIVERSITY AND INCLUSION BENEFICIAL?

Disciple: Oh Master! In today's corporate world, is there a clear understanding as to why an organization should actually pursue a D&I agenda? Is it just another fad? Is it something that the HR

Enlighten me, Oh great Master.

Master: Ananta, look around you. Nature is filled with diversity—all around you, you see beautiful differences in every form of life. A single ray of light, if it moves through the prism, shows up as seven colours of VIBGYOR. Each colour is different, diverse! Yet, all the colours need to be included to deliver that one white ray which is the form of light that we can use. Likewise, when an organization takes the effort to include different types of people—diverse by gender, age, thinking, backgrounds, education, language, culture and so on—it is able to create a vision that is more powerful than the sum of the individual parts. Have I clarified your question, oh Ananta?

In the past decade, more books have been written, more research reports have been published, about the value that D&I brings to the organization, than perhaps the previous five decades since the advent of the D&I thought. Diversity is clearly seen as the framework for bringing together diverse competencies that build a powerful workplace. The differences in thinking, problem-solving and perspectives add an indisputable value to the overall intellectual vigour of the organization. Yes, D&I is a people agenda. As such, in many organizations it is owned and managed by the HR function, but it is also a leadership imperative, hence overseen directly by the head of the company. Bringing together varied points of view is one side of the coin—the 'diversity' side. But the glue that makes the glitter stick together and become one is where 'inclusion' steps in.

Organizations hire for diversity; but after that what? The conversation that sometimes diversity hiring is just about being politically correct is a loud and strident one. In order to ensure that the hiring is effective and that the people from different backgrounds and cultures who have been brought into your culture work effectively together, it is important to focus on inclusion. Your D&I agenda cannot be just a numbers game. It cannot restrict itself to just what an organization does during the hiring and recruitment phases, but should become the cultural mooring with which the organization defines itself.

How Is Diversity and Inclusion Beneficial?

D&I is seen as a powerful strategy for growth and a key organizational competence for the twenty-first century. The organizations that instil inclusion as a principle are able to deliver big on results. Every workplace that celebrates D&I becomes a big talent magnet and has better access to creative innovation and problem-solving. Research from around the world shows that entities that embrace diversity gain higher market share and a competitive edge in accessing new markets.

DAY 9/99

WHAT IS CULTURAL BLINDNESS?

Hi, I am Mercy, a vegetarian by choice. Do you know why? When I was 15, we lived right next to a butcher shop in one of the small gullies of south Bangalore. The sight of animals being prepared to become food was a gory one and very soon I decided to give up meat-eating. My family respects this, though they are all non-vegetarians.

The other day, we had a pot luck lunch at office. Everyone brought their favourite dishes, while I carried mine—a bowl of bean salad as my contribution. We arranged all the dishes in the large conference room where we had the lunch that day. Samir, a friendly colleague of mine, known for his jokes and laughter, piled his plate with Malabar Fish curry from Anna's kitchen and the Hyderabadi Chicken curry that Jamsher had brought and sat next to me. As we enjoyed our respective lunches, Samir asked me why I, a Christian, was not having non-vegetarian.

'Go ahead, Mercy, try this fish, it is delicious! You are truly missing out. Do you know that human beings are naturally carnivorous?

We need the protein that only meat can provide. Do you see these vegetarians? They lack the strength and resistance that we meat-eaters naturally possess. And the chicken is just simply scrumptious! I cannot imagine how you are able to resist this. Go ahead and have a piece. It is not as if your religion objects to it, right?' and with that, Samir plopped a piece of fish right into the middle of my rice.

Culture—expressed through habits, beliefs, behaviour, symbols, artefacts, language and customs—is the single most important identity that a person possesses, besides gender. A popular misconception that all of us suffer from is to think that just because we know a few people from a particular ethnicity or race, we are fully aware of everyone and we understand their culture. Most instances of stereotyping occur when we broad-brush an entire community or group with a characteristic that we have seen in one individual or a few.

Being culturally blind is one of the easiest errors that take place within a group. It is simply refusing to acknowledge the culture of others. In other words, when the dominant group holds the values and norms as expectations for all people, they assume that cultural differences are inconsequential. Cultural blindness operates on judging a person or a group based on preconceived notions about the group, rigidly held beliefs that most or all members of a group share similar behaviour and characteristics. It also assumes that one race/group/ethnicity is superior to another which results in differential treatment of individuals within specific ethnic or cultural groups.

It is essential to work on cultural competence in order to interact effectively with people across different cultures. What should you be working on? Awareness of your own cultural world view, developing a positive attitude towards cultural differences, obtaining greater knowledge of different cultural practices and, most importantly, cross-cultural communication skills. Make no mistake, this will not get built overnight. It takes time and exposure. But in order to succeed in today's global workplace, cultural competence is a skill that requires sustained investment.

What is Cultural Blindness?

CROSSWORD

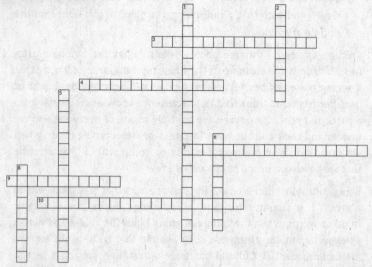

ACROSS

3 Groups who have been denied access and/or suffered past institutional discrimination. (16)

4 In an organizational context, this refers to differential treatments meted out to different groups of employees in an organization. (14)

7 Multiplicity displayed in an organizational workforce in terms of the differences amongst individuals on the basis of their thought processes and cognitive capabilities. (9,9)

9 The term used to describe the workload of women (and men) who work to earn money, but also shoulder the responsibility of unpaid, domestic labour. (6,6)

10 The extent to which a professional deploys willingness to chart his/her career trajectory. (6,14)

DOWN

1 A mindful attitude of welcoming and integrating diverse employees in an organization. (9,13)

2 The shared sense of a common heritage, ancestry or historical past within an ethnic group. (9)

5 An organizational 'snap shot' illustrating the dispersion of race, ethnicity, gender and/or disability groups for the total workforce or within specified employment, pay, award and other categories. (9,7)

6 The process of putting the concepts and practice of diversity into action by creating an environment of involvement, respect and connection wherein the underlying workforce diversity is harnessed to create business value. (9)

8 Recognition and respect of values, beliefs and behaviours that differ from one's own. (9)

SECTION 2

THE DIMENSIONS OF DIVERSITY

DIVERSITY AND INCLUSION LEXICON

S. No.	Words	Definition
1.	**Breadwinner**	A person who earns money to support his/her family, often the sole one
2.	**Cultural competence**	Set of academic and interpersonal skills that allow individuals to increase their understanding, sensitivity, appreciation and responsiveness to cultural differences and the interactions resulting from them
3.	**Cultural diversity**	Diversity among individuals based on cultural/ethnic backgrounds and the consequent cultural exposure and upbringing
4.	**Culture**	The way of life of people comprising ideas, values, beliefs, norms, language, traditions and artefacts
5.	**Ethnicity**	The shared sense of a common heritage, ancestry or historical past among an ethnic group
6.	**Gender**	A socially constructed system of classification that ascribes qualities of masculinity and femininity to people
7.	**Gender audit**	The process of evaluating organizational policies including legislation, regulations, allocations, taxation and social projects, keeping in mind their effect on both genders in a given organization

S. No.	Words	Definition
8.	Gender diversity	In an organizational context, this refers to the diversity in the workforce of an organization in terms of male and female representation
9.	Gender gap	The differences across different dimensions—social, economic, educational or political—between men and women in a society
10.	Gender identity	A person's internal sense of being male or female
11.	Gender intelligence	Ability to 'understand' the differences between men and women, not only in how they are hardwired, but in how they make decisions, solve problems and communicate
12.	Gender roles	Sets of societal norms dictating what types of behaviours are generally considered acceptable, appropriate or desirable for a person based on their actual or perceived sex
13.	Gender wage gap	The relative difference in the average gross hourly earnings of women and men within the economy as a whole
14.	Generational cohorts	Groups of people who share birth years, history and a collective personality as a result of their common years of existence, defining social, political, cultural and economic experiences
15.	Generational diversity	Diversity in the organizational workforce in terms of representation of various generational cohorts
16.	Human development index	A composite statistic of life expectancy, education and per capita income indicators, which is used to rank countries/states into different tiers of human development

S. No.	Words	Definition
17.	Intersectional diversity (or intersectionality)	The diversity created by the intersection of various strands of diversity—gender, generation, sexuality, physical capabilities, socio-economic backgrounds, etc. This calls for greater specificity in addressing individual aspirations as there are several diversity dimensions that define every individual.
18.	Lesbian, gay, bisexual and transgender (LGBT)	The diversity in the workforce of an organization in terms of representation of individuals with varied sexual orientations
19.	Linear career trajectory	A career trajectory wherein a linear progression of career happens in terms of career growth and success
20.	Maternity Benefit Act	A legislative provision that entitles every pregnant woman in India who is formally employed to a total paid leave of 26 weeks (including leave taken before childbirth)
21.	Maternity continuum	Refers to phases of maternity that a woman professional goes through in the event of pregnancy, the phases being pre-maternity, during maternity and post-maternity, in an organizational context
22.	Maternity enablement	Frameworks of support offered by organizations that allow for smoother segues of women employees through the maternity phases—pre, during and post childbirth
23.	Maternity leave	A period of absence from work granted to a mother immediately before and after the birth of her child
24.	Motherhood penalty	A term coined by sociologists who argue that in the workplace, working mothers encounter systematic disadvantages in pay, perceived competence and benefits relative to those without children

S. No.	Words	Definition
25.	Non-linear career trajectory	A career trajectory that is non-linear and non-traditional wherein career growth and success is not necessarily a function of one's career span
26.	Paid paternity leave	Refers to paid leave offered to new fathers on the birth of their child; it could also be applicable to adoptive fathers.
27.	Partially paid maternity leave	Maternity leave, over and above an organization's fully paid maternity policy, during which the new mother employee continues to be on leave but is provided a certain percentage of her compensation
28.	Pipeline leakage	Refers to the exit of professionals along the talent pipeline from employment, very often to attend to family responsibilities; it has been observed world over that the leak percentage is significantly higher for women than for men.
29.	Pyramid syndrome	Refers to the tendency of women to drop off workforce as they rise to mid-managerial and senior levels
30.	Sexual orientation	A predominant sexual attraction for the same or other sex, or for both sexes in varying degrees; few, if any, obvious identifiable mannerism exists that distinguish between individuals of different sexual orientations. Sexual orientation is not a choice, lifestyle or behaviour; it is an inner sense of identity. Sexual orientation is only one small aspect of a person's being.
31.	Transgender	A person whose core gender identity is different from his/her biological gender identity
32.	Wage penalty	The penalty a professional has to face in terms of a decrease in salary he/she draws after a career break as compared to what he/she was drawing pre-break

THE DIVERSITY
STRAND OF GENDER

It was the last working day of Mr Bhat's career. The General Manager of Thompson & Co. was a very well-respected and a well-loved man. The entire office had gathered for his retirement party. With two extensions of his service, Mr Bhat was retiring at 70 and had many protégés within Thompson & Co. The cake was cut, the speeches were made and the beautiful gift, thoughtfully selected by the organizing team, was handed over to Mr Bhat. No one was embarrassed with the tears that flowed. Mr Bhat was special and everyone knew it. As he walked down the long marbled corridor probably for the last time, Archana ran to catch up with him. 'Sir!' she said breathlessly, 'I just wanted to say a big thanks for everything that you have done for me. You have been a mentor, a guide, a godfather. I couldn't have risen to the post of Manager, Customer Care, if you had not given me valuable advice.' Her voice choking with emotion, she continued, 'I don't know what I will do without you Sir.' Mr Bhat stopped for a moment and took in the view of the beautiful lawns and the sparkling fountain that was part of Thompson & Co's Bandra office. It never failed to inspire him. 'Archana,' he said, in his usual baritone, 'Just remember this. Your success is entirely yours. You have battled more odds to be employed, to be in the workplace than any other person I know. What I have done for you is just enablement. The path was what you built for yourself. Go and conquer the world!'

Women comprise 23.5 per cent of the workforce in India as per the NSSO data of 2017. While a large number of companies, both of Indian origin and multinational, are striving to unlock the potential of increased gender inclusion, the past decade has not seen much progress. The dropout rates of women continue to be high and new measures look at how additional flexibility and routes for women to return can be set up.

It appears that firmly entrenched barriers continue to hinder the progress of women in the workplace, not in the least their own mindset. Research reveals that many women start off with high ambitions, but often sacrifice their careers on the altar of marriage or motherhood. Even very capable women often settle for less challenging roles in an effort to balance the home and the office. Among generational cohorts such as Gen X and E-Gens, there are deeply set attitudes towards household chores and childcare which further complicate the conundrum.

One of the first diversity strands to be explored and adopted by corporates—gender—still continues to be a challenge for even the most well-meaning organizations. Men and women are broadly equally distributed in the entry levels at the early stages of their career, but by the age of 30, more than 48 per cent of women drop off. Also, certain industries lend themselves more easily to greater women's workforce participation than others.

Today, India is witnessing companies with a sense of urgency to change the equation. The Working Mother and AVTAR Best Companies for Women in India initiative shows that at least 350 prominent companies and groups in India are pursuing an arsenal of measures focused on advancing and enabling women. These policies and programmes include aspects such as unconscious bias training, smoother phasebacks post maternity, flexible working and mentoring. Yet, the truth is that for the woman to succeed, it is her own intentionality that creates the difference.

THE DIVERSITY STRAND
OF GENERATIONS

Rashmi, Diversity Lead and Head of Sales HR for Trident, re-read the data analysis presentation on her laptop for the third time. She couldn't believe her eyes. With a headache that promised to become ginormous with every passing minute, she slumped into a chair in the cabin of her colleague, Asha, who headed Marketing for Trident.

'It was I who had pushed for diversity in our workplace, Asha, especially generational diversity. You know I have had held endless meetings with the business heads and the HR head to broker an agreement which allowed millennials and 50-plus professionals to be hired side by side and work together in our project teams.'

'Yes Rashmi,' said Asha. 'I am aware of all that. What happened?'

'It is this state of business survey, Asha!' replied Rashmi a little vehemently. 'It shows that the decline in productivity is due to inter-generational conflict.'

'What??' said a shocked Asha.

'Yes, Asha,' said Rashmi, her voice low with defeat.

'A majority of our employees are millennials, while their managers are Gen Y-ers. All the leaders sitting at the top setting the climate and culture are Gen X-ers. Boss (the CEO) began suspecting that the culprit causing the gradual decline in productivity was inter-generational conflict and commissioned this study. And the data reveals that Boss's gut feel is in truth a fact. Our workplace is fragmented into different groups due to the generational differences and each group has a completely different orientation towards life and work. The study shows that mutual respect and trust is missing.'

Until very recently, Indian researchers used western cohort definitions to describe generations which were not entirely descriptive of the

different cohorts at the Indian workplace. This necessitated primary research to classify and segment the Indian workplace. In two studies conducted in 2008 and 2014, the AVTAR group reported that the Indian workforce was found to be comprised of five distinct generational cohorts, namely:

1. Free-Gens (born between 1945 and 1960)

2. Gen X (born between 1961 and 1970)

3. E-Gen (born between 1971 and 1980)

4. Gen Y (born between 1981 and 1990)

5. Gen Z (born after 1990)

(Note: A cross-generational segment drawn from Gen Y and Gen Z forms the cohort that is universally known as the millennials.)

Generational diversity, especially in India, where five generational cohorts coexist, has a deep impact on workplace dynamics. Aspirational differences, different belief systems and life and career goals give rise to conflicts. Research states that these conflicts are most often an outcome of differential responses to a common strategy. There is evidence that suggests that different generations respond differently to talent management strategies. So if the strategies are to achieve the desired outcomes, it is important that underlying differences are bridged.

These underlying differences are most often (a) work values, (b) working style, (c) demonstration of respect, (d) orientation towards D&I and (e) technology comfort. Evidential research reports that managing generational diversity is only partly about knowledge and is mostly about communication. While the 'knowledge' part is about understanding and managing generational diversity especially the responses of different cohorts to the five factors mentioned above, the communication part involves (a) managing inter-generational conflict and (b) moulding a collaborative leadership style, organically.

Hiring people from different generations with different personalities and at wide-ranging stages of their career helps foster creativity and offers a range of perspectives and ideas. However, when a unifying culture is not created and when all employees are unable to understand

The Diversity Strand of Generations

their role within it, inter-generational conflict arises and takes its toll on productivity and employee engagement. Organizations that take diversity seriously and implement effective integration strategies have greater success in achieving optimal employee performance. Needless to mention, a well-oiled generational diversity strategy also enables creation of a pipeline for leadership.

DAY 14/99

THE DIVERSITY STRAND OF LGBT

Dear Diary,

Yesterday, Mummy discovered that I am lesbian. I just wish that I could have been the one to break it to her and not have her find out the note that I had written for Susan. Ever since I realized that I am lesbian, I have always put off discussing this with Mummy. Many reasons—it could be the fact that she is so religious or she always speaks about me getting married (I am just 22, yet for Mummy, my marriage is already delayed) or that I always feel that this is a conversation I would find very difficult to have with her, given her background from rural India. I thought that had it been my Daddy, things would have been different. He would have understood. He would know that being lesbian is not something I do, it is who I am. Miss you, Daddy, why did you have to die so young?

After seeing my love note to Susan, Mummy called me at college. She spoke about the fact that she knew what LGBTQ meant and that it was my life and I had to live it the way that made me happy. But, in the next two minutes, she said that this would not have to be shared with family members.

Daddy, I miss you.

LGBT challenges in the Indian workplace are a lesser problem as compared to the challenges faced by these communities in the society. While HR practices (with the IT industry being an early adopter) have been undergoing a progressive change to cater to the needs of the LGBT population, the importance of having LGBT role models can hardly be downplayed. Today, the term has expanded to include not only LGBT but also QIA to denote queer, intersex and asexual. As workers from the LGBTQIA community in India seek to resolve issues, both governmental and societal, they are assisted greatly by leaders who come out of the closet and inspire confidence in the community.

Building a safe and positive work environment for the LGBTQIA community in the workplace has benefits that are far-reaching and transformational. The greatest measures are to be taken in the space of recruitment and skilling of members of the transgender community, who, especially in lower socio-economic groups, are often victims of discrimination and isolation. Even at the workplace, more aspects leading to the inclusion of LGBT employees and creating an accepting environment will lead to organizations tapping talent from a variety of sources. Even today, workers face harassment of some kind for being LGBT and this remains a cause of great concern. While the past few years have seen more initiatives to assist gay employees to bring their whole selves to work, the same cannot be held true for lesbian and transgender employees.

From a productivity and engagement perspective, it cannot be denied that openly LGBT employees are better contributors who develop greater trust and respect for their employers than those who are closeted. It is heartening to note that as we go to print, a review of the law recriminalizing homosexuality is underway and this is sure to bring about positive change in the workplace. D&I champions focusing on creating training programmes around gender identity and sexual orientation awareness will add greater value towards LGBT inclusion at workplace.

DAY 15/99

D&I GAME: EXPERIENCING DIVERSITY AND INCLUSION

Given below are 10 statements related to situations that you might experience during the course of your work. Please tick the most appropriate answer for each given statement. Some statements may be characteristic or uncharacteristic of you. Nevertheless, try to relate each situation to your own experience and choose an answer that is most typical of you.

S. No.	Statements	Almost Never	Rarely	Sometimes	Usually	Almost Always	Score
1.	My circle of friends has people from various ethnic and cultural backgrounds.						
2.	I do not assume that others will agree with me while discussing an issue.						

The 99 Day Diversity Challenge

34

3.	Based on their upbringing, people can have very different values and beliefs from mine, and I am okay with that.						
4.	I value cultural networks; when such networks reach out and support each other, there is greater inclusion.						
5.	When in conflict with somebody belonging to a very different cultural background, I never generalize and associate negativity with their culture.						
6.	I can connect with people from any background and communicate easily—even language barriers do not deter me.						
7.	I love travelling and exploring—I believe travel is the greatest medium of getting cultural exposure.						
8.	Whenever I see another person being discriminated or biased against, I immediately speak up.						
9.	When in a multicultural group, I consciously avoid slipping into my mother tongue, even if the majority in the group understand my language.						
10.	Gender inequalities—obvious or subtle—unsettle me; I make sure I act on this as soon as instances come to my notice.						

SCORING

Please rate yourself using the following scale:

Almost never   Usually

Rarely   Almost always

Sometimes

IF YOUR TOTAL SCORE IS BETWEEN:

- 41 and 50: Congratulations! You can thrive in a multicultural environment, thanks to your high level of cultural competency.

- 31 and 40: Good! You are competent to collaboratively operate in a multi-cultural environment. You can try getting better at the game, by boosting your inclusivity.

- 21 and 30: You are in the okay zone. While you do not come across as some-body with strong cultural biases, there is definite scope for improvement. Identify your zones of discomfort in a multicultural context and work on voiding this zone.

- 10 and 20: You are in the initial stages of building your cultural competence. Greater exposure can help build your awareness towards becoming more inclusive of different cultures.

DAY
16/99

RELIGIOUS DIVERSITY

'Amma, I have received the offer letter! They want me to join by next month!' said Mohan, hugging his mother in excitement. 'Hearty congratulations, dear Mohana!' said his mother, her face wreathed in smiles of pride and joy. Taking the offer letter that was just delivered by courier, she went to the prayer room of their house and placed the letter before the Gods. Picking up the almanac, Mohan's mother quickly identified a date. 'Wednesday the 14th of December is a very auspicious day,' she said. 'If you join on that day, you will have the blessings of all our Gods.' 'But I will be going to Sabarimala at that time, Amma,' said Mohan. 'I will be barefooted, not clean-shaven and wearing black clothes.' 'Leave it to God to manage,' said his Amma.

As advised by his mother, Mohan joined InfoTechSys on 14 December. As Shantha, the HR executive finished his joining formalities, Mohan mentioned to her hesitantly, 'I have a religious requirement of wearing black clothes for the next 2 weeks. I will also not be clean shaven,' he added. 'Not a problem,' said Shantha smilingly. 'Come, let me introduce you to your reporting manager.' Shantha led Mohan into a bright cabin with lots of pictures of a happy family on it. 'Hello, I am Nizam Ahmed,' said the young gentleman seated in the cabin, wearing a skull cap. 'You must be Mohan, our new hire. Welcome to InfoTechSys!'

Religious diversity is one of the oldest forms of D&I to be prevalent in India, though it has been at the eye of several political and societal controversies. Freedom of religion is a fundamental right as per the Indian Constitution. According to the 2011 census, 79.8 per cent of the population of India practises Hinduism, 14.2 per cent adheres to Islam and 2.3 per cent practise Christianity. The remaining 4 per cent adheres to other religions such as Sikhism, Buddhism, Jainism and various indigenous faiths. Zoroastrianism and Judaism also have an ancient history in India, and each has several thousands of Indian adherents. The census states that 41 per cent of all Hindus are present in the workplace, while 31 per cent of all Muslims and 41 per cent of all Christians are part of the Indian workforce.

Religion plays a major role in the Indian way of life. Rituals, worship and other religious activities are very prominent in an individual's daily life; it is also a principal organizer of social life. Corporate India, especially in the last decade and more, specifically in its leading metros, has embraced religious diversity as one more strand of inclusion and it is quite common to see companies ready and willing to accommodate employees' religious needs.

Allowing the presence of small idols or photos of Gods on your desk at your workplace, moving joining dates to ensure sentimental alignment to auspicious days or creating spaces for prayer rooms are quite prevalent. Even in set-ups like corporate banking offices where the suit culture is prominent, it is not unusual to see symbols of religious affiliation on display. Adapting religious practices and rituals into secular events and get-togethers is also a fast-growing practice. Festivals such as Ganesh Puja, Christmas, Diwali and Bakrid offer opportunity for employee engagement activities.

Corporate leaders appreciate the value of religious diversity for the same reasons for which diversity is considered important—it helps provide different solutions and perspectives. While organizations do not have declared policies on hiring for religious diversity, several organizations mention it as one of the key diversity strands that they pursue.

DAY 17/99

SOCIO-ECONOMIC DIVERSITY

Rekha peered unbelievingly at the result in the report. She re-read the analysis just to be doubly sure. Was this true? She knew that numbers do not lie. Her heart was filled with excitement and it seemed to be a eureka moment. I must share this with Boss, she told herself. Right away, she raced to the printer and she waited for the report to emerge. As paper after paper lifted off from the printer and placed itself neatly in the tray, Rekha's mind went back 3 years when a study first revealed that hiring of candidates from lower socio-economic strata of the society yielded better retention rates. Accordingly, TOPE, the Indian back office processing arm of Trinity Bank, of which Rekha was the DGM HR, hired 300 young men and women from underprivileged families as part of their socio-economic diversity initiative. Working with NGOs and trusts across the country, suitable candidates were identified. A rigorous selection and training process had been followed, since her boss, the Director HR of TOPE, did not want this to be a token tick in the box, but a robust talent acquisition programme. Rekha recalled the many heated arguments that she had had with line managers and the finance team to secure the required approvals for this process. The on-boarding included English language training, computer skills, domain training and interpersonal behaviour coaching as well. The selected candidates were then deployed across TOPE with different business groups, under leaders who were fully convinced of the validity of this exercise. And today, the company-wide attrition and retention figures across positions had emerged. And the breaking news was that the entire set of 300 hires was intact! Even after 13 months, there was not a single dropout!

One aspect of diversity that is not often on an organization's radar is the diversity of social class or economic background. Socio-economic status is typically defined taking into account three variables (income, education and occupation) and as such broken down into three levels (high, middle and low) to describe how an individual or family can be categorized. Socio-economic classification (SEC) has several cohorts identified which are useful for consumer segmentation. The key problem in India with respect to socio-economic diversity is the fact that lower SECs continue to stay in the same classification despite several measures aimed at them. Research states that unconscious biases exist against people from lower socio-economic background, thus rejecting them during hiring, resulting in creation of even fewer opportunities for growth.

In terms of socio-economic status, one can find a lot of regional inequalities in India. The three states of Karnataka, Maharashtra and Tamil Nadu contribute a greater portion to India's GDP than 20 other states combined. Organizations which focus on elimination of socio-economic disparity and provisioning of equal opportunity to lower SEC groups have programmes which include hiring of candidates from recognized lower SEC groups, from across different states, often substantiated by a concerted CSR programme. Identifying the buying power of lower SECs (as described by Professor C.K. Prahalad in his epic book *The Fortune at the Bottom of the Pyramid*) underscores the importance of socio-economic diversity as a source of hidden potential for corporate India both as a talent segment and a consumer group.

Socio-economic Diversity

39

Success stories of organizations which have effectively integrated different socio-economic groups, especially candidates from among the lowest strata of the society often hinge on a powerful vision brought in by the leader. It also calls for substantial investment in refurbishing the hiring process, beginning with throwing the net far and wide to identify good candidates without compromising on meritocracy. It also includes devising efficient on-boarding, upskilling and induction programmes which help the new hire to perform on an equal platform with those from other SEC groups.

Poor knowledge of English, both spoken and written, is a very common barrier to the advancement of candidates from lower SEC groups. English language coaching centres and communicative English professionals are effective in bridging this gap. The past few decades have also seen the rising of finishing schools which help the candidate from a socio-economically disadvantaged background to develop those skills which will provide an equal opportunity to create a sustainable career with financial stability.

DAY 18/99

INTERSECTIONAL DIVERSITY

Sarah walked out of the appraisal meeting with her boss, her shoulders slumped and the energy deflated from her. She had been given a good rating and her performance bonus and incentives were assured, but that was not the point. She replayed the conversation she had with her boss. 'Sarah, how are things with you? Are you able to manage your projects well and on time?' began Vikram Bose, her boss and mentor. 'All good, Vikram. In fact, I am very excited about the new artificial intelligence (AI) project that we have been working on. I believe that I might really be able to add value to the analysis!' said an excited Sarah.

'And, on the home front? How are things? Your little one must be quite a handful, right?' said Vikram, looking through a few papers that were spread out on his desk, his reading glasses perched on the tip of his nose. 'Actually, things are better than I expected, Boss,' said Sarah.

'Is that so? Are you sure? Don't you think your little one deserves more of your time?' Vikram peered at her from above his glasses and there seemed to be something left unsaid. 'Why, Boss? Why do you think that way?' Sarah was never one to mince words and she dived straight into the discussion.

'Sarah, I hear that you have been working late for the past few weeks. You returned from maternity just 5 months back and I don't want any talk about how we are working you too hard. I would suggest that you take things a bit easy. Ensure that your little one gets your attention and you leave for home on time or even early. I am keen that you manage your new identity as a young mother in the same way that you look at your identity as a professional.'

'Boss, let me share something with you,' said Sarah, her voice tremulous yet firm.

'Yes, I was a young mother a few months ago. I went on a 6 month maternity leave, came back and now it's been another 6 months. My little one's first birthday is around the corner. While I appreciate that you are giving me all the support that you can in integrating my work and my personal life, I also have to tell you that that being a mom is not my only identity. I don't want to only be known as a mother. I am also many other things. I am an engineer from a Tier-III small town, who struggled to crack a placement at a company like this. I am also a woman who wants to earn well and be completely economically independent. I am an avid reader on the subject of AI and want to be known as a respected professional. And yes, I am also a mother who wants to earn and save for her

Intersectional Diversity

child. I think you are making a mistake by thinking that I am only defined by motherhood.'

The focus on D&I could sometimes lead to broad-brushing different groups of people within one major identity. For example, within the strand of 'gender' itself, one finds different categories of women professionals such as rural/urban, first-generation professional/second-gen, brought up by working mother/stay-at-home mom and so on. This has led to the concept of 'intersectional diversity' gaining ground in today's workplaces.

The *Oxford English Dictionary* defines 'intersectionality' as the interconnected nature of social categorizations such as race, class and gender, regarded as creating overlapping and interdependent systems of discrimination or disadvantage; a theoretical approach based on such a premise. Y.W. Boston further illustrates this by defining intersectionality as a framework for conceptualizing a person, group of people or social problem as impacted by overlapping identities and experiences in order to understand the complexity of prejudices they face.

The term 'intersectionality' was first coined by Professor Kimberlé Crenshaw in 1989 when she observed the following:

> Many black women found it difficult to identify with the issues of the mainstream (white) feminist movement, issues such as the pressure to be a homemaker. Black women, who often had to work in order to keep their family afloat and therefore did not have the luxury of being homemakers, did not feel as though these issues pertained to their experiences.

Although the theory of intersectionality largely grew to describe the double-whammy of racial and gender discrimination faced by African-American women, today, this concept looks at what it means for everyone to be at the intersection of varying strands of identity such as gender, generations, age, sexuality, socio-economic class and ability.

Intersectional diversity (ID) helps articulate the multiple experiences that people with different overlapping identities experience. Instead of analysing identity by using a dominant unidimensional approach whereby a single dimension is focused upon at a time, thereby leading to an exclusion of challenges caused by other identity strands, ID looks at multiple dimensions at the same time. Both approaches have their advantages and disadvantages. A unidimensional approach to D&I is much easier to implement by way of policies or programmes, but the impact is likely to be diluted and ineffective at times. By contrast, an ID approach to a D&I agenda is certainly more demanding and cumbersome, but its effect reaches the intended target audience in a much more precise and productive manner. ID has also been seen as a solution to creating a more egalitarian approach to D&I, one in which men, women, majority and minority participate equally.

IS A UNIFIED CULTURE POSSIBLE IN A DIVERSE WORKPLACE?

DAY 19/99

The Lion King Singa, supreme lord of the Jungle, sat on his forest throne, alone with his chief minister, the Elephant Gaja. It had been a long tiring day at court and the King was eager to rest. As Gaja stood up to leave, she sought permission to ask a final question for the day.

'Go ahead, Madam Gaja. I am all ears,' said Singa.

'Oh wise King!' said the elephant, 'In this hallowed court of yours, unparalleled anywhere in the universe, we have many magnificent treasures. The greatest treasures, however, are not the gems and precious stones that fill your treasury, but this great council of ministers. Under your advice, we have recently appointed all these wonderful ministers. Here, we have the agile leopard who keeps the boundaries of our kingdom safe, we have the prudent gorilla who helps us to understand the ways of humans, the intelligent peacock skilled in deciphering the weather and the astute giraffe who keeps count of all our assets. Besides these, we have the sagacious zebra, the brave tiger, the loyal bear, the sprightly deer and the strong hippopotamus.'

'Gaja, my good minister, I appreciate the wonderful people resources that we have chosen and are fortunate to have. But, what is the point of your preamble? Tell me. I am impatient to hear what you have to say,' interrupted the Lion King, pre-empting a further more detailed listing by the elephant.

'Oh benevolent monarch! It is your desire that everyone in this court bring their strongest personality to work. As an inclusive leader, you wish to have great diversity in this court, which is well reflected by the different animals present here. This means that each of our different traits will come to the fore. Am I right, your highness?' asked the elephant.

'Yes, indeed, honourable Minister. In our court, we believe that differences should coexist side by side. The right person for the right job means that we have many varied skills. It also means that each individual has a different perspective on things which helps us be better at problem-solving.'

'And that is exactly my query, Oh Lord!' interjected Gaja. 'If we have so much of diversity, how is it possible to have a unifying culture? How can this wonderful court of yours reflect 'one' value, 'one' truth? Will not the individual personalities of each of these different animals prevent the creation of one culture?'

One of the biggest challenges posed by the concept of diversity is its inherent paradox. If an organization has to perform to its best potential, it has to be unified under one culture and set of values. However, the organization, in order to be creative and adept at problem-solving has to have diverse individuals working together. So, how do leaders and people managers converge these two opposing principles? This is a question that I am very often asked. When a set of individually strong-willed professionals, successful and accomplished in their own right, come together, how can there exist one unifying culture? This is compounded by the fact that diversity in the workplace is growing at a faster rate than the organization's ability to deal with it.

The solution to this conundrum lies in leadership. More specifically, it lies in the leadership's articulation of (a) organizational culture and (b) the definition of diversity. High-performing organizations which attract successful professionals have taken this challenge head-on by creating a powerful set of shared values that guide and drive the organization as the first step. The organization's vision, mission and purpose is clearly articulated as the overarching message. The second step is to ensure that the pursuit of D&I is well clarified and communicated by the leadership. The company's D&I vision rests within the organizational value statement as one of the many enablers that contribute to creativity, problem-solving and productivity.

If harnessed correctly, a diverse workforce can transform an organization into a competitive market stronghold. However, if mismanaged, conflict can become a norm, and high employee attrition might result.

WORDFINDER

A	K	Y	Q	C	X	P	A	X	D	A	N	B	K	X	C	O	Y
Y	T	I	S	R	E	V	I	D	R	E	D	N	E	G	U	W	M
M	Y	J	R	S	M	E	T	G	M	M	G	N	N	P	L	W	C
M	U	U	N	I	T	N	O	C	Y	T	I	N	R	E	T	A	M
D	E	Y	B	R	E	A	D	W	I	N	N	E	R	C	U	N	P
T	I	D	U	A	R	E	D	N	E	G	L	R	E	L	R	H	J
T	G	A	F	S	C	O	Z	O	G	E	N	D	E	R	A	S	R
H	T	R	A	N	S	G	E	N	D	E	R	E	E	O	L	Y	T
X	S	N	V	D	X	V	S	B	N	R	M	Z	J	S	C	W	X
Y	T	L	A	N	E	P	D	O	O	H	R	E	H	T	O	M	H
V	Z	P	Y	R	A	M	I	D	S	Y	N	D	R	O	M	E	L
T	O	Q	B	I	B	B	X	F	T	W	O	F	S	F	P	C	E
E	G	A	K	A	E	L	E	N	I	L	E	P	I	P	E	L	P
E	N	A	Z	F	S	R	J	P	J	O	Z	Z	Q	H	T	A	N
K	S	B	Z	X	A	W	X	U	O	M	O	K	C	A	E	I	M
T	P	T	Y	Z	F	A	U	F	L	T	T	T	P	I	N	W	K
C	V	V	J	A	L	P	I	U	F	X	R	K	B	V	C	U	F
V	F	K	Y	C	V	H	A	H	R	L	I	P	P	R	E	Y	A

WORDS

Gender diversity	Pyramid syndrome
Breadwinner	Maternity continuum
Cultural competence	Gender audit
Pipeline leakage	Motherhood penalty
Gender	Transgender

SECTION 3

GENDER AND GENERATIONS: IMPORTANT IMPERATIVES

DIVERSITY AND INCLUSION LEXICON

S. No.	Words	Definition
1.	Early career stage	The career stage of a professional when he/she is at the threshold of his/her career and is typically aged between 20 and 30 years
2.	E-Gen	People belonging to the generation born in the decade 1971–1980
3.	Free-Gens	People belonging to the generation born between 1945 and 1960
4.	Gen Y	Professionals born between 1981 and 1990
5.	Gen Z	The generation of professionals born after 1990
6.	Gender chore gap	The difference (expressed in units of time) between the amount of housework done by women and men
7.	Generational competence	The ability to understand, appreciate and respond to the characteristics of co-workers from a different generation (younger or older) that can ensure collaborative and cohesive working
8.	Glass ceiling	The unseen, seemingly unbreakable barrier that keeps minorities and women from rising to the upper rungs of the corporate ladder
9.	Home primary career orientation	A kind of career orientation wherein the individual works but home is a bigger priority to him/her over career

S. No.	Words	Definition
10.	Intentional career pathing	The process of proactively and intentionally planning a professional's career path; the concept of intentional career pathing as a structured intervention that can guarantee career success for women professionals was first introduced by Dr Saundarya Rajesh in the year 2015.
11.	Juggling pressure	Refers to the pressure on a professional as he/she juggles the responsibilities of both his/her career and family
12.	Leaning in	The now famous phrase coined by Facebook COO Sheryl Sandberg which proposes that a woman professional be more assertive at work and not let biases keep her from pushing forward
13.	M curve	A curve shaped like the alphabet M that shows the labour force distribution of women by age with the age brackets 20–24 and 45–49 being two peaks; this concept was proposed on the basis of research on Japanese women.
14.	Mature career stage	The advanced career stage of a professional where an individual is above 41 years of age and has made significant advancements in his/her career
15.	Mid-career stage	The career stage of a professional when he/she is aged between 31 and 40 years of age and is most likely to encounter opportunities for career growth
16.	Millennials	A common term used to refer to both Gen Y and Gen Z cohorts
17.	Off-ramping	The process of stepping down from a full-fledged, thriving career

S. No.	Words	Definition
18.	On-ramping	The process initiated by a professional to make a career re-entry after a break
19.	Phase-back programme	Structured programmes for smooth reintegration of maternity returners back to their roles
20.	Pivotal generation	Gen Z that is pivoting away from the usual millennial behaviour to set its own behavioural and attitudinal standards
21.	Prevention of sexual harassment (POSH)	An organizational policy that prevents incidence of sexual harassment at work and penalizes the offender; any unwelcome sexually determined behaviour (whether direct or implied), such as physical contact and advances, a demand or request for sexual favours and sexually coloured remarks, amounts to sexual harassment.
22.	Returnee lead time	Lead time is the latency (delay) between the initiation and execution of a process; in the context of a workplace, returnee lead time refers to the time allotted to women career returnees to integrate themselves to their work.
23.	Sabbatical	A period of absence granted to an employee traditionally to acquire new skills, to rest or to travel
24.	Second-career programmes	Refers to formal company programmes towards identifying, hiring and advancing second-career women—women returning to work after career breaks
25.	Second-career women	Women who are ready to make a career comeback post a break as the reasons that previously led them to a break cease to exist

S. No.	Words	Definition
26.	Segue	The process of making a smooth transition from one state to another, unhesitatingly; the transition of a woman professional from a state of career break to that of formal employment is an example of Segue.
27.	Sexual harassment	Any unwelcome sexually determined behaviour (whether direct or implied) such as physical contact and advances, a demand or request for sexual favours
28.	Stay-at-home parent	Parent who chooses to stay at home to care for his/her children and to attend to other domesticities
29.	Untapped talent pool	A large section of people who are equipped with the necessary skills that organizations are not considering actively for recruitment
30.	Upskilling/ reskilling	The additional training to be imparted to or undertaken by an individual returning to career after a break, for him/her to meet the requirements of his/her job role
31.	Veterans	The generational cohort born between 1920 and 1945 that are rarely seen in active employment today

MILLENNIALS

[Scene: It is a corridor of an office near the coffee machine. Two colleagues, Raj and Chander, who are also good friends are talking and laughing as they are filling their coffee mugs. Another colleague of theirs, Jay, walks up to join them.]

Raj (laughing loudly): Chander, O Chander, how could you do this all the time? Unbelievable! So much shade!

Jay: Hey guys, what happened? Fill me in fellas! Chander, what did you do?

Chander (with a swagger): Just being awesome, Jay, I was just being myself.

Raj: Jay, you gotta listen to this. TD (short form for a name that the friends have kept for their boss—Targetdevil) wanted to pull Chander down a notch in public. So, he engaged him in a conversation in the middle of our bay. And then Chander…Chander (laughing again non-stop)….

Jay (slaps Raj on the back to stop him from laughing, but is unable to): Raj, man, tell and then laugh.

Chander: Jay, TD wanted to 'advise' (uses air quotes with his fingers) me about my perf. He was making a big fuss right in the middle of the floor, by analysing my numbers in front of everyone and telling me that I was not hired for just 'meeting' numbers but exceeding them. He was cribbing about my usage of social media. All this when his own targets are way below levels. Whenever I step into his office, he is busy on FB posting these cringe-max pictures of himself and his wife at all these restaurants. So, I just gave it back to him.

Raj: So Chander told him very seriously that social media is a double-edged sword and it can be used not only for topic research but also to create memes. He told TD that lots of memes are usually created by frustrated employees. TD was taken aback. After that Chander very kindly offered to change the privacy settings of TD so that he doesn't become the subject of any memes. You should have seen TD's face. My God! Brilliant! Just brilliant!

Jay: Chander, that was epic! (Does an imaginary hat tip.) TD did the same thing to me last week. He walked into our team station, and in front of Prabha and the girls, told me that I am taking off a lot for the eco society. He doesn't own my time. YOLO, right? People of TD's generation have screwed up the environment and don't care two hoots if we inherit a dead earth. He doesn't understand that a single tweet can make him the laughing stock of the entire office.

Chander: I told him sorry, but not sorry. The problem with these guys is they know nothing other than their own jobs, and even that they do so horribly. Someone has to tell them that we millennials like gigs, we like to focus on one thing at a time. We like a positive environment and we like mentors, not stupid bossy superiors.

Raj: Cool! Absolutely on fleek, man!

In a few short years, as per global census data, millennials will be the largest generation in the workplace. Not only would they be the most prevalent in numbers, they will also be the most influential cohort, given their ability to use technology and their fluency in creating networks. There is a veritable battle for their talent, as they form a substantial portion of the entry level and entry-to-mid employee segment. As such, it is absolutely imperative to understand what motivates millennials and how the office can be restructured to be truly inclusive of their expectations.

Millennials are a generational cohort that care as much about money as they do about values. A company culture that embraces their ideals, a top management team that is authentic and aspirational and a leadership style that is more mentor-like than hierarchical—these are the big asks of this generation, according to research. The urban–rural divide between millennials is a very thin line and instant transformation happens when a rural millennial gets to live in a metro, even for a short while. Connected as they are by a plethora of social media platforms, information sharing is seamless and instant. Their ability to form opinions is therefore rapid.

Millennials are known for their ability to build strong relationships, their need for access to transparent and high-tech communication, and a very high prerequisite to integrate work and life, the last being a gender-agnostic requirement. Most millennials seek professional growth that is wide-ranging, which includes the opportunity to develop specialized skills and also emotional maturity. One of the prevalent charges against them is that they seek a 'parent' in every boss.

Organizations that have a well-engaged millennial population demonstrate an astute awareness of the career advancement methods popular with this audience. Such environments present lots of opportunities for upskilling and education and have a coaching style of leadership blended into the culture. As such, the millennials are a generation that need to be won over not just with a banal job description and a CTC, but with an exhaustive culture change at every level that blends with their standards. Many organizations find the engaging of millennials to be a daunting aspect, simply because of the complexity of managerial styles that are required to engage with them.

AGE DIVERSITY

Hi, I am Srini, 46 years old and the latest hire at XFS, the 'cool' digital marketing solutions company. Most of my colleagues are under 25 and well, I am not ashamed to say this, my boss is a solid 12 years younger than me. Why was I hired, you ask? Because I am a damn good sales guy, the best in the business. But then, I have to fit in. For me to perform, I have to feel included and respected. Right now, this emphasis on 'coolness' is kind of getting to me.

I am not being paranoid. Listen me out. All my friends—in this age group of 45–50—are quite wary about making a career change, that too to a company which has such a wide age range of people— the millennials, the Gen Zs, the Gen Ys and all the other alphabets! Even when I applied in XFS, I was cautioned to critically examine the JD to find out if they were not subtly discriminatory against my age. To my knowledge, I could not find anything like that, but when I joined this team, my boss introduced me, very impressively, I must admit, but she used the word 'digital new grad' to describe me and everyone laughed. What does this mean? Am I like some kind of raw apprentice in the digital world?

In the last one month, I have thought more and more about the concept of 'ageism'—am I being discriminated against unconsciously? You see, the team is a really nice set of people, including my boss. They all are creative, driven and result-oriented. But sometimes I find myself being the butt of a few jokes, which involve things like my fluency (or the lack of it) with technology, the fact that I have a college-going son and the apparent humungous length of my work experience. When this happens, I just feel like telling them, 'If you don't know something about me, don't assume, just ask respectfully and I will answer. Be honest, but don't be rude.'

Even during meetings, I find a strange sense of ganging up that takes place. It's as if I am the outsider, the guy who doesn't 'get it'. This is really a strange feeling as compared to how I used to be in my previous company—the boss guy. Here, my jokes seem to fall flat and when I make references to certain instances (like the dot-com revolution) or certain objects (like the telex machine), it just does not gel. Not just this, even work values are so different. I find these kids asking for help all the time! If you spend so much time in just 'learning' how to do it, when will you actually get down to doing the job? It won't take too much time for me to flip the argument and say that all these young kids have such a strong sense of entitlement. I can also point out that they are 100 per cent of the time fiddling with their phones and their productivity would be a lot better if they focused. But I won't do it; if I did, then what would be the difference in maturity between them and me?

With advancement in medical technology, lifespans have increased considerably, leading to the phenomenon of age diversity in the workplace. In a typical office, over four generational cohorts work shoulder to shoulder and this brings about unique challenges which were not observed even as recently as a decade ago. In the previous eras too, such as the industrial era and the information technology era, diversity in the ages of the employees was a reality, but today, with the advent of technology and the resultant ease of information distribution, the complexity of managing a multi-age workforce is very high. Age diversity is defined as the ability of an organization to include workers of different age categories and ensure that a positive and productive work environment results.

Most industries have employees of different age groups and this presents huge opportunities when leveraged properly. Matured professionals bring in perspectives that are rich with the learnings of their practical experience, while younger employees add that zing of energy and creativity which comes from fresh, unjaded viewpoints. Organizations that have adequate age diversity in their workforce are positively primed to exhibit robust decision-making skills. The enhanced capacity to solve problems is a direct benefit of age-diverse workplaces as also is the opportunity to create out-of-the-box solutions. However, if these differing styles and identities are not merged and included smoothly in the same business environment, it can lead to friction which destroys the basic trust and respect in the culture.

Powerful communication skills and a discerning leadership style are the first requisites for managing an age-diverse team. Creating mutual understanding and respect, a standard communication guideline which is decipherable by all and an involvement in working towards the same goal lead to a workplace that positively benefits from age diversity. Lack of mutual interests, ego problems arising from strong opinions and misunderstanding caused by poor interpersonal interactions are some of the challenges mentioned by organizations which have had a rough experience while integrating different age groups. The different approaches to a problem which emerge from varying age perspectives can cause conflicts when people lose sight of the goal. Even the very definitions of what constitutes success, what is meant by professionalism and how wins are celebrated might lead up to tension.

When leaders and managers are trained in promoting inclusion in age-diverse teams, the results are powerful. There is no one right answer to dealing with challenges that arise from diversity. Having regular age-diversity conversations and training sessions can yield positive returns in the form of eliminating biases, uniting teams around common objectives and creating a sense of oneness. When members of all generations come to realize that they have more in common than they think—be it fears, dreams, weaknesses or strengths—then respect and trust emerge. When younger and older managers exhibit mutual respect, humility and learnability, such a workplace obtains the best of age diversity.

KNOWLEDGE TRANSFER IN GENERATIONAL DIVERSITY

Asif rang the bell to his mother's apartment at the senior citizen's community. Even today, after almost 5 years of his mother moving there, he still missed Ammi deeply and wondered why he had agreed to her living away from him and his family. But Ammi had convinced all of them. She had pointed out that this way, they would all enjoy each other's company even more and she would not be a burden on them. Despite Asif's protests, Ammi had been resolute. Thankfully, she lived in the same city as he did and that helped.

Why do I miss Ammi so much, pondered Asif to himself. It's because of her amazing ability to be a source of advice, he reflected. Maybe I will obtain a response to my problem today, just simply by chatting with her, he thought.

The door opened and Asif was surprised to see a young girl answering the door. 'Hello, you must be Asif Sir,' she said. 'Your mom is waiting for you. I was just keeping her company,' she said as she gathered her things before leaving.

'Do come tomorrow, Shruthi!' said Ammi and gave a hug to the girl. 'Shruthi is quite amazing with technology. She is my Guru as regards my laptop and my mobile!' she added with characteristic enthusiasm. 'And how are you Asif? How is the new division coming along? Settled well into the new role after your promotion?'

'Hmm, alright, Ammi. I should say that I am taking things slowly and kind of observing people,' said Asif as he poured himself a tall glass of water flavoured with lemon zest that Ammi always kept in the fridge.

'Well, that's a rather uncharacteristic reply coming from you, Asif,' observed Ammi with a smile. 'What are you going through?' she asked directly.

'Oh, Ammi, you are just amazing!' said Asif, his shoulders instantly relaxing as he settled into a chair in front of her. 'How do you know that there is something on my mind?'

'Go on, tell,' said Ammi.

'Well, it's like this. This new division has people of very different age groups. I have at least 20 per cent of the workers due to retire in the coming six months and it would be very difficult to replace all of them with young people. Sometimes my sales people, who are in their 50s, end up selling to very young customers and the fact that they are not very tech-savvy creates a lot of issues,' said Asif.

'Well, it does not seem very different from what we are doing here at the community,' observed Ammi with a smile.

'Shruthi who just left, is a 22-year-old who is learning recipes from the 60-year-old me. She edits a popular blog which she has named *Rukku's recipes* (after Ammi's name, Rukshana). I believe they have a lot of requests for traditional recipes, so I find that I am actually doing something useful! And for her part, Shruthi ensures that she keeps my mobile updated and does all the troubleshooting for me. I think what you need is a way in which the Shruthis and the Rukkus of your office are connected to each other to build something together.'

In a workforce that is increasingly becoming age-diverse, knowledge transfer (KT) is a crucial building block of competitive edge. When knowledge is shared between employees of different generational cohorts, it leads to the pooling of substantial intellectual capital, which in turn impacts performance and productivity of the organization. The unique competencies, experiences and life-learnings that each cohort possesses become the secret sauce for problem-solving and innovation.

The key to ensuring a systematic and organic KT mechanism lies in the creation of a culture that demonstrates collaboration, motivation and a sense of shared achievement. This is not an easy goal since there are multiple instances of inter-generational differences derailing the growth stories of organizations. The advent of the millennials, the retiring of Baby Boomers (known as the Freedom Generation in India), the small numbers of Gen X-ers and the fast integration of Gen Zs are some of the watershed events which already have and will continue to impact the workplace mix. When this is overlaid with the blistering pace of change in technology as well as the dominance of social media, the workplace is ready for a transformation like never before.

KT, therefore, becomes not just a routine process that mines and stores information, but also an expanding repertoire that includes the understanding of values, language, mindsets, motivation and biases. It, therefore, becomes important for employees across the generational spectrum to acknowledge and appreciate the differences in skills, perspectives and decision-making styles in order to facilitate the progress of seamless KT. It is not just the millennials who will be required to adapt to the work environment which they are entering as freshers, but also the older generations which will need to understand younger cohorts genuinely and with empathy, rather than observing them like an alien species.

KT is successful when the leader demonstrates the value that mentoring can be both ways. Learning has neither barriers nor an expiry date. When older and younger professionals align with one another and decide that they will not be victims of popular media stereotyping, then the scales fall from their eyes. They begin to see each other as possessing the same goals, the same desire to be respected and trusted and the similar need to be accepted and included. Thus, people from different generations become trusted advisors for each other, demonstrating openness in sharing information.

D&I GAME: EXPERIENCING DIVERSITY AND INCLUSION

MASTERMINDING SOLUTIONS

Please use this checklist to identify challenges that your team or organization is currently facing while trying to recruit diverse categories of people. Suggest possible solutions to overcome these obstacles in the solutions column.

S. No.	Obstacles	Solutions
1.	Women don't apply for certain positions, so it is difficult to source candidates. The hiring and talent acquisition teams find it difficult to source the right kind of CVs.	
2.	Most managers think that certain positions are not suitable for people with disabilities or women as some of these positions often require overtime or working in night shifts.	
3.	The organization wants more aggressive and competitive employees who can consistently meet targets and often women get overlooked while recruiting for these positions.	
4.	Having a woman manager to manage a predominantly male team often causes problems related to stereotypical mindsets and attitudes.	
5.	Since certain technical roles can be played very well by youngsters, they are actively recruited for these positions because of the perception that millennial generation is very tech-savvy. People from other generations usually lose out on such opportunities.	

S. No.	Obstacles	Solutions
6.	There are no women role models to lead the way for other women to move into management or technical positions.	
7.	Women generally lack the right qualifications for the job. When it comes to technical specifications, the general belief is that men are more convincing and effective.	
8.	Having a single woman technical employee in a predominantly male team would make her life difficult. So it is difficult to both recruit and retain female employees in such teams.	
9.	Male managers often find it difficult to give proper feedback to female colleagues. They are often worried about women getting emotional.	
10.	After the POSH Act became a law, there is a certain reluctance in male managers to mentor female employees. They are worried about the perception of others and wonder if their reputation will take a hit.	

Dear Diary,

Today will be my 18th year of working! Yes, 18 years! Unbelievable, right? I didn't even think I would enter the workplace, forget working for so long. I still remember the day when Amma and I went to the local engineering college to get the application form. When I got selected to do the course, she was super thrilled, more than I was. Till then, I had only studied in all-girls schools. Engineering would be my first co-ed experience. Grandmother was not too happy with it and ensured that I was duly informed of the perils of 'losing my focus' while at college. But I did not mind all that one bit. What excitement! In the entire joint family, I would be the first engineer! Appa was full of sombre advice, as usual, but I know that even he was secretly thrilled. All my cousins and aunts and uncles were there to see me off on my first day, as if I were going on some expedition.

Even during my 4 years of engineering, the family had started talking about getting me married off. I was so grateful that I got to do the course of my choice that I did not mind this. And then, I finished the course and got campus placed at Kadayur Computers Ltd (KCL). Again, another first! Among all my cousin sisters,

I was the first who was 'allowed' to go for a job. In that one month, so much happened! Appa had shortlisted Arun's horoscope from the several dozens that came in response to his advertisement in the *Hindu* matrimony column. He particularly liked Arun's distinguished family, his bank job and also that his wheatish complexion would nicely match with my fair skin. Arun came to 'see' me, liked me and the marriage was solemnized without further ado.

I must admit that the 18 years have not been an entirely easy ride. I have had so many battles to fight, both with my own as well as with Arun's family, beginning with things like whether it was morally right to put a child in a day care, to how it was not hygienic to have a cook at home, to the fact that in our homes, we did not make the men work. It is indeed a wonder that I have managed to survive all this and I am still with KCL, as General Manager—Business Solutions, no less. And I am equally the traditional daughter and daughter-in-law. I still celebrate all the important festivals, make sure that my children appreciate the relevance of our culture and visit all my relatives from time to time. But do you know what I appreciate most in my life? You may be surprised, but it is Arun's transformation.

While he started off as a conservative husband who did not want his wife to work (we have had huge fights about this), he slowly changed when he saw how important a career is to me. Initially, his support just meant not criticizing me or putting a spoke on my decisions, but in the past few years, it has actually moved way beyond this. Arun is today an equal contributor at home, helping me not only with the home-related work and taking care of the children, but also being very understanding of my work pressures.

I would give him a larger share of the credit in who I am today than even to myself.

Why? Simply because, while I am propelled by all the new opportunities around me and the support that I get from the work environment, Arun has had to overcome not just decades but generations of conditioning. He would often be questioned by his relatives as to why he is 'allowing' his wife to work. He would have to explain to the school PTA, why he was attending instead of me. He has attended my office get-togethers and been called Mr Anuradha by my KCL colleagues. Why is all this so important? Because, each time, Arun has to repel the voices in his head—that of his father's, his grandfather's, his cousins'—which were orthodox and old-fashioned and had very set views on the role of women.

If Arun had not changed, I would be yet another statistic of a woman who started off promisingly, but dropped off from the workplace somewhere in the middle, clueless about the real cause of her unhappiness. Thank you Arun!

We can define first-generation women professionals as people whose parent or parents did not pursue a professional career. The first-generation Indian woman professional is somewhat unique as compared to her counterparts around the globe. She is not just battling cultural mores and the onslaught of patriarchal value systems, she is also bearing the brunt of walking a lonely journey, without the path being previously lit by role models close to her. She is probably the first to complete a professional course in her family, is very often academically bright and definitely the first daughter that secures a job. She is most often full of ambition and expects the workplace to also be a simple, linear excursion just like her academic achievements. It is only a few months or perhaps a year into the job that she realizes that it is not just hard work, but also professionalism, intentionality and other critical skills which will allow her to pursue her aspirations.

While the Indian woman professional, whether first-generation or otherwise, will require to learn a lot of different skills in order to be successful in the workplace, the other dimension—namely, how the workplace treats her—is also equally important. In order to ensure that the first-generation woman professional is fully empowered to succeed, it is imperative that her identity is understood. As the workplace trains its attention even more keenly on D&I, the first-generation woman professional has a lot more in common with marginalized talent pools than with the average woman professional. Being a first-generation is somewhat of a professional Achilles heel when the woman employee does not obtain requisite support to learn and share her experiences. The lack of a role model at home results in a lower sense of professional expectations, a lack of self-confidence and a higher instance of the so-called imposter syndrome. Even more confounding is dearth of support from the family while also being isolated at work.

Many organizations have comprehended the challenge that the first-generation woman professional faces and have created a lot of programmes that enable and support her. Policies that allow flexibility and crèche services, sensitizing sessions that teach coping skills and networking and the presence of mentors who prove to them that they are not alone—all of this goes a long way in alleviating the anxiety of the first-generation and creating confidence. Special network groups also provide support to encourage the first-generation to access shared resources, provide valuable perspectives and contribute to the creation of a truly inclusive workplace.

THE PHENOMENON OF SECOND CAREERS FOR WOMEN

It was 2007–2008 and we were conducting a series of second-career assessment centres for Future Group. Meeting, interviewing and assessing over 10,000 women at cities such as Bangalore, Hyderabad, Pune, Kolkata, Mumbai, Ahmedabad and Kolhapur, we hired more than 1,600 second-career women who became part of the store operations team for the many retail outlets of Future Group. It was one of India's very first second-career programmes and the visibility was immense. It gave all of us at AVTAR an amazing first-hand view of how women shaped their careers after a break and what this phenomenon of second careers was all about.

The city was Kolhapur and the crowd was large. Future Group had aggressively advertised this programme, calling out to women who had taken breaks in career to come forward and apply and we, AVTAR, were their partners in organizing the selection process. A woman around 35/36 had applied for a position at the backend and one look at her resume told us that she would not make the cut. However, she was very persistent and observing her energy levels and intentionality, we decided to shortlist her for an interview with the client.

After a series of meetings, she did land the job. She was one of 150–200 women who were given a re-entry opportunity that day. After receiving the dossier containing the letter of intent, she left. A couple of hours later, she was back, this time with a young boy in tow, about 8 years old. They waited while we interviewed the other applicants and it was soon time to close shop. However, Geeta (that's what we will call her) did not leave. She sent word through one of my colleagues that she wanted to meet me and hand over something to me. I replied through the same colleague that we did not accept gifts and this was part of our job and we were very happy for her.

Demonstrating the by now characteristic perseverance, Geeta waited till the last person was gone. Then she came up with her son. There were tears in her eyes. 'Madam, I was a middle school teacher. After the birth of my son, I was asked to leave my job. Here in Kolhapur, we don't have many options. I have waited almost 10 years to get back to a position where I will earn money. My son and I wanted to thank you for creating this opportunity for us,' she said, and her son handed over a sheet of notebook paper in which he had drawn a bouquet using crayons. Underneath it were the words, 'Thank You for giving Mummy job.'

This is one of my most treasured mementos, which will always remind me of the angst that the Indian woman professional goes through in her attempt to pursue a sustainable career.

Career breaks are a very common occurrence in the life of the Indian woman professional. Research states that close to 48 per cent of all Indian women under the age of 30 take a break in career at least once due to marriage, maternity or childbirth. However, only 18 per cent of the women who take breaks actually end up returning to the workplace. In 8 out of 10 cases, these re-entries are possible not only due to the woman's own grit and diligence but also due to the specially crafted second-career programmes offered by discerning corporates. India's first ever recorded re-entry programme was in 2006 when SCOPE International, the back-office operations of Standard Chartered Bank, in partnership with AVTAR, hired over 200 women who made a career comeback after wide-ranging breaks.

Second-career programmes for women in India have become a very popular choice for companies to hire from this pool of sustainable talent. Depending upon the type of industry and the roles offered, it would be a safe estimate that over 30,000 women have made a re-entry through AVTAR's efforts in the past decade. Organizations such as SHEROES, JobsForHer and BD Foundation too work in this space and are involved in ensuring that women who take breaks are not penalized for it. The success of these programmes, as a talent strategy to win the war for talent, has had a ripple effect with over 40 per cent of the Working Mother & AVTAR 100 Best Companies for Women in India designing structured hiring programmes to recruit second-career women.

Companies are also following the internship route wherein prior to taking up a full-time job after the break, the woman professional undergoes a period of work where the focus is on reskilling and building her competencies. Second-career internship programmes are very popular in the IT and BPO industries where the woman is able to bring her skills up to speed. One of the huge reasons for the success of second-career initiatives is the high offer-acceptance and joining rate by women, which in the case of AVTAR-led programmes is as high as 95 per cent. Similarly, the length of tenure of the returning women professional is also 65 per cent higher than a regular hire. Data such as this enables organizations to focus and invest on this talent pool, through which double benefit is yielded—India increases its per capita income levels while the Indian industry is able to leverage the value of trained resources who return with greater intent than before.

INTENTIONAL CAREER PATHING FOR WOMEN

DAY 28/99

Interviewer: Ms Samyukta, as per this report, you spent a huge amount of money, accounting to almost 2 per cent of your annual revenue this year, on gender diversity programmes to increase diversity in your workplace. And when you analyse that at the end of the exercise, the ratio of women remains almost the same, it appears to be an erosion of shareholder value. As the Managing Director of Serene Enterprises India (SEI) do you have anything to say about this?

Samyukta: At the outset, I have to say that these funds were spent not just in one financial year, but over a period of 3 years. This is an investment whose returns will only be perceived in the long run. It is not a plug-and-play mechanism whereby a sudden jump in women's workforce participation happens. I am confident that over the next few years, we will see a dramatic increase in gender ratios at SEI.

Interviewer: Is it really possible to change the gender ratios in the workplace by aggressive hiring?

Samyukta: Gender ratios can be changed significantly, but it will not be only because of targeted hiring. It will be a combination of various initiatives.

Interviewer: Could you name some of these initiatives?

Samyukta: At the outset, a company needs specific hiring programmes. This year at SEI, we have introduced the concept of hiring second-career women. We have also begun hiring women from specific campuses, and also first-generation women professionals. Not stopping just with hiring, we are also creating a positive, enabling environment by providing the women with policies that help them manage their life and work better, such as flexible working, telecommuting and work-from-home facility. At SEI, we have one of the city's best day care centre which is in-house. Our women don't need to travel far away to drop and pick up their children at the creches. They have the freedom to check up on their kids anytime they wish.

Interviewer: And all of these facilities are for the women alone?

Samyukta: Not at all. All policies at SEI are gender-neutral.

Interviewer: And these policies will result in an increase in women's employment at SEI?

Samyukta: I am not finished—there are two critical aspects that are absolutely required to ensure that not only are women hired in large numbers, but they also stay the course to build their career and eventually rise to leadership. Number 1—the support and mentoring they receive from men. This is very critical and is often the game changer when it comes to having a robust gender balance at the workplace. However, it is the second aspect that I believe is the reason for the amazing success of women in the workplace.

Interviewer: I am very curious! Is it maternity leave, is it the phase-back programmes or is it sensitivity training?

Samyukta: It is the intentionality of the woman herself! Unless and until the woman is deeply intentional about her career, all these support systems will not play their part. She has to believe that her career is as important a part of her identity as her personal self. She will have to build those skills necessary to help her in the workplace and also learn how to differentiate herself as a professional. More than anything, the woman has to give up the feeling of being a victim and should place the locus of control for her success firmly in her own hands. This intentionality will enable her to not only rise to her full potential but also effectively utilize the support systems that the organization provides her. Ultimately, the woman professional's growth and sustenance are not a game of snakes and ladders with everything being manipulated by the luck of the draw. It is a game of chess where she controls the moves.

What is career intentionality or intentional career pathing? In research terms, it is the extent to which professionals deploy intention in charting their career trajectories. A concept that has been created and curated by AVTAR, after a longitudinal study consisting of over 2,700-plus subjects across their early career, mid-career and matured career stages, career intentionality is the ability to focus on your career by nuancing it as a series of strategic decisions. The concept of intentionality is gender-neutral but it assumes great significance in the case of women because it makes all the difference between the woman professional staying engaged with a career and dropping off. Career intentionality training includes a set of skills that every woman professional is required to cultivate in order to achieve her professional goals.

Basis a 2015 India-wide study on gender variance in the career intention-ality of Indian professionals by AVTAR, there were three important findings:

1. Women do not invest in careers the way men do. Getting a job is a natural event to most young women, but taking strategic decisions to further it rarely is. Her investment in a career would at best result in hiring domestic help to manage the home front and not involve creating mentors or sponsors. Having to prove herself as career-oriented at work and family-oriented at home is a double whammy.

2. Women seek less of non-family support for careers than men. Indian women, post marriage, often relocate to their husband's hometown. With the joint family system still in prevalence, the woman is expected to rely on her immediate relatives for support. There are few friends, colleagues or neighbours she would discuss 'work' with. She tends to neglect chances for networking that would help her manage her career and home better and could have a positive spin-off on all aspects of her career.

3. Women in early career stages have a narrower perspective of business than men. Many women see their career as a series of temporary jobs especially when burdened with managing home and work commitments. The concept of a long-term career calling for intentional commitment is often missing. They also take more time in developing a strong rapport with their managers which if effectively built could work to their advantage.

The solution to the above challenges lies in the woman professional's acquisition of a diverse set of skills as part of her career repertoire. Most of these skills such as networking, negotiation and communication are not in-born; they are learnt. Research states that men employ these skills almost like second nature, while the socializing of women as caregivers and little else creates a need for them to learn these consciously and mindfully. Secondly, intentionality helps one in strategic decision-making by pursuing fulfilment. The objective is not balance or perfection; it is fulfilment while leading an intentional career. And finally, the third core of intentionality is the ability to change what requires to be changed.

It is the capacity to invest sufficient introspection, collecting sufficient information to arrive at a well thought out decision.

Several organizations have introduced the concept of intentional career pathing to the women professionals in their workplace in order to create greater focus. This has resulted in higher levels of engagement in combination with decreased attrition rates. Women who have turned intentional about their careers display maturity and application that ensures purposeful engagement with their workplaces.

POSH: A FOUNDATION

DAY 29/99

[Scene: It is an office get-together in the evening, and colleagues Prabha, Mona and Raj who work for PP Ltd are standing together holding their plates of snacks. Their boss, who they refer to as TD (Targetdevil) arrives on the scene.]

TD (shaking his head and laughing): All three devils are right here! So, what is cooking, folks?

Prabha (surprised that the boss who is referred to as Targetdevil should himself call them devils): Err, nothing Sir. We were just enjoying these snacks.

TD (turning to Mona, placing his arm around her shoulder and speaking in a hoarse whisper): What snacks are these? If you want something really good, you must come to my house. I have the best collection of wines from across the world.

Raj (realizing that Mona is uncomfortable): Boss, you should invite Chander, me and Jay someday. We will give you good company.

What is the point in inviting these girls? They don't drink, especially Mona. She is very uncomfortable with these things.

TD: That is probably because nobody has taught her the right way. I am very good at teaching girls these special skills. In any case, so what if they don't drink? It's always more interesting to have girls at a party than you boring guys. [He does not remove his arm and Mona is now visibly in discomfort.]

[Chander walks in and immediately notices this.]

Chander: Sir, I have to show you something, just see this. (He points to his mobile phone to get TD away from the place.)

TD (Ignores Chander. Turns to Mona, while leading her away from the group): I have been wanting to discuss about your performance scores. You should drop by my house sometime (smiles and winks). We can have a detailed chat. Maybe even dinner later.

Mona (decides she has had enough. Extricates TD's hand and speaks in a clear loud voice for all to hear): Boss, thank you so much for inviting me to dinner. But, before we speak about my perf. scores, I wanted to know if you have attended the POSH training?

TD (seems quite hassled and looks at her in surprise): Why? Why are you asking?

Prabha (hears Mona's voice and realizes the play. Reaches the spot where Mona and TD are standing): Boss, it is a very nice, interesting new webinar—details very clearly what happens to people who indulge in unwelcome behaviour. You are always so concerned about us, you will be happy to know that our office has adopted a zero-tolerance policy towards sexual harassment. (Turns to Raj and involves him in the conversation) You have heard about this, right, Raj?

Raj (joins them): Absolutely, Prabha! In fact, just yesterday Chander and I were speaking about how things like passing inappropriate comments, innuendos and uncomfortable physical behaviour can actually lead to a person getting thrown out of his job.

[The four colleagues form a sort of circle around TD.]

Mona (returns to take her place within the group): We would really like your take on this, Boss. Like you just said, you are a great teacher and it would be wonderful to learn about POSH from you and also what can be done to prevent it.

TD (pulls out his mobile phone and begins speaking to an imaginary caller): Hello, hello, yeah, speaking....

The advent of large numbers of women into the workplace has necessitated the creation of stringent laws that ensure their safety and protection. Research states that a sense of susceptibility and defencelessness is a huge impediment to women at work, not only interfering with their performance but also becoming a critical reason for attrition. Sexual harassment is one such egregious obstacle which severely affects the woman professional and puts her through untold physical and emotional suffering. In the larger context, this also leads to a decrease in women's social and economic capital, resulting in poor per capita income.

In India, a focus on the safety and security of women from a harassment point of view was first brought into effect with the establishment of the Vishakha Guidelines in 1997, when the Supreme Court of India recognized the term 'sexual harassment' for the very first time in a landmark judgement that subsequently led to the creation of the guidelines. While the principle of gender equality is enshrined in the Constitution as a fundamental right, it was only after the promulgation of the guidelines that the topic of sexual harassment entered the organizational discourse. Organizations that were serious about the welfare and safety of women in their workplaces created codes and processes to ensure the establishment of a protected and safe environment.

In order to further strengthen the focus to establish the importance of protection of women and eliminate gender-based discrimination, the Union of India created the first ever legislation to specifically address the issue of workplace sexual harassment and outlined the definitions for what constituted sexual harassment. Through an Act titled the

Sexual Harassment of Women at Workplace (Prevention, Prohibition and Redressal) Act, 2013 (also known as the POSH Act), the legislation sought to set in place measures to address and prevent crimes of a sexual nature against women workers. The aim is to remove the insecurity and hostility that emanates from a work environment where women feel vulnerable to sexual advances.

The POSH Act was further reinforced with the amendment of the Criminal Law (Amendment Act) in 2013 which criminalized offences such as sexual harassment, stalking and voyeurism. The statute has as its objectives the creation of a safe and dignified work environment and also provides guidance on the efficient redressal of complaints about all forms of harassment. As per the POSH Act, 'sexual harassment' includes unwelcome sexually tinted behaviour, whether directly or by implication, such as (a) physical contact and advances, (b) demand or request for sexual favours, (c) making sexually coloured remarks, (d) showing pornography or (e) any other unwelcome physical, verbal or non-verbal conduct of a sexual nature. The Act also necessitates the setting up of an Internal Complaints Committee (ICC) which takes care of the proper process for enquiry and redressal.

The effectiveness of the POSH Act in the workplace lies in awareness creation and also engendering a sense of confidence in the woman to open up about her victimization. The #MeToo phenomenon in which millions of women across the world revealed the instances when they had faced sexual harassment was a shot in the arm for the POSH movement. Training sessions which sensitize people on the definition of sexual harassment, the repercussions of indulging in it and consequences that follow are essential in bringing about a paradigm shift in the culture of workplaces. Very importantly, in areas where the patriarchal mindset still abounds, the Act is an important tool to prevent instances of sexual harassment.

CROSSWORD

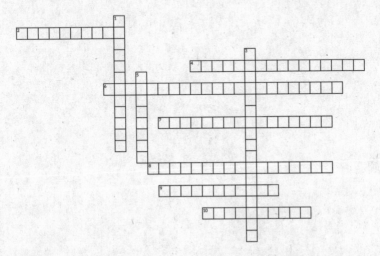

ACROSS

2 A period of absence granted to an employee traditionally to acquire new skills, to rest or to travel. (10)

4 Refers to the stress on a professional as he/she shifts between the responsibilities of both his/her career and family. (8,8)

6 The ability to understand, appreciate and respond to the characteristics of co-workers from varied age groups that can ensure collaborative and cohesive working. (12,10)

7 Lead time is the latency (delay) between the initiation and execution of a process. In the context of a workplace, returnee lead time refers to the time allotted to women career returnees to integrate themselves to their work. (8,4,4)

8 The advanced career stage of a professional where an individual is above 41 years of age and has made significant advancements in his/her career. (6,6,5)

9 A common term used to refer both Gen Y and Gen Z cohorts. (11)

10 The now famous phrase coined by Facebook COO Sheryl Sandberg that refers to the process of a woman professional being more assertive at work and not letting biases keep her from pushing forward. (7-2)

DOWN

1 The unseen, seemingly unbreakable barrier that keeps minorities and women from rising to the upper rungs of the corporate ladder. (5,7)

3 Defined by the media, this particular group of millennial sets its own behavioural and attitude standards. (7,10)

5 The generational cohort born between 1920 and 1945 that are rarely seen in active employment today. (8)

SECTION 4

INITIATING THE DISCUSSION
AROUND DIVERSITY

DIVERSITY AND INCLUSION LEXICON

S. No.	Words	Definition
1.	Annual hours contract	A flexible work arrangement wherein employers and employees agree they will work a given number of hours during the year, but the pattern of work can vary from week to week
2.	Backup dependent care	Refers to guaranteed dependent care that is used not on a regular basis but when other forms of care are not available. This does not include resource and referral and is separate from backup childcare; dependents needing care can include elderly family members, partners, terminally ill family members and adult children with special needs.
3.	Break-free career	A continuous, uninterrupted career with no incidence of breaks
4.	Day care services	An enabler for professionals that refers to facilities of childcare, which are reliable and affordable
5.	Peer group network	A professional's network (organized or informal) comprising his or her colleagues
6.	Product diversification	Process of expanding business opportunities through additional market potential of an existing product

S. No.	Words	Definition
7.	U-curve	A curve shaped like the alphabet 'U' that denotes the job satisfaction levels of employees at various career stages; according to this curve, the satisfaction is at a peak during the early career stage, dips significantly towards the mid-career and rises again as the professional enters the mature career stage.
8.	VUCA	Acronym used to describe or reflect on the volatile, uncertain, complex and ambiguous world where today's businesses operate in unpredictable conditions

PROBLEMS OF A DIVERSE WORKPLACE

DAY 32/99

Disciple: Oh Master, we have many research reports and empirical proof that diversity is great to improve creativity at the workplace. But is not homogeneity better to arrive at decision-making?

Master: Oh Ananta, you seem to be alluding to something. Come clean. What are you referring to?

Disciple: Oh kind Master, it is impossible to feign ignorance before you. I am referring to the spat between our Senior Brother and Junior Brother that took place yesterday. They are two ends of the spectrum. One is old, the other young. One is from the North, the other from South. One has come here on his own seeking the truth, while the other has been part of our organization through his family connections. As such, they never agree on anything. Whereas our two brothers in the food preparation duty are so alike, they could be two peas in a pod. I find that they often arrive at decisions very quickly and easily. They even complete each other's sentences. Thus, I ask—Is not homogeneity better for faster decision-making?

Master: Ananta, conflict is part of diversity. After all, when two people are different, it means that they will have differing views. If you want quick decisions, it's better to put together a team that is similar. But then, if you want effective decision-making, you will for sure need a diverse team.

Scott Page, in his bestseller book *The Difference: How the Power of Diversity Creates Better Groups, Firms, Schools and Societies*, speaks about how the most important purpose of enabling diversity in the workplace is to ensure robust decision-making. He does not deny that this is difficult, but he argues that without diversity, the uncompromising nature of a well thought out decision is lost.

A study in the US centred around a 100-year-old organization which employed very similar people revealed that quick decision-making was one of the areas of strength of the senior leadership team. While the value of this metric, that is, speed of decision-making, was high a few decades ago, recent researches show that it is not just speed of decision-making but also the quality which is important. A decision that leads to sustainable growth is far more critical to an organization than a quick decision taken in haste, leading to disaster. A diverse group of individuals take longer to arrive at a decision but the likelihood of their having discussed more facets of the problem than a homogenous group is high.

While the concept of diversity has won accolades for being a great USP, a fabulous competitive edge for an organization, it is not true that if you merely put together a diverse team, productivity and efficiency will automatically result. Companies that have very heterogeneous team members find that it takes longer to come to a decision, which can be quite frustrating for the people concerned. In order to improve business performance, it is not just enough to bring together diverse groups of people, it is essential to create a culture, under an impactful leader, where idea generation, brainstorming and decision-making is managed well. There are studies which have discovered that while diversity can lead to innovation, it can also lead to 'detrimental team dynamics' if not carefully managed.

DIVERSITY IN A VUCA WORLD

**DAY
33/99**

Hi, I am Sunitha. I just had to share this. I have been working at Manprotech for the past 11 years and was recently promoted as Senior Manager—HR. When our company launched its D&I agenda 7 years ago, I had volunteered for the job of running the women's network group. I have been doing a really good job, even though I say so myself! By itself, it is actually not a big headache, we have an events calendar and I run the four or five events that we do each year with the help of the enthusiastic new joinees in the engineering department, and the feedback is always very good. But of late, I am finding it very difficult to manage the network group. The issue is this—every day, we are facing newer and newer business challenges. These challenges are in the form of various issues and problems. One day I have to manage a communication problem, the next day we have to sort out an issue between head office and the branch sales office and another day I have to sit on the ICC committee to provide resolution to a complaint and so on. There is just no pattern to my day. I have to learn new things every day, because without that knowledge I cannot do my job. And the most important thing is I am not able to run the women's network group as easily as before. With the new questions and concerns being raised by all, young and old alike, I am just not able to focus. Frankly, I am wondering if I am even suited to this new workplace.

There is no denying the fact that we live in a VUCA world—volatile, uncertain, complex and ambiguous. More and more businesses are operating in unpredictable environments. There is disruption in every aspect, especially with how businesses are run. Competition emerges from unforeseen areas. Business models change every day. Customer expectations shift constantly and the hyper-connectivity brought in by technology only serves to put the locus of control away from predictable management styles.

VUCA-ness also manifests itself in the world of people management with specific focus on D&I. New world dynamics create new levels of unprecedented change in how processes and programmes are managed. In this brave new world, the relevance of inclusion and diversity rises to never-before heights, simply because of the increased advantages that organizations obtain of being agile and adaptive. The inclusive organization which is capable of harnessing a broader set of perspectives, heuristics and truths is infinitely better placed to manage the constant flux of this new normal.

In this VUCA world, the D&I agenda takes on a different level of relevance. Leaders who drive D&I from the very word go—who demonstrate real executive commitment to create inclusive workplaces—are the key differentiators. Seeing an inclusive environment as more than a culture or people agenda, as a business process transformation opportunity, is the truly inclusive leader's take. Realizing the value of D&I as a learning facilitator and an agility-enhancer allows the leader to impact business delivery at a very integral level. The inspired, discerning leader looks at D&I not as something that is at the periphery of business, but as something embedded deeply throughout the organization's core functions. This perspective enables the organization to work on programmes and policies that are themselves disruptive, thereby providing very contemporary and relevant ideas.

Organizations which understand that the world is changing each minute and that status quo isn't an option anymore, adapt the principles of inclusion and diversity in a much more effective and purposeful manner. Allowing different voices to be heard across the organization and enabling new approaches to problem-solving are ways in which inclusion manifests itself as a powerful competitive advantage. When inclusion is provided a platform of influence, suboptimal styles of using old, hackneyed methods are avoided. Not only do today's VUCA conditions require fresh perspectives of inclusion, they also need to be implemented with agility.

Leaders who attract diverse talent, who then inspire and engage that talent, are able to leverage the full force of inclusion. They are able to drive innovation and are able to produce exceptional results. For these leaders, the antidote to the VUCA world is creating an environment of inclusion, driven by adaptability and agility. These leaders have renewed their commitment and focus on D&I, making it even more germane for a VUCA world.

D&I IN SMALL AND MEDIUM ENTERPRISES

DAY 34/99

'Sir, are you in town, can we meet for coffee?' Vikas's voice was as usual friendly and energetic.

'Great to hear from you Vikas! Yes, I am very much in town. 5:00 PM at the Grand Latte?' Anand was careful about choosing the point of meeting. It had to be a nice coffee shop, yet not too ostentatious, as that would put off Vikas.

'Done, Sir! I will see you at 5:00,' said Vikas as he disconnected the call.

Anand looked at the time. It was 3:00 PM and he still had some of his writing to complete. A retired marketing professional, Anand had once facilitated a brainstorming session for Vikas's business networking club in a Tier-III town which turned out to be a huge hit. Since then he had been invited to return year on year and had ended up becoming a de facto mentor of sorts for the small group of second-generation businessmen. Vikas and his friends looked for more excuses to invite Anand to visit the small town upon their request since he was deeply respected as a practical and sensible advisor. And, expectedly, to some, he became more than a business advisor —he was a sort of personal sounding board, a moral compass.

And Vikas was one of the few that considered Anand to be more than a mentor. He discussed personal matters with the older man, spoke about skill-development courses that he could take and even discussed holiday options with him! Anand realized that Vikas, who had taken over the family business, was caught in the warp of change that usually results when the son takes over from the larger-than-life first-generation entrepreneur father. He empathized with Vikas and this formed a strong bond between them. Whenever Vikas made a trip to the city on business, he made it a point to meet Anand Sir.

'Sir, I have something specific to discuss with you this time,' said Vikas after the first half hour had passed pleasantly with both them sharing updates from their respective lives.

'Tell me, Vikas.'

'Sir, I keep hearing about this concept of D&I—about how hiring different kinds of people will help in increasing productivity, etc. Is it true? Will it even work for a small company like mine?'

'Vikas, you employ over 800 people in one of the biggest pump manufacturing organizations of your town. How is that small by any standards?'

'Sir, you know what I mean. Most of my employees are on the shop-floor, in the foundry shop, the grinding shop, the painting lab, the testing bench or the assembly shop. I have just a handful at my office. My question is whether these techniques like D&I will only work in the large IT companies or consulting MNCs or will it also be useful for a small-scale hydraulic pump manufacturer like me?'

'Vikas, do you know what the essence of D&I is? It is the simple philosophy of trust and respect. If this is actively present in your workplace, then you can assume that the starting point for D&I has already been achieved. Let me ask you a question—why do you hire people from your own community in the key roles at your office? Yes, it is because you trust them. What if you could learn to trust people different from you? What if women could do the job as well as the men? The most important thing is to not get blinded by assumptions that have got handed down decade after decade. When you include new and different people and also ensure that their ideas and perspectives are fully taken into consideration, then you are fully leveraging the power of D&I.'

D&I is often perceived as an organizational tool that can only be implemented by some organizations or certain industries. It is also seen as a cost-intensive measure with large organizations being able to allocate sizeable budgets in creating D&I programmes. However, even small businesses with just a handful of employees can leverage the benefit of a diverse and inclusive workplace to drive productivity and performance. In fact, it is in a small-sized operation that the full benefits of D&I can be unleashed with clear correlation.

Several small business owners often wonder how to get started on the D&I journey. For these entrepreneurs, the challenge lies in getting the ball rolling. In fact, once created, it is a far easier proposition to manage and monitor an inclusive culture in a small group, as compared to a large set-up. To start off, the first step would be to become self-aware about one's own biases and work towards eliminating their negative influence both from organizational decisions as well as the workplace in entirety. The leader or owner-manager is a powerful influence in a small or medium enterprise and his/her behaviour and language has a deep and abiding impact on the work environment. Becoming a role model who demonstrates how biases can be removed and how his/her particular business process can benefit from a conscious, mindful approach is a critical start to the journey. This behaviour is witnessed, absorbed and internalized by the group that constitutes the employee base and in turn it gets translated into the culture of the organization. Here, scale is of no essence. Consistent, authentic practice is.

The second part of the implementation is in creating a work environment where employees can bring their whole selves to the workplace. It is in the conscious encouragement of differing preferences, which in a small group can be positively incorporated. Acceptance and inclusion of different backgrounds, work styles and thinking processes ensures that the workplace is seen as a talent magnet, allowing the amalgamation of various perspectives. This 'inclusion' is a great competitive advantage for small- and medium-sized businesses since it generates very positive word of mouth, leading to top talent acquisition. In fact, for a company that is operating at a small or medium scale, engendering a diverse and inclusive work culture is a magnificent selling proposition.

The third part is in the setting up of policies and programmes. Inventive inclusion policies that drive flexibility, collective decision-making and acceptance of differing choices of life are a great way for small and medium enterprises (SMEs) to create powerful employer branding. Engaging employees as D&I champions who will not only decide on the way in which D&I gets practised and manifested but also promote the values by their own behaviour is a wonderful method to ensure engagement. In a small business, it is possible for every policy to be viewed through the D&I lens and to make positive changes. Innovative ways of inclusion can be ideated by a group and implemented to communicate that every employee is deeply valued. In an SME, when an inclusive way of thinking becomes habit, it enables the identification of the diverse needs of customers and ensures that new markets are tapped.

The most potent success secret for D&I to work in the case of a small/ medium enterprise is when the business owner makes it personal. When it is a clear personal priority for the leader, D&I comes alive, becomes a vibrant energy that resonates in every action. For this, the owner-manager does not need to be responsible for implementation; rather, his/her presence and consistent demonstration of the value of inclusion are sufficient to make a strong mark on his/her work base.

D&I GAME: EXPERIENCING DIVERSITY AND INCLUSION

This is both an individual and a group activity.

Go through the diverse categories of people mentioned in the left-hand side column of the following table. Schedule 30 minutes for this activity in your team/organization and invite people from the below-mentioned diversity strands. Ensure that there is at least one member from each diversity strand in the group. Once the team members are ready, handover printouts of the table to each person. Ask each person to try to envisage what could be the top three challenges faced by people from each diversity strand at workplace and write these in the right-hand side column. Allocate 10 minutes for people to fill their sheets. Every person in the group has to do this activity. For example, what do they think are the top three challenges faced by women in the team/organization?

Once every person has filled up the sheet, ask them to sit in a circle and discuss the challenges written by each person, and clarify the same with people from the respective diversity strand. For example, every-one would have written about the challenges faced by women. Clarify these with the women in the group and find out if the challenges written by others are just perceptions or reality. Carry forward these discussions for all the diversity strands from 1 to 10. Once the discussions are over, ask the team members to reflect on the following questions:

1. Which group did you learn the most about?

2. What challenges mentioned here surprised you? Why?

S. No.	Diversity Strand	Top Three Challenges Faced at Workplace
1.	Women	1. _____ 2. _____ 3. _____
2.	Different race	1. _____ 2. _____ 3. _____
3.	LGBTQIA	1. _____ 2. _____ 3. _____
4.	Persons with disability	1. _____ 2. _____ 3. _____
5.	Different cultural background	1. _____ 2. _____ 3. _____
6.	Vegetarian/non-vegetarian/vegan	1. _____ 2. _____ 3. _____
7.	Different language	1. _____ 2. _____ 3. _____
8.	Persons working in shifts	1. _____ 2. _____ 3. _____
9.	Different generation	1. _____ 2. _____ 3. _____
10.	Different country	1. _____ 2. _____ 3. _____

OBTAINING THE BUY-IN FOR A D&I AGENDA

Snow White began running. Stumbling over sharp stones and thick bushes, she ran for as long as she could. Dark tree trunks stood like frightening giants in the spooky wilderness. She realized what a narrow escape she had had a few moments ago. Thanks to the kindly huntsman, her life had been spared. He had disobeyed the evil instructions of her diabolic stepmother, the Queen, and left without killing Snow White.

Just when she felt that all the breath in her body had been knocked out, she chanced upon a beautiful small cottage. A house in the midst of this dense jungle! Everything about the house was tiny and seven in number—seven small beds, seven little chairs around a table, seven plates with bread, seven cups, seven glasses of milk. It looked like a slightly bigger version of a dollhouse.

Her hunger overcame fear and gulping down some slices of bread and downing a couple of glasses of milk, Snow White chose the largest among all the seven beds and instantly fell into a deep sleep.

At sunset, the seven dwarves who were the occupants of the little house came home. Doc, the leader of the dwarves along with Grumpy, Happy, Sleepy, Bashful, Sneezy and Dopey walked in and were shocked to see their food eaten and their milk gone. While they all wondered who could be responsible for this, Dopey, the seventh dwarf, looked at his bed and found a young girl lying there asleep. Crying out in amazement, he called out to the other dwarves and all of them looked at beautiful young Snow White.

Hearing their voices, Snow White woke up with a start and seeing the seven odd people gathered around her, screamed in fear.

'Don't worry, lass,' said Doc kindly. 'We are honest hard-working miners and will not harm you. Who are you?'

'I am Snow White,' she replied and looking at their faces, decided to trust them. She shared her sad story. The dwarves were shocked to hear that the Queen of their land could be so wicked, in trying to kill her own blameless young step-daughter. 'What a cruel woman! Don't you worry, Snow White. We shall take care of you,' said Doc.

'Doc, Doc!' called out Dopey in an exaggerated whisper. The Dwarves got into a huddle.

'Are you serious? Do you want her to live here?' asked Dopey.

'But what do we do?' said Happy. 'She looks so sweet and innocent. Our home will be a better place.'

'We don't have space in our home to accommodate one more person, that too a big human like her,' said Grumpy, his mind made up to send Snow White out.

'But it is the right thing to do. She is so young! Where will she go in this harsh forest? She could get killed,' said Bashful, his cheeks already turning red at the sight of a stranger.

'Hachoo!' began Sneezy, true to his name, and then continued in a rush. 'Forget about doing the right thing. Tell me, why should she be here? What use will she be for us? We have to make so many adjustments to have one more person here. Why should we? What if she harms us?'

'She will not,' said Doc firmly.

Taking courage from his words, Snow White decided to speak up. 'Kindly Sirs, I heard you talking about me. I promise you, if you let me stay here, then I will keep house for you, make your beds and clean the floor, cook your breakfast, lunch and supper, wash and sew your clothes!'

'We already do all of that. We don't need another person to do what we are already doing,' said Grumpy.

'Oh, wait! I can tell stories. I can tell the most enchanting stories you have ever heard,' said Snow White excitedly.

'That settles it,' said Doc. 'You can stay here.'

D&I has become an important part of the culture of many discerning organizations. The push for this usually comes from the leader—business or HR—whose focus is not just from the obvious ethical and moral viewpoint but also because it's good for business. A diverse workforce that feels engaged and committed to the organization's goals is a must-have today. This, therefore, leads to the setting of ambitious D&I targets.

Very often diversity enthusiasts look for concrete and credible reasons for why D&I is important for the organization. This is to ensure that the push for D&I is not just event-led but moves beyond to become part of the company culture, permeating even the small acts of workplace behaviour. Most often, driving D&I projects is not a full-time day job, it would be a second hat worn by folks passionate about inclusion. When employees are inspired by the cause of D&I, their buy-in is genuine and they demonstrate a willingness to go the extra mile.

Astute D&I leaders emphasize a plethora of positives while obtaining employee buy-in for an inclusive workplace. The return on investment (ROI) on diversity often features prominently and most leaders include a financial statement that points out the returns, not just financial but also from an engagement and productivity point of view. Strategizing the rewards emerging from D&I for all segments of the audience becomes necessary. Companies on a start-up mode could look at high employee engagement which could add to cash flow, while steady-state organizations will focus on how D&I creates shareholder value.

Senior HR leaders who have become passionate advocates of inclusion are able to articulate perfectly the key requirement on the CEO's mind and therefore obtain buy-in, both top-down and bottom-up. D&I is communicated as not an HR tool but a business solution. The inclusion strategy has to be presented to decision-makers as a solution to the challenges faced by business and not merely yet another tick in the box for HR. For this, data becomes very important and organizations seek benchmarking data in order to present their case accurately. Hard-nosed business leaders of large conglomerates will not support D&I just because it is trending within the HR community—it has to have data-backed logic which will lead to a big business change. The benefit of the transition has to be squared down to organizational success.

While the senior leadership team is most often thoroughly convinced about the necessity of a diverse workplace, the success or failure of its D&I agenda is in the gelling with the middle management team and employees down the hierarchy. How people managers and individual contributors pick up the thread of D&I and drive the chosen projects is what ensures the true success of the programme. For this, the D&I team needs many allies across the length and breadth of the organization. Seeking the help of influencers, functional heads who are opinion leaders, ensures that key decision-makers are on the side of D&I which allows their team-members to participate wholeheartedly in the process. When heads of horizontals are kept in the loop regarding D&I initiatives, it provides greater perspective and D&I is often seen as a business solution. Well-planned implementation of activities also leads to trust being created within the company.

DIVERSITY AND
TEAM DEVELOPMENT

Dear Diary,

Today is my second week at Inspirion. My team is a very interesting one—or so I feel. It could also be challenging! I have been placed in a team that is diverse in every possible way. We have two Americans, a Korean, an Indian single mother, a young millennial of 24 and, finally, me—gay, out and proud of it! What can I say, last week was a revelation. So many different approaches to work! I came to know that we did not really have a boss who managed us and that the work was just split and assigned to each of us as per our availability and workload. The team kind of self-manages itself and we each have our own deliverables to action. Our office is a beautiful multi-level, co-working type of space, verdant and green and with nice piped music in the common spaces. Hey, even our loo has music!

Yesterday was one of those very interesting days. I have worked in creative hotshops before, but this was something else. I began the draft of the marketing campaign for our marquee client and in the afternoon, we had a team huddle. I received several valuable insights and perspectives and it was wonderful to know that you could jam with people so different from you and yet reach a common decision. I am just really high on the energy and the diversity. I hope I am able to manage the conflicts also.

You see, I am not under any illusion that diversity always only means the positives. In my last job, we were just three of us in a team and boy was it conflict-filled! We each had our own unique point of view, we did not want to give up our ideas and it always ended with a huge fight. You know what, I am even okay with the out and open fights. What I cannot handle are those passive aggressive silences. You just don't know what to do and you feel so utterly alone. I really hope Inspirion is not one of those places.

Lee Gardenswartz and Anita Rowe in their book *Diverse Teams at Work* speak about the big myth that 'Potential for conflict is greater with diverse teams.' This is indeed a myth, since conflict is universal among all kinds of teams. Heterogeneity or homogeneity has nothing to do with the prospects for conflict that a team has. It is true that diverse teams are not specifically more conflict-ridden than non-diverse teams.

There are the more obvious, visible aspects of diversity such as gender, age and ability. And there are the largely invisible, 'below the iceberg' type of identity aspects such as the style of working, of thinking, cross-functional aspects and work experience, which cause an equal amount of conflict in teams that on the surface appear to be cohesive.

In truth, it is easier to manage any conflict that arises out of diversity. Let me explain. In organizations where the source of conflict has clearly been seen to emerge from diversity—either gender, culture or ethnicity—the solution too is quite simple. It calls for education. Companies that have embarked upon a journey to gender inclusion, for instance, have found sensitivity training to be very effective. This means that both men and women undergo sessions on gender intelligence, informing them how to most effectively work with people of the opposite gender. Similarly, cultural/ethnic intelligence can be created by providing information and insights on how people from different backgrounds work and function. This paves a path to better understanding and ensures that people from different ethnic groups, languages and cultures are able to effectively work together.

DIVERSITY AND PROBLEM-SOLVING

The Lion King Singa strolled into the green glade where his council of ministers, led by the able Prime Minister, she-elephant Gaja, were deep in discussion. Without wanting to disturb their thought process (which always seemed to get disrupted upon his arrival and veer off-course), Singa quickly stepped back into the grape vine arbour where he could observe them without being discovered.

Mayil, the peacock, was speaking animatedly. 'And so, Madam Gaja, my point of view is that we should look at the trees which have fruit right at the top and begin protecting them from the winter-worms. The tress which are at eye level are anyways easily managed by us.'

'And that is where the conflict lies, Mr Mayil,' interjected the Chief Treasurer, Cerf, a handsome white-tailed elk. 'What is eye level to you might not be at eye level for everyone else.'

'But, Sir Cerf, what I am suggesting is for the benefit and well-being of all, not just those animals and birds of my build or stature. I am merely pointing out something that is seen by me, due to my height, but which might not be visible to all. But the problem is a common one, which impacts all of us.'

'It appears to me, Mr Mayil that you are only focusing on the problem which is seen by you. What about the other challenges seen by others? For instance, Commander Snake has been complaining about the sharp cracks in the earth which might be very dangerous for all!' said Cerf, raising his voice a decibel higher than normal.

Just as Singa decided to intervene, he heard the calm yet firm tones of Madam Gaja. She had not been elected Prime Minister for nothing. 'Mr Mayil and Treasurer Cerf, both your points are valid. And both bear merit discussion. As a team, we have the advantage of diversity. This is our strength. We are therefore able to draw upon different points of view brought by each of you. What we now need to do is finalize which decision is more critical and time-bound for the well-being of the entire forest. Mind you, all points are important—just that they are not urgent all at the same time. Keeping this is mind, we can prioritize our action points.'

Singa entered the glade to listen to the decisions being taken.

One of the most important benefits of encouraging diversity in your team is the big advantage it brings to problem-solving. In order to fully leverage the power of diversity, it is critical to ensure that inclusion is practised. Inclusion ensures that every member of the team is fully engaged, is concerned about solving problems for the team and is unafraid to bring his or her perspectives to the table.

A diverse team that has a good combination of people with different approaches to issues, life experiences and work backgrounds has a much higher probability of solving problems faced by business than a highly qualified homogenous team. The same holds true for creativity and out-of-the-box thinking. For businesses that rely heavily on creative solutions to problems, it is imperative to cultivate the capability to encourage diverse discussion.

As Scott Page says in his book *The Diversity Bonus*, a diverse team is often compared to an investment portfolio put together by an astute fund manager, yet it is not the same at all. While a fund would perform as well as the average, the diverse team performs as optimally as its best. When diverse team members share ideas, the team catalyses the ideas and make them even better.

The role of a leader, thus, is twofold—(a) to create a diverse team carefully and (b) to ensure that the team has a conducive working environment and culture to be able to share all its members' ideas for the benefit of the team

DIVERSITY AND PROFITABILITY

DAY 39/99

Interviewer: Ms Mahmoud, as the Global HR Head of EarthStyle, you must be thrilled with your 2018 annual report which states that the company has delivered greater profitability than before. And what's more interesting is that this research (points to a report) on your performance shows that it coincides with a higher number of women candidates hired by your company. I think is it safe to say that we can put all concerns about 'selling' diversity to your leadership at EarthStyle to rest. If diversity and profitability are so deeply linked, then, we can just leave it to your board and shareholders to insist that there should be diversity in the company! Am I right?

Ms Mahmoud: Well, I believe that diversity is such a powerful cultural tool that it should not need laws or policies or even profits in order to unleash its positive influence. It is the most impactful concept to have hit our workplaces in the past couple of decades. Diversity helps various aspects of the business. Instead of trying to force-fit an explanation as to how diversity has helped performance, I would suggest that we actually look at the business value offered by the diversity of the team.

Interviewer: How so?

Ms Mahmoud: Diversity, in order to deliver its best possible outcome, requires to be allowed to influence all your HR policies. The hallmark of a successful diversity agenda in a company is the extent to which each employee is enabled to perform to the fullest of his or her potential. Articulating which aspects of your business are impacted by a diverse team is the next step. Subsequently, you must think how your team can achieve different business goals through their unique diverse talents. Let us not assume that every member of your team knows their value and the special strength they bring to the team—it is the job of the leader to clearly identify the many skills that a diverse team brings to the table. This includes both cognitive diversity as well as identity diversity. For instance, we discovered that there was a significant segment of our customer base which consisted of the 'silver' generation of people who have just retired and also soon-to-be mothers. The head of our product development team got his team which consisted of both gender diverse as well as generationally diverse individuals to draw upon their personal experiences with these cohorts and understand how to serve them better. Thus, these two strands of diversity have directly led to better business insights, which has enabled to post higher levels of profitability!

In the past decade, we have seen the emergence of specific research that states the correlation between higher levels of diversity in the workforce (especially gender and race) and profitability. An analysis in 2016 by the Peterson Institute of Industrial Economics is among the most comprehensive, looking at global data pulled from 21,980 firms across 91 countries. This study, along with others by McKinsey, Sodexo and BCG, suggests that there is a strong correlation between the presence of different forms of diversity (such as gender, race, ability, minorities, underprivileged and LGBT) and the profitability of the organization.

This profitability is demonstrated to be not a causal relationship, which means that the sheer presence of diverse talent is not sufficient to lead to profits, but a correlation linked to factors such as creativity (more new products created per annum), better problem-solving (ability to remain resilient during crises) and improved innovation (different customer segments addressed). Researchers found that greater gender diversity for instance led to an improvement in the firm's skill diversity.

However, the contra-view also states that other factors which positively correlate with better profitability such as firm size, industry and national attributes also are related to greater diversity in the workplace. As such, it is important not to hard-sell diversity as a direct influencer of profits. The change in culture and behaviour brought about by the presence of diversity is the leading indicator that must be focused on. Take the case of enhanced decision-making, which diversity promotes simply by encouraging greater debate and access to more perspectives. This, in turn, leads to robust customer focus, solid business practices and astute risk-taking, thereby impacting profitability.

Even more critical for today's talent managers is the fact that a diverse workforce is seen as the hallmark of a successful, contemporary and 'cool' place to work. Thus, it has a direct effect on the war for talent. Ensuring that your workplace is a talent magnet for all types of diverse candidates is the surest way to create a successful and, therefore, profitable organization.

WORDFINDER

Z	W	L	P	S	L	B	B	B	Y	R	P	H	L	R	B	D	W	W	G	I	W
V	E	E	R	X	Q	O	K	C	G	Q	E	Y	D	F	M	F	E	A	W	Q	F
N	A	V	O	C	B	Z	C	K	J	C	E	H	E	W	E	R	U	T	L	U	C
Z	N	R	D	U	Y	B	Q	V	J	Y	R	F	J	I	F	F	A	S	E	O	B
N	S	U	U	N	Y	S	B	I	B	F	G	S	K	G	X	J	N	C	T	I	K
E	N	C	C	N	G	S	I	H	G	Y	R	F	Z	F	E	B	N	S	V	I	H
C	E	Z	T	Z	D	M	S	N	B	U	O	C	N	Q	D	P	U	T	X	B	A
A	G	U	D	C	Z	F	X	W	Y	R	U	T	B	J	N	R	A	B	I	J	G
R	L	J	I	S	E	Q	S	W	U	E	P	S	F	N	I	G	L	G	U	Y	I
L	E	Z	V	O	V	Z	V	S	X	E	N	O	U	C	Y	I	H	W	V	Z	H
W	E	L	E	O	X	V	M	E	X	R	E	E	B	M	T	A	O	G	O	A	R
F	R	H	R	F	H	T	U	L	Y	A	T	K	N	U	I	W	U	O	R	G	S
P	F	G	S	E	P	X	Y	O	L	C	W	J	B	N	S	K	R	H	V	X	X
T	F	A	I	Y	K	V	E	R	J	E	O	W	W	Y	R	O	S	J	H	E	F
W	P	D	F	S	W	A	O	R	J	E	R	E	U	T	E	Q	C	D	T	A	A
K	F	C	I	P	Q	A	K	E	S	R	K	Q	G	A	V	X	O	Y	O	V	G
D	P	K	C	Y	M	U	J	D	V	F	V	Q	P	C	I	P	N	S	A	D	G
Z	J	I	A	D	P	E	E	N	R	K	G	Y	O	B	D	L	T	L	W	K	J
S	L	D	T	Q	E	V	M	E	S	A	V	H	U	W	S	Z	R	A	U	P	G
R	O	F	I	L	C	R	G	G	F	E	E	G	V	F	A	R	A	Q	Y	Y	H
Q	K	Z	O	L	W	N	A	Q	S	R	P	D	B	Q	Z	O	C	X	F	Y	J
N	K	W	N	W	K	M	J	G	U	B	E	I	D	X	O	T	P	I	G	P	

WORDS

Peer group network	Product diversification
Annual hours contract	Gender roles
Culture	Break-free career
U-curve	Free-Gens
Race	Diversity index

SECTION 5

DEMYSTIFYING DIVERSITY IN YOUR WORKPLACE

DIVERSITY AND INCLUSION LEXICON

S. No.	Words	Definition
1.	D&I champions	Organizations which are strong advocates of the concepts of diversity, inclusion and equality and have achieved significant milestones in the D&I space through specifically targeted initiatives
2.	Diversity capability	The ability of an organization to embed diversity in its organizational culture
3.	Diversity consciousness	An attitude of welcoming and integrating diverse employees in an organization
4.	Marginalization	Social exclusion; the placement of minority groups and cultures outside mainstream society
5.	Minority	Refers to a person who has historically been in the demographic minority in the overall population sample
6.	Pay disparity	Unequal pay distribution amongst individuals in the workforce who are on the same job role

Hi, I am Shiva. I am an MT at Parson & Fibro (P&F), working in the Group Corporate HR department for the past four months. I was damn thrilled when I got selected on campus, because P&F is one of those companies that is a true-blue Indian icon. It was on my dream-company list, no less! After induction, I got posted in Group HR, which is brilliant, because I get such a comprehensive view of what is happening. It is tough sometimes, but overall I would say the learning has been great. But you know what? The best part of my job is that I am working on the D&I agenda at P&F.

You see, there's a bit of context I need to share. P&F like some of India's other distinguished conglomerates has been busy expanding its footprints. So much has been happening over the past couple of decades, that I personally think (and don't quote me on this) that P&F has kind of got left behind in the D&I game.

Not that it is a game that needs to be won, but the problem is that while P&F might be known for things like going abroad to secure assets such as mines or creating cutting-edge intellectual properties, they are not seen as a contemporary, inclusive company.

I think it has to do with the culture here at P&F. After growing organically for many years and having presence in all important Indian markets, P&F got into a tie-up with the European MNC, Arulette, and now suddenly we have offices and manufacturing units in 26 international locations.

And that is where the problem lies. All of a sudden, we are thrust into a global environment and everyone is speaking terms such as LGBTQ, generational diversity and inclusive growth, and we don't know what's happening. So, this cross-functional team has been created to drive the agenda for D&I. I report to this team and our job is to suggest the best possible route for P&F to become 'D&I compliant'. I have been clocking 17-hour days, trying to put the data together. I have so much data that I could just do a PhD on what it means to be a diverse and inclusive company in India.

But here's my problem. All this data will not work if we don't have an inspiring leader to charge us with motivation. Our CEO is a great guy, very successful, a role model, a home-grown hero of P&F who joined here as an MT (like me) and is today the CEO. But somehow, he does not speak the right language. He still seems a bit conservative, says these off-colour jokes in meetings and seems to want a lot of convincing.

I feel we need a D&I champion—a person who is respected, whose opinions are valued and who actually lives the value. For you see, D&I can't be just an organizational agenda. It has to be something that the person is deeply, personally, passionate about. But then again, it should not be like he/she is evangelizing it. Then it will come across as some kind of social activism and that will obviously not gel at P&F at all. We need someone who is very good at business, understands the purpose of D&I, but at the same time is not doing it just as a dry must-do. Yes, it's going to be tough.

Several organizations embark upon an ambitious D&I agenda only to find it running out of steam pretty soon. The D&I implementation team could be full of excited, enthusiastic folks who are keen on driving positive and measurable change within the organization and focusing on multidimensional solutions. A solid measurement plan could be in place. Yet, some organizations are able to quickly get the benefits of D&I to be visible and palpable within the workplace, while others struggle for a long time with no apparent progress. To achieve true organizational D&I, the efforts need to go beyond the action points.

Here is where senior leadership makes a critical difference. When senior leaders become champions of D&I and commit to both personal and organizational change, it sets the tone for the rest of the organization to follow suit. On the other hand, when the C-suite treats D&I as yet another low-impact engagement jamboree, it fizzles out even before it has a chance to create change. Mid-level managers who are truly passionate about the potential that an inclusive workplace can bring soon become frustrated and discouraged at the lack of resonance of D&I with senior management, and all the effort is wasted.

A D&I champion is usually a senior leadership representative, from any of the functions of the organization. The CEO herself could be the D&I champion, but here, the key requirement is not the weight of the position, but the fact that there is a certain amount of personal commitment that the leader brings to the table. The D&I champion is a secure role model focused on the action, not interested in empty sloganeering or hogging the limelight. Instead a lot of his/her work gets done behind the scenes, mentoring, rather than monitoring. He/she is comfortable dirtying his/her hands with the last detail of the action plan, yet holds a certain amount of magical hope that the success of an effective diverse and inclusive culture is more than just the numbers. He/she is particular about who is part of the D&I action team, aware of his/her limitations and, therefore, seeks to bring complementary strengths into the picture.

The effective D&I champion is a keen teacher, eager to pass on what he/she has learned to others. In a world filled with sceptics, he/she is thrilled and excited about the possibility of change and his/her enthusiasm overcomes even the most jaded cynic. But this cannot just come from mere words; the track record of the D&I champion in other areas, in his/her own functional role, is important. His/her credibility in making things happen is the first qualification to bring him/her into reckoning as a D&I champion.

Identifying the perfect D&I champion for your organizational voyage could be the most critical piece in the puzzle. The process can sometimes be slow and intimidating, but the success of a D&I champion is not just in recruitment or retention numbers, but when every employee in the organization feels included and hence empowered to take individual accountability. When co-workers begin noticing biases, then your D&I culture is well and truly alive.

Facing objections that D&I is yet another HR spin, the D&I champion focuses on real and measurable change, with his/her 'propaganda' detector firmly in place. He/she is authentic, has a log-term perspective and speaks from the heart. The jargon is used sparingly, the corporate mumbo-jumbo rejected and the tired clichés eliminated from the mission. The true D&I champion is practical and positive.

DAY
43/99

HALLMARKS OF AN INCLUSIVE COLLEAGUE

Dusk had just fallen in the forest and the last drops of rain filtered through the golden light. The hypnotic rhythm of the pattering rain which had dominated the atmosphere receded slowly and allowed the other sounds of the forest to gently fill the silence. Birds which had rested till then began singing from a distant tree, while the persistent squirrel chattered away.

Singa, the Lion King, stood majestic and proud next to the gigantic mountain cave that was his abode during the monsoons. The warm scent of the wet earth mixed with the dense carpet of foliage rose like fragrant smoke. Singa was waiting for his Prime Minister Gaja, the elephant, to arrive. She was, uncharacteristically, a bit late. 'The sudden downpour would have held her back,' he thought to himself.

Just then, he heard the sound of branches snagging and the squish of damp leaves underfoot. 'My sincere apologies, Oh monarch!' said Gaja a bit breathless as she arrived at the glade. Singa smiled and welcomed Gaja in. It had been some time since the King had held court. Every rainy season, he loved to take a retreat at this cave, watching the rain dance in the valley. And it was Gaja's responsibility to update him from time to time on what was happening at his court. In that sense, she was the de facto leader in his absence.

'It's alright Madam Gaja. I realize you must have got caught in the rain,' said Singa kindly.

'On the contrary, the rains, I love, your highness. They cleanse everything and I would not mind getting completely drenched. And I have to say that no rain has the power to stop a herd of elephants from crossing. That was not the reason for my delay. I was held back in an orientation that I was giving to our new minister for the treasury, the Turtle.'

'You have a new Treasury Minister, again??' Singa sounded incredulous. 'But you just selected another treasury minister not even five seasons ago! You seem to be losing a lot of people in that role, Madam Gaja. Have you thought about it?'

'Yes, your highness and that is the reason for this orientation,' answered Gaja before continuing. 'I realize that our court is not exactly welcoming of new people,' she said a little sheepishly. 'A lot of the newly appointed ministers and courtiers who arrive at your court are often left to sink or swim by themselves.'

'Sink or swim!' Singa's voice came close to an angry growl. 'Are we talking about children here? Ours is a respected court adorned by great warriors and strategists. All adults, not children. We are led by the laws of the jungle. To sink or swim is a choice that the newly appointed functionary has to make. Doesn't he want to perform well? Justify his selection? Why should anyone else be responsible for his job??'

'Things are changing, Oh wise Lord,' said Gaja carefully choosing her words. 'There is a labour crunch in the jungle. And if we do not ensure that our new employees feel included, we will continue to lose more people.'

'Madam Gaja, you have been a young minister at my great father's grand court. Today you are my Prime Minister. Did anyone

109

"orient" you? Everyone is here because they possess certain traits or qualities. They and they alone are responsible for how they fulfil their responsibilities. This is how it has been at the grand court for as long as I can remember. The jobs are demanding and nobody has the time to orient new people.'

'Pardon me, My Lord, but that is the reason we are having such a turnover. Our court is not inclusive. Our ministers do not know how to be inclusive colleagues.'

'I agree Madam Gaja that times are changing. But what do you propose to do? Change everyone's thinking?'

'I hope to create a court, your Highness, which will demonstrate both "belongingness" and "uniqueness". Everyone—not just new recruits—will have to feel that they are part of a group, but still special on their own. For this to happen, our court will have to learn the skills of being inclusive. Every courtier has to be an inclusive colleague!'

The twin attributes of 'uniqueness' and 'belongingness' are the hallmark of a truly inclusive workplace. Research proves that when employees feel a sense of being included on account of both (a) their special uniqueness and (b) by being part of the larger collective, they will go above and beyond their defined KRAs. In organizational behaviour terms, this is known as the demonstration of 'discretionary effort'.

In the mix of actions directed towards 'diversity' and 'inclusion', the latter takes pre-eminence. While diversity is achievable in a relatively shorter time frame through focused efforts, it is not sustainable in the absence of inclusion. Mere diversity may even result in a tower of Babel style dissonance, when the glue of inclusion is missing. Leaders who are unaware of the power of small, hardly noticeable actions in the line of inclusion are often surprised by the rate of attrition of their employees, in spite of having a highly visible diversity agenda.

Support and belongingness ensure that inclusion is fostered in the workplace. Apart from a clear objective that allows every voice in the room to be heard, inclusion also ensures the coming together of various forces of diversity, young and old, gay or straight, thinkers and doers, senior and junior, black and white, extrovert and introvert, male and female. Inclusion, when inculcated assiduously, proves to be the headwind against organizational politics.

An inclusive workplace focuses both on a long-term commitment as well as short-term everyday behaviours. Active listening in teams is the first hallmark of an inclusive workplace. Apportioning of individual responsibility, creation of trust between team members, the absence of rank-pulling and a clear process for conflict resolution are other significant features.

An inclusive colleague is a perceptive one. He/she is sensitive to the emotions and moods of her teammates and is keenly observant of any changes in behaviour. He/she has an intuitive knack for sensing the motivations and needs of his/her colleagues. Often, such a co-worker is able to gain insights from what appears to be unrelated occurrences. He/she demonstrates the uncanny ability to manage complex social situations with elegant grace and confidence.

Today, the competency of inclusive workplace behaviour is considered an important arrow in the quiver of organizational must-haves for growth and progress. D&I training helps to foster the spirit of inclusion in the workplace. It provides employees with an opportunity to extricate themselves from day-to-day preoccupations and work on the essential skills of inclusion and empathy. Most employees find themselves naturally inclined towards inclusive behaviour. But here's a caveat—this is possible only in an environment where inclusion is actively pursued and encouraged as a workplace value and behaviour.

Disciple: Oh Master, I would like to seek your permission to visit the village.

Master: Ananta, may I know why you would like to go to the village which we consider a distraction from our duties and our discipline?

Disciple: Master, I wish to confirm something for myself by observing it in the village. It is for this purpose that I wish to visit the village.

Master: Ananta, I bid you to explain this to me, without further ado. You know that I get impatient when people beat around bushes.

Disciple: A thousand apologies, oh venerable Master! Let me explain my line of thought. I have been observing that our two new students—Gita and Kumar are very alike. They belong to different genders, of course, Gita being a young girl of 13 while Kumar is a year older and a boy, but both have the very same approach to everything. In fact, yesterday, I had asked the class to sort out the palm leaf manuscripts and noticed that both Gita and Kumar decided to sort them from oldest to newest, without looking at the subjects in the manuscripts. I found this quite fascinating. In spite of their coming from different families, different social backgrounds and of course, different genders, it seems that by virtue of their upbringing in the same village, they both think alike. I want to observe children in the village and decide if they have the same influences which make them think alike.

Master: Wonderful, Ananta! I am delighted with your discovery! Yes, you are right. It is possible for people who are different on the outside to be similar on the inside, due to the same influences that they go through while growing up. Thus, people who belong to different generations or genders or socio-economic classes might share similar perspectives. As such, the diversity they bring to a team might actually not be diversity at all! However, Ananta, I must warn you that the opposite is also true. People who are different on the outside also turn out different on the inside. For instance, people from the same ethnicity might share common ideas which might be different from people of other ethnicities. Two women might have more in common than two men. Have I made myself clear, Ananta?

Over the past few decades, the increased focus on the benefits of having a diverse workforce has resulted in many organizations starting off the diversity journey. When companies embark upon a diversity agenda, the first steps are usually to focus on increasing diversity of gender, age or ability. These are the 'visible' aspects of diversity or what is referred to as identity diversity.

The aspect of diversity which lies unseen is known as cognitive diversity. This has been defined variously as the differences in perspective, problem-solving behaviour or information processing methods that individuals possess. When speaking about cognitive diversity, we refer to the way in which people think about and relate to different situations. The full range of analytical, computational or conceptual differences that a set of people bring to a discussion defines the cognitive diversity of the team.

Research shows that the correlation between identity diversity and cognitive diversity has still fully not been proven. While in the early stages of the diversity focus, organizations can find great benefits from simply emphasizing identity differences, over a period of time, cognitive diversity appears more useful for leveraging the full benefit of diverse learning styles and experiences.

Cognitive Diversity and Identity Diversity

D&I GAME: EXPERIENCING DIVERSITY AND INCLUSION

DIVERSITY BIODATA—DEMYSTIFYING DIVERSITY

This is both an individual and a group activity. Please refer to the frame fan that follows (Figure 5.1). It has several aspects related to the identity of an individual. It represents the various traits about our personality, that is, our diverse self. This activity will take approximately 30 minutes.

PART 1

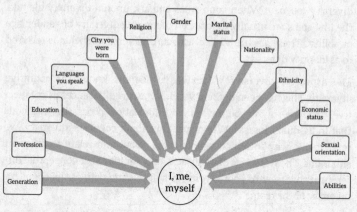

Figure 5.1. Diversity Frame Fan.

Source: Dr Saundarya Rajesh and Nisha Chandran.

Please take photocopies of Figure 5.2 (illustrated in the next page) and share it with your team members. Using Figure 5.1 as a reference, please fill up Figure 5.2 with various aspects related to your diverse self. Once every team member has completed filling up his/her sheet, discuss the following questions:

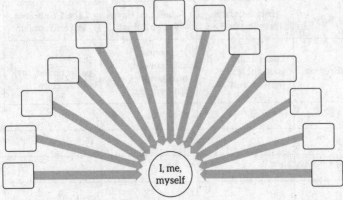

Figure 5.2. Diversity Frame Fan.

Source: Dr Saundarya Rajesh and Nisha Chandran.

1. How many team members have certain traits/aspects that are similar to yours?

2. What new aspect did each person discover about another team member?

3. How is the diversity within your team contributing towards diversity of thoughts, creativity, problem-solving and innovation at the workplace?

Once every person has spoken, move on to Part 2 of the activity.

PART 2: LABELS

Labels refer to the words and phrases we use to describe other people. It can have a positive or a negative connotation.

Please take photocopies of the following table, distribute it to people in the group and ask them to fill it. Each person has to write about what kind of labels others have assigned to him/her, starting from their childhood, later on during adolescence/college life and then at the workplace. Similarly, each person has to write about what kind of labels they have given others. Lastly, write about what labels each person has assigned himself/herself.

S. No.	Labels Others Have Put on You	Labels You Have Put on Others	Labels You Have Put on Yourself
Example	Lucky, bully, good girl, stupid, perfectionist, etc.	Hypocrite, disorganized, transgender, different, etc.	Brave, perfectionist, introvert, etc.
1.			
2.			
3.			
4.			

Once each person has filled his/her sheet, start discussing each column. The following questions can be used to start the discussion:

1. Going back in your life's journey, how did you feel when you realized that others have given you a certain label, especially when you were a child? What did you feel when you were labelled by others during your adolescence/college life? How did these experiences affect your outlook towards others and life in general?

2. When you labelled another person in a certain way, what were your thoughts behind that? How do you think it would have impacted the other person?

3. When you assigned certain labels to yourself with a negative connotation (consciously or unconsciously), how did it affect your thinking and your potential? Did it lead to self-limiting beliefs or thoughts? How did labels with positive connotation affect your mindset, attitude and outlook towards life?

Dear Diary,

Today, I obtained a very different definition for D&I.

Like in the past four days, today also, my team and I were sitting out of the 13th-floor conference room at our Ahmedabad office, working furiously on the machine learning product launch. Non-stop 9 hours, none of us had even taken a break for lunch. It was evening and a beautiful sunset displayed myriad colours and reflected off the gorgeous waterfront of Lake Kankaria. Even though we all were very stressed out because of the terrible deadline we had to keep for the project, the pleasant evening made us all relaxed and reflective.

Shalaba and I went out to get coffee and cookies, and as soon as we got back, all of a sudden, the talk turned to education and the low numbers of girls from underprivileged families who were graduating from colleges. Ujjwala spoke about how the 17-year-old daughter of her home help ran off with a 40-year-old man who was abusive and alcoholic and wondered whether a good education could have prevented this.

That was when Deepak suddenly became all passionate and emotional. He mentioned that our company's focus on diversity was all skewed. He said that what we meant by D&I was all about conducting events and having fun and this was of no use really. Even in the best of companies, D&I was just a mere tool for organizational productivity enhancement, whereas it had to be more.

Santhosh tried to calm him down by saying that inclusion itself was a great cultural framework and very few organizations were truly inclusive. Deepak didn't agree and said that these days, companies look at diversity as being about demographics and identities, while in reality, it should be about caring for the society. Santhosh countered that organizational inclusion is equally important and it is all about leveraging diversity to achieve superior performance. It looked like they both would argue for quite a bit.

That was when Deepak began speaking about social justice. He mentioned that there was a very high incidence of young teenage girls being married off in the slums of India. 'D&I has to work on managing the problems of the society,' he said. 'It can't just be about creativity and employee engagement.' And then he started speaking about this NGO that he volunteers for, Project PUTHRI, which works with young adolescent girls and skills them on career intentionality.

At the end of the conversation, I felt what Deepak said was absolutely true. Should not D&I be about lifting the moral fibre of the organization?? Yes, it's indeed correct that D&I has brought attention to the idea that having different people in the workforce with divergent views is good. But should it stop with merely looking at productivity and employee engagement as the outcomes? Should it not lead to the creation of an environment of respect and trust? I feel D&I should actually make the organization a better, nicer, fairer place to work in. And Deepak is right. It should not stop there, it should extend its arms out into the society and make sure that the community is engaged in creating better outcomes. D&I should actually have social justice as its goal.

The vision of a fair and just society emerges as one that is accepting of all kinds of people and provides everyone an equal opportunity to grow. In fact, a truly just society is one which focuses on equity (customized measures of support for each individual) than equality (the same support for everyone, notwithstanding their background and context). Research states that when systems become inclusive, they lead to growth and development for all, not just those sections which are required to be included.

Most of the time, the strict standard which is easily accepted into any system, be it organizational or social, is one that looks at the able-bodied, young, conventionally intelligent, successful, attractive, thin, preferably male stereotype. It appears that society expects everyone within the bell curve to conform to the middle. Those who fall outside the range are seen as not just divergent, but abnormal too. Diversity practitioners know that heterogeneity and not homogeneity is the real norm. Yet, from a societal point of view, all inclusion is tough and difficult to achieve because of the enormous amount of bias and prejudice which permeates the majority.

Today, many large corporate groups define D&I not just as something to be achieved within the workplace but also as an effort to influence the ecosystem around the organization. To these discerning establishments, social justice in the form of inclusion of all marginalized groups of people is not a destination, but a continuous process which recognizes the dignity of each individual and accords the necessary respect and inclusion within its framework.

[Scene: It is a narrow staircase. Raj is running up the stairs to a class that he has signed up for on AI. He enters the class, to find that he is late and all the students are already seated with the trainer addressing the class.]

Trainer: So, as I said, the Bayesian probability method is one of the main systems... (noticing Raj) Hello! Mr Gupta, am I right?

Raj (Shuffling embarrassedly): Yes, Mr Starsky. I am so sorry. I thought the class was starting only at 6:30 (and noticing Chander, quickly gets seated in a chair next to Chander).

Ross: Chander! Chander! (He whispers hoarsely, but Chander appears to be immersed in the lecture.) Why did you not text me before starting?

Chander: Wow! Convenient. Listen Raj, the texting was supposed to be done by you.

Raj: Me? (Looks puzzled and then confounded.) What the hell? Didn't we decide that we would text each other before getting to class? I distinctly remember that we agreed to this last night during dinner.

Chander: In my defence, it was late and you said you would text!

Raj (sadly): I thought you were my buddy.

Jay (who is sitting across the aisle from Ross): Raj, you did say that you would text us all. (This time angrily) And am I not your buddy?

Raj (in a louder whisper): Jay! Even you didn't text me. It's so unfair. What about the girls?? Did anyone text them?

Chander: Mona, Prabha and Ranjana are all here and no one texted them. They just landed up text-less.

Raj (he searches for the girls and find that all three of them are seated directly behind him): Hey, hey!!

Jay: Come on, it's not like we ordered pizza without you.

Raj (addressing the girls): Girls, girls! None of you texted me.

Prabha: Come on Raj, you are in quality control, you are supposed to be persistent.

Chander: Next time, remind me with an email on www.i-don't-care-that-much.com.

Mona and Ranjana: Stop talking! The trainer is watching.

Raj (after sometime): Well, not all of us are alike. Some of us like being texted to. Some of us like being 'inducted' into the system, reminded, made feel a part of the group. Some of us want our buddies to keep a watch on us, tell us from time to time what to do, how it is done, when it is done. It's a new place. I, for one, like to have a reliable buddy around when I am in a new place. I feel included!

Trainer: So, Mr Gupta, would you like to share with the group your thoughts on 'the probability trap'?

D&I is a cultural factor to be experienced from day 1 in the office environment. While most new hires begin their first day on the job with a sense of excitement and anticipation, this can easily be diminished if they don't feel a sense of belongingness. Companies which use buddy systems to create a positive first impression and answer FAQs have discovered that this is a great way for new employees to get a first-hand sense of an inclusive environment.

The buddy is usually a peer who is able to build a personal connection between the organization and the new hire. When inclusive action is brought into play, the buddy is more empathetic and sensitive and goes beyond the basics to ensure that the new recruit gains confidence. The essential qualities of inclusive behaviour call upon the buddy to provide support beyond the formal orientation period and even underscore the positive impression that would have been created during induction.

The selection of a buddy, therefore, becomes important, since the ideal buddy is someone who is well-integrated into the system and understands the culture of D&I well enough to demonstrate it. Some organizations also have training programmes for buddies where apart from the routine FAQ information which is provided, a reinforcement of the D&I thought also takes place. Large organizations prefer this as it ensures consistency in the way the buddy system is managed through the workplace.

In the triumvirate of mentoring, coaching and buddy systems—all three of which help the employee to feel engaged, learn better, stay motivated and perform effectively—buddy mechanisms are probably the most important touch point for driving a sense of inclusion. Even the simple act of answering questions can be an experience in creating a feeling of non-judgemental acceptance. The buddy helps the new employee understand the system better, provides inputs on how concerns can be voiced and gives a peer's viewpoint of the systems and processes that drive the organization in a manner that reflects inclusion.

DAY
48/99

D&I METRICS

Kumar had taken over as the Diversity Point of Contact at Saswat & Co. This was double hatting; his day job was that of the AVP— Sales (North region), yet he did not feel burdened. On the contrary, he had actually put up his hand and asked for this role when the Diversity Council announced it. This was the first time that D&I as an initiative was being rolled out at Saswat. The council was a high-powered one on which a few of the board members sat and of course his MD. This was a super opportunity to learn new things, experiment and actually quell the ennui of his routine daily role, Kumar thought. And last but not the least, a fab platform to impress his super bosses! He was excited as he read up on the trends of diversity. The excitement turned into reflection and reflection into concern as he realized that this was an ocean. Two weeks later, at the inaugural Diversity Council meeting, Kumar was slightly nervous as he presented his vision for what he hoped to achieve. As the meeting progressed it was clear that this was not something to be taken lightly. The council asked a lot of questions, but the one question that stayed with him was what Ms Abha, Senior Lawyer and Independent Director on the Board of Saswat, had to ask—'How do you actually measure something as fundamental and esoteric as diversity? What metrics can you use to quantify the change in a person's belief system??' Kumar pondered the point. 'What do I expect out of D&I?' he thought to himself. 'Is it a mindset change, or an actual difference in the workforce composition or is it both? Should I present a plan that looks at recruitment and advancement or at workshops and sensitization programmes? What if my line of thinking was totally flawed and resulted in absolutely no change at all?'

The start of a diversity journey means setting of goals for your organization. Like the old adage goes—what gets measured gets managed. Metrics for D&I initiatives are usually a combination of both the soft and the hard. While numbers and targets are essential to show a 'visible' difference in your organizational demographics, it is equally important to also look at what cannot be seen—the inside of your employee's mind. To put it simply, numbers and quotas are your 'diversity' goals, while programmes that enable your colleagues' mindsets and thinking to change are your 'inclusion' objectives. The one will not work without the other. Whatever be the 'age' of your D&I journey, it is very important to begin with both these ends in mind. Diversity goals refer to who is in the room; inclusion goals measure if each of their voices is heard.

A good first step to diversity metrics would be to obtain all data around your organizational demographics—men versus women, recruitment and advancement of each, employees who fall under various diversity clusters (such as persons with disability, generational cohorts and LGBT population), etc. This will provide a great state-of-organization reality check. Going a little deeper into the culture of the company, by way of focus groups and audits will help to peel away the top layer and point to what lies below. Armed with this data, you can begin setting your D&I metrics.

D&I ACTION PLANS AND BUSINESS GOALS

The Kurukshetra war between the 5 Pandava brothers and the 100 Kauravas had just finished with the former winning the encounter and establishing the rule under King Yudhishtra. It had been a bloody battle with huge losses on both sides, but more than the lives that were lost, the many treacherous and wily incidents left a truly nasty aftertaste. Uncles and cousins turned betrayers, while mothers watched their young children get killed mercilessly.

A few weeks passed in which everyone allowed the weariness of battle to slowly ebb out of their systems, replaced by a sense of philosophical melancholy for the cherished relationships that were destroyed. Arjuna, the third among the Pandava brothers, who was closest to their first cousin and mentor, Krishna, sought solitude in the forest as he reminisced the many events that together created the Kurukshetra theatre of war.

He heard the soft rustle of leaves and suddenly Krishna was there, dressed as usual in his yellow silk robes, with the single peacock feather tucked in his headband. 'I see you are alone,' said Krishna, stating the obvious. 'When you are here, how I can be alone?' replied Arjuna, matching Krishna's logic.

'But now that you are here, may I ask you a question?' Arjuna's voice held a tremor as he wondered how Krishna would react to his question. 'Even during the thick of battle, I paused to answer the most existential of your questions, dear Arjuna. Nothing that you ask will ever perturb me. Go ahead,' said Krishna reading his mind.

'I know that the purpose of our efforts was to win the war. We needed to achieve our objective and we needed to achieve it at any cost. And we did. But I feel we sacrificed many of our values while doing so. My question therefore, dear Krishna, is this—What is our purpose? Is it to live our values or win our wars?'

'Arjuna, the answer lies in your own question. "Living" values is what you do with your entire life. "Winning" is just a part of it.'

'So, Krishna, is it then a king's responsibility to demonstrate his values, even at the expense of winning a war?'

'Arjuna, who said that the two are mutually exclusive? Winning a war need not be at odds with living your values. Observe what comes at the start of your journey, Arjuna! It is the setting of values. That is the thread of life, the purpose of your existence. Day-to-day events such as quelling skirmishes, waging wars and fighting battles to protect your boundaries are what happen subsequently. The successful king is one who establishes the "how" and the "why". The "what" is merely circumstance.'

Many corporates at the beginning of their D&I journey often ask this question: 'What if my D&I values are at cross-purposes to my business goals?' In other words, there is a certain level of tension within the organization as to what should take precedence—is it the setting and following of cultural mores (which includes D&I) or the relentless pursuit of business objectives? When you consider that training is one of the cost heads that immediately comes under the scanner during times of low revenues, this question is natural.

The answer lies in understanding why the organization pursues D&I. If it is merely for the purpose of showcasing a diverse workforce, then the focus simmers down to the acquisition, training and adapting of diverse employees to the workplace. This by itself is a very restricted and nearsighted objective. On the other hand, if we looked at the real purpose of D&I in the long-term journey of the enterprise, then the vision becomes clear. There is no false urgency to action a set of short-term fixes. D&I actually transforms into an opportunity area and not a problem to be solved.

Some of the best ways in which organizations have ensured that D&I gets actioned as something coherent with business and not in conflict

D&I Action Plans and Business Goals

with it is by moving the D&I function out of human resources. Needless to mention, the highly visible aspects of D&I are processes such as recruitment, training and retention. By default, most of these activities are 'cost centres' whose immediate benefit is not apparent. As such, when D&I is aligned to HR or CSR or even more narrowly to employee engagement, it typically limits the huge growth opportunities that the practice can provide.

It is imperative that the D&I function should be in the business of making the company not just a better place within but also a competitive and sustainable organization without. As such, it should be able to impact the organizational horizontals both from a language and culture perspective. D&I impacts decision-making, it impacts the choice of priorities. When people are at the centre of your organizational strategy, then D&I becomes not a series of short-lived tactical to-dos, but a way of conducting business that fuels growth and innovation.

Discerning, far-sighted leaders have realized that today, successful businesses are those which allow people to define who you are rather than vice versa. When D&I stops becoming a tool to make statements, but is an integral part of the organization, running like a central thread, connecting functions, processes and outcomes, then, it is able to create trust, transparency and an entrepreneurial mindset. In this avatar, D&I goes hand in hand with the attaining of business goals and is no longer at cross-purposes to it.

CROSSWORD

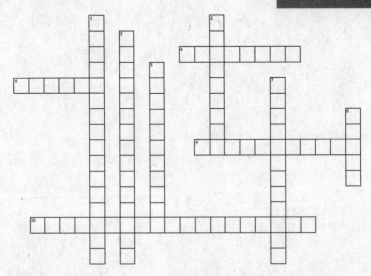

ACROSS

4   This refers to a person or a group who historically has/have been in the demographic lesser group in the overall population sample. (8)

6   A curve shaped like an alphabet before N that shows the labour force distribution of women by age with the age brackets 20–24 and 45–49 being two peaks. This concept was proposed on the basis of research on Japanese women. (1,5)

9   The additional training to be imparted to or undertaken by an individual returning to career after a break, for him/her to meet the requirements of his/her job role. (2-8)

10 The ability of an organization to embed diversity in its organizational culture. (9,10)

DOWN

1   Structured reintegration plans for smooth reintegration of maternity returners, back to their job roles. (9,7)

2   The differences across different dimensions—social, economic, educational or political—between men and women in a society. (6,3)

3   Also termed as social exclusion—the placement of minority groups and cultures outside mainstream society. (15)

5   The penalty a professional has to face in terms of a decrease in salary he/she draws after a career break as compared to what he/she was drawing pre-break. (4,7)

7   Unequal pay distribution amongst individuals in the workforce who are on the same job role. (3,6)

8   The process of making a smooth transition from one state to another, unhesitatingly. (5)

SECTION 6

THE ROLE OF LEADERSHIP AND STRATEGY IN DIVERSITY AND INCLUSION

DIVERSITY AND INCLUSION LEXICON

S. No.	Words	Definition
1.	Corporate dropout	An individual who voluntarily drops out of a successful corporate career to either pursue personal interests or hobbies or to be the primary caregiver of the family
2.	Corporate ladder	A conceptualized view of a company's employment hierarchy in which career advancement is considered to follow higher rungs on a ladder, with entry-level positions on the bottom rungs and executive level positions at the top
3.	Career success	The professional success that an individual has achieved by means of his/her career; career growth is an indication of this success.
4.	Career trajectory	The path an individual's career takes as he/she moves ahead in years; while a linear progression is most desired, the trajectory might also include career breaks or other occasional dips in a professional's career due to unforeseen circumstances.
5.	Career sponsor	A senior, successful professional who believes in another high-pot professional's (sponsee) career potential and actively sponsors his/her career growth by introducing him/her on relevant platforms and nominating him/her for appropriate high-growth roles
6.	Career stage	The three active stages, namely early, mid and mature, that an individual passes through in his/her career span

S. No.	Words	Definition
7.	Career priorities	The priorities a professional assigns to various aspects of his/her career
8.	Career longevity	The length of an individual's professional existence
9.	Career motivator	The individual(s) a professional idolizes and one who inspires him/her to conquer greater career heights; this could be political leaders, corporate icons, social activists, actors, etc., amongst others.
10.	Career orientation	The relative importance a professional attributes to his/her career as against his/her home
11.	Career plan	The plan a professional adheres to in order to attain career growth that can result in professional and personal development
12.	Inclusion maturity	Organizations' level of commitment towards inclusion, also indicative of their progression in the inclusion journey
13.	Inclusion readiness	An indicator of an organization's readiness to embrace inclusion that is a consequence of best practices to embrace people from a wide range of needs, abilities, interest and backgrounds
14.	Succession planning	Refers to a process of systematically and deliberately preparing for future changes of leadership in key positions; this process may involve identifying potential replacements and/or providing strategies for developing or hiring individuals to meet future needs.

INTERLUDE: THE TALLEST LIGHTHOUSES CAST THE LONGEST SHADOWS

The sound of the water sprinkler keeping the lawn of his beach house fresh and green was meditative. Bharat leaned back in the rattan chair on the large first-floor verandah that overlooked his garden. The backwaters flowed within visible distance of his house and in the light of the setting sun, he could see the golden brown silhouettes of the fishermen standing on the slim row boats, gently rowing towards the centre where the catfish swam. The Saturday breeze wafted in with the voices of Moti, his old gardener, in conversation with the cook. Moti was plucking tender coconuts from the trees that lined the garden.

His mind drifting to other days and times, Bharat found himself reflecting about a summer vacation he had had with his dad several decades ago. How time has changed! He realized that while he was a celebrated CEO whose interviews were featured as cover stories of every popular business magazine, he would always be his father's boy. Dad's guidance and many pieces of advice had always kept him in good stead. Having lost his mother at an early age, Bharat had been raised by his father single-handedly. 'I was never a rebel teenager,' thought Bharat to himself with a smile. He remembered that he was scheduled to have a video-chat with his father that night. He was delighted that his dad had taken to smartphones easily and had now mastered WhatsApp and Facebook.

It had been a few weeks since he began the 99 Day Diversity Challenge and Bharat realized that each topic impacted him in a different way. It had been an experience like no other. He had gone through the manuscript hurriedly at first and then began reading and absorbing parts of it with more relish. The comments and notations on the sides of the pages provided interesting insights and Bharat wondered who had written them. A thorough search on the internet on the '99 Day

Diversity Challenge' had yielded nothing. Not wanting to engage Advaita in another conversation about the antecedents of the book, Bharat quelled his curiosity and continued reading the tome. Much to Evita's surprise, he had even brought it with him to the beach house.

They were expecting guests, and Evita and the kids had gone to the village to buy fresh vegetables for the night's dinner. The beach house was Bharat's retreat, his haven, the place where he travelled to for peace, quiet and reflection. He sometimes invited friends or partners over for discussions, and today, he was looking forward to the conversation. His mentor, Paramita Acharya, was driving down.

Paramita was Bharat's predecessor at AcceLever. It had been a short stint, but in the brief time that Bharat had known her, Paramita, a small-made pleasant lady who reminded you of your favourite aunt, seemed more like a coach than a CEO. While Bharat had been a career AcceLeverite, having joined as an MT and working his way over 25 years to a senior management position, Paramita had been a rank outsider. She came from a completely different industry background and was even considered a maverick. Her three previous stints had been hugely successful but each had ended with a buy-out or a public issue. Paramita was a makeover artist and seemed to have been brought in by the board as part of a compromise to infuse fresh blood into AcceLever.

Initially Bharat had resented Paramita as did most of the tenured team at AcceLever. Paramita was alien to the culture, the way things worked at AcceLever. Her soft-spoken manner was a complete antithesis to the sharp, aggressive style that was typical of AcceLever. The fact that she listened more than she spoke seemed in contrast to the AcceLever old boys club, where the guys in charge did all the talking. It appeared as though Paramita would always be the outsider, the unfamiliar X factor, and everyone waited to see if her methods would fail.

Nothing speaks louder than success and Paramita's was no different. Over time, Bharat learnt to trust her. He accepted that the older woman's methods may be different but they worked. Paramita's thinking seemed more suited to a social enterprise, but the results they gave ensured that the board felt vindicated in their choice. Which was why it came as a complete surprise to Bharat when Paramita shared with him that just after 13 months, she would be leaving AcceLever.

'I am recommending your candidature to the board, Bharat. I would like them to name you the CEO,' she had said to Bharat's great delight. As a fast-tracker and a career-primary professional, Bharat knew he would become CEO one day, if not of AcceLever but certainly of some company, but he didn't expect it so soon. The opportunity to lead a business, define customer expectations, create new products and solutions, pick up CSR as a focus area—Bharat foresaw an exciting future but also realized that he would need Paramita's guidance and mentoring. 'I will accept the position, but only on one condition, Paramita,' Bharat had said. 'I want you to be my mentor.'

Paramita happily agreed. Once the board accepted Paramita's decision and named Bharat the CEO-in-waiting, the duo swung into action. Paramita spent two hours each day for the next two months, guiding and counselling Bharat. In those 60 days, Bharat learnt more about managing people than he had in his entire career. He also realized that behind the soft façade of the Type B, Paramita was a sharp thinker and keen observer of human behaviour.

That was more than two years ago and the two had stayed connected, friends. 'If there's one person I would like to talk to about inclusion, it is Paramita,' thought Bharat as her car pulled into the driveway.

Paramita and her husband Shekar stepped out of the car, their faces wreathed in smiles. Each time Bharat looked at the couple, he could not but reflect on the utter contrast between husband and wife. Shekar, his bearded bespectacled visage with a prominent nose, was reminiscent of a young Tagore. His lean 6-foot frame in a pair of jeans and a loose-fitting sweatshirt looked every inch the relaxed, retired man, while Paramita, 4 feet 11 inches tall, dressed in a crisp cotton saree was a small dynamo of energy and enthusiasm. One could never imagine her being retired.

'Ah, the beard is even more luxurious than I remember!' laughed Bharat as he shook hands warmly with Shekar and gave Paramita a tight hug.

'Bharat, how have you been? How's Evita? How are the kids?' Paramita handed him a large cloth bag filled with fruit. 'We harvested this morning. Mangoes from the farm.'

Bharat opened the bag and breathed in deeply the fragrance of ripe Alphonso. 'Hmm, divine.'

'Great to see that the farm is shaping up well. How are you and Shekar enjoying the farm life?'

'It's a labour of love. And as all good work, as you sow, so you reap,' drawled Shekar, as enigmatic as ever.

'Well, Shekar's current obsession is with the betel vine at home. He is trying his best to get it to grow exactly the way he wants!' laughed Paramita.

'All I am doing is giving it a few gentle nudges to change direction. It is trying to latch on to the tree jasmine, I want it to be independent!'

'That's Shekar for you! If I do the same thing at the NGO, he asks me not to be fussy! I split time between the NGO and the farm—don't know which is more demanding!' said Paramita.

The friends walked inside and the evening turned mellow. Between the laughter, the catching up and the hot dinner served by Evita, the talk turned to Bharat's work.

'Ah, I have to tell you this,' said Bharat, once they were settled in the verandah with bowls of freshly churned home-made ice creams. 'I am reading this book—I don't even know if I can call it a book, it is more like a manuscript of reflections. It is called the 99 Day Diversity Challenge!'

As soon as he had shared this, Bharat noticed the couple promptly exchange glances. Shekar adjusted himself a little more comfortably in the rattan settee, while Paramita leaned forward a little and asked, 'And how do you find it?'

Bharat looked at the couple incredulously. This was not the question he had expected from Paramita. He thought she would ask, 'What is the 99 Day Diversity Challenge??' Instead she was asking about how he found it! Did she know about the book? But how could she? Was it not strange to them? Had they too read it before? But it did not seem like a published book.

A million questions racing in his mind, Bharat asked the first that he could articulate. 'But, but... how do you know about the book, Paramita?'

'Because I wrote it,' said Paramita simply.

While Bharat's expressions revealed that he was finding it difficult to digest that bit of startling information, Paramita began softly. 'Advaita is our niece. You have met her a couple of times at my house parties....'

As Bharat looked even more astounded, Paramita continued. 'Bharat, I always felt that AcceLever was at a huge disadvantage when it came to D&I. In fact, one of the primary reasons that I left the organization was because even at the very top, the culture was very non-inclusive.'

'But, how did Advaita...' before Bharat could complete, Shekar piped in with a broad smile. 'Advaita is my sister's daughter, Bharat. Didn't you recognize our prominent family heirloom?' laughed Shekar, pointing to his own nose. With a start, Bharat realized what he had found familiar about Advaita. She was a female version of Shekar!

As Bharat joined in the laughter, Shekar continued, 'She finished her MBA and got campus placed last year at AcceLever. Even we did not know that she was applying for an MT's position. It is only after she got through and mentioned that she had met you that the idea was born in Paramita's mind!'

'I had been wanting to speak to you about inculcating a culture of inclusion at AcceLever, Bharat,' said Paramita, this time her voice serious with intent.

'Inclusion is something that has to begin at the very top. It is not a culture change that you should attempt with a bottom-up strategy. To use an analogy closer to this beach house of yours—the tallest lighthouses cast the longest shadows. Leaders create cultures. A culture of inclusion and diversity has to be driven top-down. You—the leader—have to internalize it; you have to make it cool, make it part of the organizational DNA. And you need to approach it in your usual intellectual manner, not emotionally. That is why I made sure that Advaita worked really hard on the report before sending it to you!'

The revelation was astounding and Bharat shook his head in surprise and amazement. 'The 99 Day Diversity Challenge is a compilation of my thoughts on the subject. I urged Advaita to give it to you and if you did not take it, to just leave it in your office!' continued Paramita.

'Oh and over the last one month, she has been dying to call you and ask you how you found the book!' said Shekar, again with a huge laugh, while Paramita quickly added, 'It was a surprise and delight that you called us for dinner today! I was wondering if you would at all bring up the topic of the 99 Day Diversity Challenge and even if you did, whether you liked it ....'

Bharat stood up suddenly and took Paramita's hands in his own— 'Thanks for never giving up on me, Paramita!' he said wholeheartedly. 'The 99 Day Diversity Challenge is the most thought-provoking thing I have ever read. It has made me reflect and revisit many of my decisions and behaviour. I have just completed about a third of it and already I find myself thinking differently. But why did you not just call me up and ask me to read it? Why the whole cloak-and-daggers thing with Advaita giving me the report and all??'

'Because I did not want you to do it just because I said so,' said Paramita staring into her ice cream bowl for a second before looking up and facing Bharat squarely. 'I wanted you to see the importance of it, the necessity of it. I wanted you to buy the "business case". Which is why I asked Advaita to prepare the document. I asked her to minute the meetings that she sat in, collect information that was publicly available on the sales results and the contributions made by individuals. I wanted her to build a strong and powerful argument. And then, I asked her to write to you. And knowing the kind of thorough guy that you are, who is a logical and systematic thinker, I knew that you would take the bait!'

Bharat smiled at how well his mentor had predicted his own behaviour. 'Have you shared the 99 Day Diversity Challenge with anyone else, Paramita?'

'No, not yet. You were always my first option. I wanted you to not just read it, but also make sure that you live the values, Bharat. You were a soft target for me!' laughed Paramita.

'I know the incredible influence you have within AcceLever,' she continued. 'Not just with your team but also among your peers, your own age cohort. That's why I backed you for the role of the CEO, because I know that you are a truly charismatic, influential leader. And that is the reason why I wanted you to be the first to read the 99 Day Diversity Challenge.'

'Thanks again, Paramita. I am deeply grateful to you,' said Bharat rather emotionally.

'No thanks needed, Bharat, I said this before and I will say it again—the tallest lighthouses cast the longest shadows,' said Paramita, getting up quickly from her chair and pacing around the room. 'Having worked in the corridors of power, I know exactly how much influence you wield. When you decide to adopt inclusion as a behaviour, you impact scores, even hundreds of other influential leaders. Your behaviour is observed, it is discussed. You are the subject of much thought. Which is why I wanted to start with you. I want inclusion to be a leadership competency. I want it to be your signature trait. And knowing the kind of leader you are, you will ensure that your team follows your example. Because...' and this time, Bharat joined in 'the tallest lighthouses cast the longest shadows....'

THE CEO IS THE CIO

Hi, I am Jane and I am the General Manager of Red Star, a financial consulting company. We have over 300 employees and I am very conscious about building an inclusive workplace. Lately, I noticed that things are not going fine between Sarah and Amit, two of my team members. Sarah reports to Amit, who leads a five-member team. One of Amit's star performers is Mumtaz, a young woman who is 6 months pregnant with her first baby. I have often seen Amit permit Mumtaz to work from home and also leave office early. At a recent informal office lunch, I was observing Sarah's interaction with Amit and it seemed as if things had hit a new low. I called Amit to my office to ask him about this.

Jane: Amit, what's the issue between you and Sarah? She is usually a warm and friendly person, but today at the lunch, I noticed that she seemed kind of put off and irritated. I also noticed that when the rest of you in your team sat down together to have lunch, Sarah went away by herself. What's happening?

Amit: I think Sarah is behaving rather immaturely, Jane. She feels that I am partial to Mumtaz. As you know, I allow Mumtaz to work from home occasionally and leave early if required on account of her pregnancy. Sarah had asked me if I could also allow her to leave early since she has a weekly Church meeting near her home. I refused. Now she is all miffed and acting like a childish teenager. She has actually gone and told Abel that I am prejudiced against Christians. Such rubbish!

Jane: But why did you not allow Sarah to attend her weekly Church meetings?

Amit: Jane, I constantly assess the performance of all my team members. Mumtaz is an exceptional performer and I am happy to allow her flexibility as per her needs. However, Sarah requires a lot of supervision and constant monitoring. I am working with her to improve her output. If she reaches a particular benchmark, then I am fine to cut her some slack, not now when she has not even touched average. In my opinion, just to retain an image of being an 'inclusive' leader, I am not willing to compromise on productivity. After all, the company exists to deliver results to our stakeholders, not merely to be inclusive, right, Jane?

Jane: Amit, the hallmark of a truly inclusive leader is effective communication and understanding. It is important that you communicate to Sarah the reason behind your decision. Also, it would be good to occasionally allow her some flexibility in order to motivate her. Telling her that you are working with her to ensure her productivity and performance is bettered and also making her feel that you both are in this together is true leadership. You have to take her emotional well-being also into account. Diversity is not merely what is seen outside. Apart from what is visible, such as gender, ability, appearance, race, religion and age, there is a wealth of diversity below the surface. True inclusion means looking at both the visible and the invisible.

The leader of the organization is the most effective role model for inclusion. Hence, it is often said that the CEO is the Chief Inclusion Officer (CIO). An inclusive leader observes all his/her employees and carefully includes the contributions of all stakeholders. Thus, it is most important for the leader to be involved and at the table at all levels within his organization. Inclusive leadership creates an organizational culture that not merely looks at number-based results, but also focuses on the well-being of all stakeholders, with the deep realization that both of these are interminably interlinked.

An inclusive CEO consciously practises the attitude of involvement by being fully responsible for the productivity and contribution of every teammate. He/she does this by being internally dedicated to assessment and development of the organization while demonstrating a visible commitment to a culture that looks at bringing everyone to their fullest potential. An effective leader is by default an inclusive leader, who is able to get the team to work together not only because the members are committed to the same goal, but also because they each can approach the problem differently. When team members feel included, their confidence in sharing thoughts and ideas increases and this leads to innovation.

Mere diversity in the form of numbers is hardly enough to add value to the organization. The potential that emerges from inclusion is the secret sauce that makes diversity work. And the leader is the fulcrum who gets the magic mix to deliver its results by leveraging the insights, knowledge, identity and culture of the team to create a trusting, confidence-building workplace.

Leadership by inclusion really translates into a deep and abiding investment made by the leader in learning about the complexity of his/her team. He/she actively demonstrates his/her passion in everyday behaviour. He/she genuinely understands the benefits of the diversity that each member brings. In a way, inclusive leadership is about reposing sustained confidence in every teammate with the realization that demystifying the various layers of their identity is not easy. It is about asking difficult questions, working through conflicts and communicating powerfully. Thus, for a truly inclusive leader, inclusion is a way of life; it is not merely an organizational tool.

CREATING AN INCLUSIVE BUSINESS ENVIRONMENT

DAY 54/99

Disciple: Oh Master, may I have your permission to speak?

Master: Ananta, you have already spoken.

Disciple: I was just requesting your permission, Master.

Master: And by doing so, you spoke.

Disciple: A thousand pardons, Oh Master. I will remain quiet if this is not the appropriate time to speak.

Master: Now that you have established that we are conversing, we might as well. Go ahead. What did you want to state?

Disciple: I find that our new brother from the mountains is very different from others. He thinks differently. He finishes his tasks very differently. For instance, his manner of cutting vegetables in our kitchen is vastly different from how we do it. I don't know whether to tell him that we do it differently or to just ignore it. Also, he is more modern than the rest of us. He knows how to use computers. Maybe we can remove him from the kitchen and use him only in the office?

Master: But why should you tell him that he is cutting vegetables differently?

Disciple: So that he fits in with the rest of us. So that he can cut vegetables the way we do. So that we can all be alike.

Master: Should we all be alike, Ananta?

Disciple: Oh Master, as usual, I am stuck. I do not know the right reply to your question. I am afraid that if I say the wrong answer, I will invite your anger upon me. Kindly shed light on this yourself, benevolent Master!

Master: Anger? No Ananta. There is no anger, merely exasperation. Anyway, here are my thoughts. The question that you need to ask is why have we been cutting vegetables in a particular way? Is there an inherent reason for it? Does it make the flavour come out better? Does it cook easily thereby conserving fuel for us? Does it save time so that we can do other tasks? If our new brother from the mountains cuts vegetables in a manner that satisfies our objectives or has its own special benefit, there is no need for him to change, just because we do it in one particular way.

Disciple: Oh, I understand! The value that a different approach or background brings to us gets diluted if we make everyone adhere to the same rules of functioning. But what about putting him in the office where he can make good use of his computer skills?

Master: That is the problem when we highlight differences, Ananta. You are then unable to look beyond their 'difference'. They get pigeonholed into one category and are unable to learn further. Yes, we benefit from his different skill, but won't he feel exploited? Our new brother from the mountains might have many other ideas to make our place better, which he might not share if he is thrust into doing just one type of job.

Disciple: Then what is the solution, Oh Master?

Master: Frank and open communication is the answer, Ananta. If we have to create an inclusive environment, then we must encourage candid discourse. What we need here is an inclusive environment where everyone gets to practise their faith in their own way. When we try to make everyone adhere to a common way of doing things, which has no logic, then we send out a message that we do not value everyone's opinion.

Disciple: But won't that mean that people will say things which are conflicting and there might be difference of opinions?

Master: Yes, there will be and the purpose of our abode is to ensure that everyone feels safe to express their opinions. Just like you did.

Inclusion, when put to practice, adopts fairness as its primary hallmark. At the beginning of the diversity journey, many organizations usually look at the ideas of (a) 'assimilation'—making everybody act and behave the same, or (b) 'differentiation'—highlighting everyone's difference. True inclusion lies in the middle.

An inclusive business environment must emphasize the importance of a unifying culture while at the same time provide breathing space for every individual to bring their different selves to work. Each employee has special qualities that make him/her unique—both in the form of identity diversity as well as cognitive diversity. And this is the gift that he/she brings to the workplace—his/her uniqueness. Your teammate's past experiences have moulded him/her to be the person he/she is and this in turn influences his/her behaviour at the workplace. One's singular identity shapes his/her behaviour both with his/her colleagues as well as customers.

An inclusive business environment is created almost entirely with the power of communication. For example, in an environment where a multinational has set up a new business and its staff do not speak English fluently, inclusion takes the form of bilingual managers who ensure that all decisions are clearly communicated to the staff in a manner and way that demystifies and provides clarity. Likewise, in a situation where older people are employed in a largely millennial-dominated work environment, inclusion is that manager who diffuses potentially explosive situations by encouraging conversation and dialogue.

As such, making your workplace a safe space for expression of dissent becomes paramount in the journey to inclusion. An inclusive manager is accessible. He/she is a coach, a guide. His/her leadership combines the seemingly contradictory twin priorities of business efficacy with empathy. When an employee is hired, an inclusive business ecosystem ensures that he/she is steered towards productivity and ownership to respond to business challenges. When a workplace is inclusive, it throws open the doors for innovation to work its magic, to discover hidden knowledge and create a cohesive community.

Inclusion in business is that unifying force which actively involves every teammate's experiences and ideas to lead to business success. The inclusive organization exists to achieve its targets and goals in a way that involves maximizing every individual's potential. And this is done in a manner that is natural and organic and not forced or contrived. An inclusive business environment sets the same if not higher standards of accountability, measurement and ambition as a purely commercial enterprise, the key difference being in the engagement with which employees commit to their goals.

D&I GAME: EXPERIENCING DIVERSITY AND INCLUSION

INCLUSIVE LEADERSHIP: SELF-ASSESSMENT

Inclusion and leadership are no longer mutually exclusive workplace variables. To manage, nurture and grow organizations, it is important that leaders of today and tomorrow are inclusive, stay inclusive! Take this self-assessment to find out how inclusive you are.

Please tick the most appropriate answer for each question. Some statements may be characteristic of you, some may not. Nevertheless, try to relate each situation to your own experience and choose an answer that is most typical of you.

1. Inclusion is a two-way bridge. As much as it requires mindset change and acceptance from a leader's end, it is not going to get anywhere, if people continue to exclude themselves.

    a. I have felt so innumerable number of times, especially when new members are inducted into my team.

    b. While this thought has occurred to me occasionally, I have never let it curtail my efforts at inclusion.

    c. This thought does not resonate with me. I firmly believe that if one's efforts at inclusion are genuine, he/she will be able to break all shells of exclusion.

2. Chaotic team meetings are the result of too many incoherent thoughts flying around. Team meetings are best conducted if one or two members of the team take lead.

    a. Team leads in my team are super-efficient. They seldom let chaos into a meeting room.

    b. Key agenda meetings need to be conducted in an organized fashion. When it is a casual brainstorming session, chaos is fine.

    c. I love such meetings. Some of our best ideas were products of chaos.

3. The concept of 'career sponsorship for women' is very overrated. Today's Indian woman professional does not endorse preferential treatment.

   a. In the capacity of a leader, I have always ensured that our policies stay open and inclusive. I haven't pushed my people to pick up the cause for any one 'gender'.

   b. I have often faced stiff resistance from men in the team when sponsorship tracks were rolled out, and I have ended up questioning the 'sponsorship rationale'.

   c. We aren't yet at a zone where equality reigns. Sponsoring women's careers cannot only result in more women role models but also can foster a culture of male allyship.

4. Poor business results are a direct consequence of improper planning and blind strategies. When faced with such situations in the past:

   a. I have most often attributed it to market inconsistencies/VUCA-ness which we do not have any control of.

   b. I have accepted the failure, never being able to give concrete explanations for it.

   c. I have taken ownership and sat down with my team for failure analyses.

5. Collaborative efforts are almost always brokered. In today's workplaces, there is so much of diversity, right down to the individual level; clever brokering strategies are necessary.

   a. This has worked well with my team, in several occasions in the past; only that strategies need to be revisited from time to time, based on the diversity profile of the 'current' team.

   b. I can't see any harm in indulging in this 'brokerage', occasionally. The results of collaboration are far more important than the methods.

   c. This isn't sustainable. An environment rooted in trust and respect and one that enables constructive communication is what can sustain collaboration.

SCORING

For:

- every 'a', you ticked, give yourself a score of 1.

- every 'b', you ticked, give yourself a score of 2.

- every 'c', you ticked, give yourself a score of 3.

IF YOUR TOTAL SCORE IS BETWEEN:

- 5 and 8: You are yet to embark on the journey of being an inclusive leader. While you may be an efficient leader, consistently producing results, mastering the art of inclusive leadership can up-league your leadership abilities.

- 9 and 12: You are on the path of being an inclusive leader. While you strongly believe in the tenets of inclusion, there is visible scope for improvement towards bettering yourself in inclusivity in leadership.

- 13 and 15: Congrats! You are an inclusive leader—your conviction has been built and you are able to look at the bigger picture. Continue your efforts at staying inclusive, also creating an army of inclusive leaders.

OBJECTIVES OF A D&I AGENDA

DAY 56/99

I was once invited to work with the senior leadership team of a chemical manufacturing company on their D&I agenda. Led by a deeply passionate, visionary leader who wanted to change the culture of his organization to one that was gender-inclusive at all levels and functions, this organization, however, struggled to get its plan together. Reason—they did not know how to begin.

147

The intent was there—'to become a gender-inclusive company which leverages the full potential of every member'. The vision was clear—'to create a workplace where every individual is enabled to rise to the fullest of his or her potential'. Yet, carrying a 50-year-old legacy, where diversity had not been one of the success secrets, the leadership team wondered how they would assimilate it. As we began diving into the data, analysing the slice and dice of their demographics as well as hiring and advancement patterns, one thing became very clear—'inclusion' would not be a challenge, but 'diversity' would. The HR Director of the company was confident that she would be able to change the culture of the company to one that was inclusive and accepting of differences, but she was not sure of meeting diversity targets: 'I can get the inclusion piece, Dr Rajesh, but the diversity part—the actual hiring, the ability to get our women numbers to go up to double digits—that is going to be a challenge,' she shared as an aside.

Organizations embark upon the diversity journey usually for one of three reasons: (a) The leader at the very top of your organization is deeply passionate about it and wants it, (b) Your global headquarters has mandated that it be practised and followed, (c) Your successful competitors have institutionalized it and are speaking about its positive influence. Of course, there are other reasons too. Depending on which reason drives you, the end objective could be (a) diversity, (b) inclusion or (c) both.

When an organization focuses mostly on 'a', that is on diversity, it directly relates to the numbers—the talent acquisition piece. It means that the organization wants to see a visible difference in its workplace composition. For companies which operate in industries such as manufacturing, chemical, pharma, logistics and FMCG, this is a challenging task, since the universe of diversity candidates is itself small. Lateral hiring (hiring from your competitors) becomes difficult as well as futile. Thus, for the diversity journey to become meaningful and purposeful, many role model companies have focused on creating the talent pipeline by influencing the source—educational institutions. Companies also identify alternate talent pools such as women returning to a career after a break or alumni of the same organization.

To an organization focusing on 'b', the end result is to ensure that the culture of the company becomes a more inclusive and accepting one. Workplaces which already have reasonable diversity would like to centre their journey around increasing the inclusion mindset. This begins with the basic accepting of differences and grows to become a celebration of diversity.

Today, I find several organizations focusing on 'c', that is both diversity and inclusion to ensure that the one is not sacrificed on the altar of the other.

YOUR D&I BRANDING

DAY 57/99

I was having a chat with a journalist friend of mine when she asked me something that surprised me, even shocked me a little. 'Dr Rajesh, don't you think companies get into this whole diversity thing more as a branding opportunity than genuine intent?'

It was surprising to me because a question relating to branding came from a journalist. 'Diversity is also a branding opportunity, Selvi,' I replied. 'But if it is created only to be that, then it totally loses its value. Sometimes when companies run programmes and events just to get eyeballs, I am not comfortable with that.'

'Then, do you suggest that companies that undertake diversity initiatives should not speak about it?'

'Not at all. But I feel that your workplace has to speak louder than your ads. Your current employees must be your biggest brand ambassadors for diversity, their referrals must ensure that you add more diversity to your workforce. In today's hyper-connected world where social media rules with an iron fist, if you are not unaffectedly genuine, then you stand to lose a lot.'

'Is diversity then a tool to get the word out about how cool your organization is? Is it to close deals with that pesky customer who appreciates diversity and therefore wants to see it in your pitch?'

'How the D&I thought is brought into the organizational mindset is not important. It could be a customer, it could be an employee or even a competitor. What is important is whether the practice is pursued genuinely.'

'I come back to my original question, Dr Rajesh,' said Selvi, not giving up. 'I find us receiving a lot of press releases that speak about how so-and-so company is making waves by hiring returning women, by providing flexibility, by sourcing people with disabilities and so on. So much of tokenism, I feel. To me, it appears that the branding intent is even greater than the true benefit to the employee.'

'Diversity is not just beneficial to the employee, it is very beneficial to the company too. What might appear as tokenism to you is making a big difference to the person who got hired by this company when the other companies rejected him/her. Even by hiring people with differences as an experiment, it is making a significant change to the workplace. Just like how quality circles and Six Sigma trained the focus on quality, D&I is shining the light on culture. In today's VUCA world, the survival of the corporation is at stake. Companies are trying their best to reinvent themselves and if they have discovered the power of D&I, what is wrong in that? So many events have changed our world view. We are operating with a new normal that seems to require a greater emphasis and attention on the acceptance of diversity and the practice of inclusion. D&I is at work whether one likes it or not. Just like how millennials are challenging the slow-moving, hierarchical, conventional approach to management and decision-making, there are several identity factors which are more critical today than ever before. And if a company wants to speak about what it is genuinely attempting, why not?'

Today, businesses are in quest of cutting-edge solutions for the new challenges which they face. They are searching for ways to increase innovation, problem-solving skills and intrapreneurship. They look for talent that demonstrates engagement, ownership and prompt delivery of KRAs. And they seek these new competencies not from outside but to be embedded within their culture. The philosophy of inclusion and diversity is one that solves this conundrum and is revamping the workplace, allowing the unleashing of hidden talents.

Talent acquisition and people management are therefore among the most critical items on the plate of leaders. Every business, whether start-up or steady-state, appreciates the fact that people are their most valuable asset. Hence, creating a culture which allows them to fully utilize their skills, experiences and perspectives is a must-have. A diverse and inclusive work culture therefore has many benefits, and economic growth is not the least of them.

The key to this lies in a comprehensive, well-considered D&I strategy. A strategic approach to D&I ensures that the enterprise does not end up merely creating hype without a solid logic backing the implementation. Companies truly committed to an inclusive workplace have leaders who emphasize the strategic nature of diversity and begin building it into the very DNA of the organization. They set hard targets for including different candidates into their ranks and drive change management programmes to modify culture. They conduct townhalls and dialogues and ensure that the transformation is driven into the very gut of the company. Many of these initiatives are not known to the outside world but are quietly conducted with only the end goal in mind.

When a company decides to promote its organizational culture in order to attract the best talent, D&I branding is irrefutable. Companies use tools such as participating in events, conducting events of their own, sponsoring events, creating innovative hiring fairs, etc., to combine the benefits of branding with D&I. All these initiatives lead up to the creation of positive word of mouth generated both by mainstream and social media. Such programmes are very effective not only to send out a message to the external audience that the company is serious about its culture, but even more importantly to its own internal audience.

Several organizations build D&I into their people strategy, while a few others look at it as a business imperative. In both cases, the long-term benefits of what D&I can deliver to the organization are kept firmly in mind, employer branding being one of them. However, the danger sometimes lies in considering the tactical action points, say for instance, employer branding, as an end by itself, which defeats the very purpose of what D&I is all about.

DAY 58/99

CREATING A D&I VISION STATEMENT

Captain Kuruvi, unmatched pirate of the Red Seas, charismatic leader and rakish seafarer, peered at the golden key. It seemed heavy and shiny. 'And this be the key to our treasure, mate?' he asked doubtfully, swaying a little addressing his question to Bomma who had given the key to him.

Bomma, the fearsome one-eyed pirate who shared a love-hate relationship with the Captain, plucked the key off Kuruvi's fingers irascibly and turned it around pointing to a groove on it. 'This here is the magic combination that makes this the original key. For certain, this little clog here is the key to Jhoomla's treasure.'

'Aye, aye! As my learned colleague suggests, this would indeed be the real one,' said Kuruvi, sombrely addressing the small group gathered there. Kannamma, Pottu and Kaka—the motley team that was part of Captain Kuruvi's shipmates waited for his next words, while Kuruvi searched for something in his pockets, oscillating as if already aboard an imaginary ship. 'And we have my beautiful vessel—the Grey Diamond, my trusted friend the monkey and me mates. But I am missing something.'

'What are we missing?' questioned Bomma impatiently. 'We have our ship and we have these gizzards to sail, we have the rum for the way and we have the key! Look alive and let's set sail, men!'

'Set sail? How? Tell me my dearie, how do we sail?' Kuruvi was enjoying this.

'For sure, as we always do. What are you getting at, Kuruvi?' said Bomma, clearly on the edge.

'You know, for all the cleverness in you, you are not very impressive with your thinking,' said Kuruvi squinting at Bomma and the rest. 'We know what to do, but do we know how to get there? What will guide us to our destination, the place where we need to be?'

Bomma lost his patience. 'Stop those bloomin' riddles and say what you got to say, you infidel! Or by thunder I'll burn your precious ship down!'

Captain Kuruvi, on the other hand, was still as cool as a cucumber. The smile widening upon his visage, he said, 'The answer, my man Bomma, is, a map!' And turning to Kannamma, Pottu and Kaka, he said, 'A map, my hearties! You know maps? Those drawings and squiggles that show the real world on a much smaller scale? We need one of those. A map is a picture of the place you wish to go to, a picture so clear and strong it will make you want to go there! Even if you got your key, your ship and your men, you most certainly need a map. What has a pirate's life taught me? Yes, that if you need to get somewhere, you need a map to guide you. It gives you direction, even provides inspiration! It points the way, my mates! That's what maps are for!'

A diversity vision statement is like a map that points the way to your destination. When the D&I agenda has been thought through exhaustively and a strategy formed, it needs a powerful articulation of the intent. The vision statement should communicate effectively to the audience—both internal and external—the organization's commitment to D&I. The vocabulary of the statement is important and should not sound dry and business-like.

The purpose of a diversity vision statement is to inspire the community at large, which includes present and potential employees, the larger ecosystem in which the organization conducts its business and anyone who visits their website or their office. An organization genuinely committed to inclusion perceives the value of reiterating its vision. Incorporating the key action points of the D&I agenda into the vision statement in a way that resonates with the audience is imperative. As all effective visions statements go, the ideal D&I vision statement too is pithy, motivating and is used to reinforce the repeated focus on individual behaviour and organizational systems. It is simple, focused on grounded reality and not a buzzword-laden sermon.

Following are a few D&I vision statements by leading organizations.

UNILEVER

To accelerate progress in equality and women's empowerment, because they are central to both our social impact and our business growth. That process starts with building a gender-balanced organization with a focus on management.

Source: https://www.unilever.com/sustainable-living/enhancing-livelihoods/opportunities-for-women/advancing-diversity-and-inclusion/, accessed on 24 August 2018.

ACCENTURE

Our ambition is to be the most inclusive and diverse company in the world. We believe our diversity makes us stronger and more innovative—and we embrace diversity as a source of innovation, creativity and competitive advantage. Inclusion and diversity are fundamental to our culture and core values at Accenture. We believe that no one should be discriminated against because of their differences, such as age, disability, ethnicity, gender, gender identity and expression, religion or sexual orientation.

Source: https://www.accenture.com/in-en/company-diversity, accessed on 24 August 2018.

IBM

> *Innovation comes from seeking out and inspiring diversity in all its dimensions. IBM recognizes the unique value and skills every individual brings to the workplace.*

Source: http://www-03.ibm.com/employment/inclusion/inclusive-ibm.html, accessed on 24 August 2018.

MAHINDRA GROUP

> *Together We Rise. We celebrate the uniqueness of every individual by fostering an environment of inclusion and empowerment.*

Source: http://www.mahindra.com/riseforgood/empowering-our-people/diversity-and-inclusion, accessed on 24 August 2018.

TATA GROUP

> *The group respects the uniqueness of each individual employee. The diversity and inclusion (D&I) culture across Tata companies enables employees to achieve their full potential without being discriminated on the basis of factors such as religion, age, gender, ethnicity, race, and physical and mental ability. The D&I strategy of the group has been further strengthened with the launch of Tata LEAD, the group D&I initiative.*

Source: http://www.tata.com/careers/sub_index/diversity-and-inclusion, accessed on 24 August 2018.

JOHNSON & JOHNSON

> *Diversity and inclusion are integral to the way we work at Johnson & Johnson. We embed them in our businesses, promote equal access to opportunity for all our employees, and have leaders who hold themselves responsible for the growth and success of every team member. Our culture allows our employees to change the world without changing themselves.*

Source: https://www.jnj.com/_document/diverse-inclusive-workforce?id=0000015c-a1ad-d443-a55d-b9af73ce0000, accessed on 24 August 2018.

Creating a D&I Vision Statement

SODEXO

> *Leveraging the Power of our People: Strengthening our Business through Diversity & Inclusion. Diversity and inclusion differentiates us in the marketplace and contributes to a culture of inclusion in the workplace. It drives our ability to identify and develop the best talent, create an engaged and committed workforce and enhance Quality of Life for our clients, customers and the communities we serve. Our commitment to diversity and inclusion promotes growth within Sodexo and cultivates external partnerships.*

Source: https://www.sodexousa.com/home/corporate-responsibility/a-responsible-employer/diversity-and-inclusion.html, accessed on 24 August 2018.

EY

> *At EY, we believe that only the highest-performing teams, which maximize the power of different opinions, perspectives and cultural references, will succeed in the global marketplace. Our focus on diversity and inclusiveness is integral to how we serve our clients, develop our people and play a leadership role in our communities.*

Source: https://www.ey.com/gl/en/about-us/our-people-and-culture/diversity-and-inclusiveness, accessed on 24 August 2018.

DELOITTE

> *We are all unique. Each one of us is different from anyone and everyone else. All those differences that make each of the individuals working at Deloitte Touche Tohmatsu Limited and the member firms unique represent many dimensions of diversity—and this diversity is Deloitte's greatest strength.*

Source: https://www2.deloitte.com/ug/en/pages/about-deloitte/topics/global-diversity-deloitte-is-diversity.html, accessed on 24 August 2018.

P&G

> *Everyone Valued, Everyone Included, Everyone performing at their PEAK.*

Source: https://us.pg.com/who-we-are/our-approach/diversity-inclusion, accessed on 24 August 2018.

> *PepsiCo believes in respecting and encouraging diversity and makes it a point to encourage the intake of people with diverse backgrounds. The company believes in building a workforce that reflects the diverse consumers and communities they serve. Diversity and engagement is core to the company's values and how they operate as a global corporate citizen.*

Source: http://www.pepsicoindia.co.in/careers/why-work-at-pepsico/we-nurture-differences.html, accessed on 24 August 2018.

WHAT IS THE ROI ON DIVERSITY AND INCLUSION?

DAY 59/99

John (Quality): Hey, you have a min?

MS (Strategy): Sure, go ahd.

John: Prepping fr CFT (Cross-functional Team) mtg. What r these nos on D&I recrtmt?

MS: Current yrs' perf on D&I. To measure ROI on D&I spends.

John: We measure ROI on D&I???

MS: LOL, yes of course.

John: Sorry, was not aware. Thot it was just culture and stuff. We have a strategy on it?

MS: Not just strategy, but vision & milestones also.

John: Wow. Will you be presenting all this?

MS: Yep.

John: Anything I need to be aware, specific to quality?

MS: Ha ha, don't worry, all depts. are tracked, using people data.

John: What sort of data? Sry, lots of qustins.

MS: NP. Event budgets, engagement scores, hiring and retention patterns.

John: So, only people data, is it?

MS: This yr, since it's our 1st yr, starting off with people data. Nxt yr, we will track productivity, innovation and problem-solving.

John: Cool! Frankly didn't think ROI on D&I could be tracked so much in detail.

MS: Just a beginning, got to see if it will make sense.

John: With you at the helm, it sure will.

MS: Hey, thaaanx! Ok, GTG. TTYL.

One of the most frequently asked questions by organizations, early in the journey of D&I, is how ROI can be calculated on the spends. This is an important question, for it means that D&I is a strategic priority whose effectiveness and value is subject to the rigour of measurement. While D&I has been a hot topic in the workplace for the past few decades, it is imperative from a business perspective to show ROI from D&I, mainly to measure its impact and efficacy. Even more importantly, a focus on ROI is critical to demonstrate its purpose to the top leadership. Measuring the contribution that D&I has on profitability and growth of an organization is the holy grail of ROI calculation.

Diversity ROI is calculated in many ways, depending upon the stage of the organization along the D&I continuum. Many companies adopt a smart strategy of splitting 'diversity' goals and 'inclusion' goals and there-fore apportioning separate budgets and investments for each. For globally dispersed organizations, there might be a challenge in the form of a lack of uniformity in reporting, due to differing local regulations. It begins with listing all the possible spends that are planned under the D&I agenda, including items such as (a) cost of conducting a D&I event—both internal and external, (b) cost of recruiting specific diversity talent pools such as women, returning women, persons with disabilities or seniors (depending upon the D&I strategy), (c) cost of participating in external D&I programmes such as conferences or symposiums,

(d) cost of special D&I sensitivity training that is offered to the employees. This is not an exhaustive list and could include other budgetary items which the organization spends under the heading of achieving the D&I objective.

Once the different expenditure aspects are determined, they can be split into one-time and recurrent expenses. One-time costs or 'capital expenses' are incurred only at the beginning of the D&I voyage, by way of establishing the focus. Items such as the cost of a visioning offsite for the senior management team to finalize the D&I strategy will not be a repeating expense. Similarly, branding and marcom spends around D&I will also not be recurrent. Recruitment and training, on the other hand, are likely to recur right through and will be treated as regular D&I expenses.

As such, once the 'investment' options are finalized, the 'return' part can be determined. The ROI in D&I can be calculated with hard quantitative metrics such as the number of persons hired, retention rates, length of service and projects completed. Other aspects too could be brought into the picture such as engagement scores, increase/decrease in team productivity and happiness index.

The decision to measure the ROI of D&I spends is an important one that ensures that organizational commitment is reinforced from a very logical and data-oriented standpoint. Traditional ROI formulas where you take the total ROI and subtract the original cost of the investment and arrive at an ROI percentage will probably not apply. However, ROI on D&I can be calculated as a profitability ratio over time, once the organization has completed a few cycles and is, therefore, clear on the value and purpose.

What is the ROI on Diversity and Inclusion?

WORDFINDER

S	I	U	Q	G	F	B	K	Z	T	Q	S	C	O	X	E	B	Z
Q	N	E	D	N	N	I	N	T	T	K	Q	D	G	Y	C	F	T
E	C	M	R	I	A	D	I	P	M	U	I	T	S	S	A	I	U
V	L	T	W	N	L	Y	J	E	M	C	P	X	L	T	R	H	O
A	U	V	H	N	P	A	N	B	L	A	C	R	P	C	E	T	P
E	S	G	A	A	R	O	U	E	P	R	N	H	P	A	E	O	O
L	I	R	U	L	E	U	X	H	G	E	Y	L	D	R	R	C	R
Y	O	P	A	P	E	F	R	S	O	E	T	G	H	E	P	E	D
T	N	E	U	N	R	H	S	J	O	R	L	W	Y	E	R	E	E
I	M	K	L	O	A	S	A	V	L	S	A	Z	U	R	I	R	T
N	A	Q	P	I	C	M	C	H	K	U	N	T	K	S	O	J	A
R	T	H	N	S	Y	I	A	N	D	C	E	I	N	T	R	N	R
E	U	C	L	S	D	M	W	X	K	C	P	C	U	A	I	R	O
T	R	G	J	E	J	M	V	K	P	E	E	E	O	G	T	D	P
A	I	P	R	C	I	C	N	F	W	S	G	X	S	E	I	Z	R
M	T	S	X	C	T	Z	X	J	K	S	A	B	Q	Z	E	H	O
O	Y	Y	F	U	T	D	D	Z	J	J	W	O	L	M	S	A	C
S	Y	G	M	S	L	R	T	N	L	V	A	G	M	B	S	N	Q

WORDS

Corporate dropout	Career success
Career stage	Career priorities
Inclusion maturity	Succession planning
Career plan	Gen Y
Maternity leave	Wage penalty

SECTION 7

ACTIONING YOUR D&I VISION

DIVERSITY AND INCLUSION LEXICON

S. No.	Words	Definition
1.	**Diversity readiness**	An organization's capacity and preparedness to foster diverse viewpoints, support employees and partner organizations through inclusive and equitable practices and culture
2.	**Diversity management**	Initiatives that an organization spearheads to efficiently manage a diverse workforce to sustain diversity through recruitment, retention, talent development and related best practices
3.	**Diversity competence**	The ability to understand, appreciate and respond to the characteristics of co-workers from a diverse background that can ensure collaborative and cohesive working
4.	**Inclusivity index**	A measure of the degree of inclusivity in organizational practices
5.	**Mentoring**	A professional relationship in which a subject matter expert (called the mentor) helps a junior professional (the mentee) in developing specific skills and knowledge that will enhance his/her professional and personal growth; the mentoring process is mostly one-to-one and is continual and evolving in nature.
6.	**Underutilization**	The state of not being used enough or not being used to full potential

'Mom, Hi Mom!!' Saro's voice was both excited and tensed as she heard her mother's voice on the other end of the phone.

'Hello dear!' said her mom. She seemed to be in the middle of something. 'Hold on, Saro,' she said before addressing someone nearby. 'Let it marinate, don't remove it so soon. The spices have to seep into the vegetables. Yes, that's it. Mix it well and let it rest.'

'Mom, who are you teaching?' asked Saro.

'Who else but our new cook Raji. She knows only very basic cooking; hence, I have to teach her almost everything. But I am thankful that at least I have her to take care of the day-to-day work,' she said with a laugh. 'Ok, you tell me. How are you? And to what do I owe the pleasure of this out-of-the-ordinary call, that too on a Friday morning? Usually, I will only get to speak to you on a Sunday, if at all.'

'Mom...come on,' said Saro sheepishly. 'It's not like I don't speak to you frequently. I text you every day, don't I?'

'Just joking my dear, I know you are busy, what with setting up your house and the work and everything. How is Rahul?' asked Mom, her voice filled with love.

'He is fine, Mom. Listen, I need your help.'

'Tell me.'

'Rahul and I are hosting our first ever dinner tonight. His colleagues are coming over. I am so worked up. Imagine! I am hosting a dinner in my new home with my husband. Oh God, I have adulted so fast. Mom, it's crazy!'

'First of all, relax. Have you planned what you are going to cook?'

'Mom, why do you think I am calling you? I don't have even the faintest clue. It just got decided and I am freaking out! We have been living off Swiggy and Uber Eats for the past 3 days, ever since we came back from the honeymoon.'

'May I ask you then why you agreed to host this dinner if you are not prepared for it?' Mom's logic hit hard and Saro's voice sounded exactly like a 6-year-old's.

'Mom…, we were chatting, Rahul, me and his friends on our WhatsApp group and suddenly they began planning this. You know that IPL is going on and there is a CSK match tonight. So Rahul suggested why don't they all come home and I suggested the dinner part. It seemed like fun, because all these are super cool folks and they all have so much fun together and most of them are working away from their native places and yearn for home-cooked food and so I can't just order out; it will seem weird, so I have to make dinner,' Saro finished in a rush.

'Calm down Saro, catch your breath!' laughed Mom. 'It's not that big a deal. Listen. For a dinner to be successful there are six elements: the ambience—the place where you serve dinner; the starters—the first thing that you serve; the drinks; the main course; the dessert; and most importantly, the group that comes together. Decide what you will make and what you can buy. It has to be a good mix. But, in my opinion, the group is the most critical ingredient. You can plan the fanciest dinner ever, but if the group that comes together is boring or does not gel, then your dinner will not work. If you have an interesting, spirited group, then even the simplest of meals will be a lot of fun! That way, your dinner is already a success!'

Once the D&I vision statement is created, the broad elements of the D&I agenda are put together. These would include the following: (a) The definition of D&I from your own organizational standpoint—How does the practice of D&I stand uniquely positioned within your culture?

(b) The need articulation or the 'why' of D&I—Why does it become imperative that the culture of D&I is followed and practised? (c) What are the goals or objectives that the D&I agenda must achieve? These could be short term, medium term or long term. (d) What is the governance model? How is decision-making enabled both from a macro and a micro perspective? (e) How do we ensure that adequate control is maintained by leadership while still not removing from the actual implementers their skin in the game? And finally, (f) What is the universally understood mechanism for calculation of ROI?

A simpler method would be to use a marketing analogy by asking the following questions from a D&I outlook: (a) What is my current situation from a talent and culture perspective? (b) Who are the target audiences for whom I am building this agenda? (c) What are my milestones and goals? (d) What will be the most effective communication and implementation strategy? (e) What will be the scaling up method and what can I look at as stretch goals? (f) How do I measure progress?

A D&I agenda creates a tangible and measurable plan which everyone involved is able to clearly articulate. It establishes a causal relationship with the achievement of business goals and is devoid of intellectualism. The pre-work required to set the objectives clearly is not to be underestimated, since a robust D&I plan cannot fall apart under logical scrutiny. While innovation in the form of new and unchartered D&I objectives is nice to have as a marcom differential, it would be wise to look at the basics of what D&I is essentially meant to achieve and pursue the same, even at the cost of being repetitive or monotonous.

Also, for those organizations embarking upon a D&I journey, it is beneficial to allow some organic change to take place in the objectives, to allow a trial and error method of reaching the most ideal plan. Preventing opacity and ensuring clarity in the setting of objectives are critical to the successful attainment of D&I.

A HIERARCHY OF D&I PRIORITIES

An organization, let's call them 123Inc, had reached out to me after hearing my talk at a conference. Their need was simple. They wanted a diverse and inclusive workplace, but didn't know where to begin. After a series of calls, meetings and discussions, I was asked to travel to their Asia Pacific HQ in Singapore to meet with their senior leaders. The India Geography Head for 123Inc got the meeting together and opened the floor.

He presented the data on the representation of different diversity groups within 123Inc India and the plans for the future. His diversity council, a cross-functional team of senior management professionals, went up next and spoke about each of their ideas for the company's D&I agenda. Finally, the APAC regional CEO turned to me and asked, 'Dr Rajesh, are we on track?'

I replied, 'Mr Po, in my experience, D&I action can happen in two ways. There are two directions from which this can be led—from the top or from the bottom. When the D&I agenda is driven from the top, it takes the form of events, new policies, programmes, training, etc. This is what I see in the presentations made by your team. But when the D&I focus begins from the bottom, it means that a need for change has been felt at the individual employee level. That translates into small behavioural differences with 'inclusion' becoming more visible. For instance, it is in the way work gets done in your logistics department or your product development hubs. That, in my opinion, is more sustainable.'

In a valuable report on understanding the maturity of D&I agendas of organizations, PwC speaks about four key differentiators that set apart companies which create effective diverse work environments. The four differentiating steps are: (a) understanding the facts of today, (b) building

an inspirational strategy, (c) developing leadership engagement and (d) creating sustainable movement.

These four steps are essentially the key elements of the D&I strategy. These, in turn, (a) enable the organization to delve deeper into obtaining and analysing data around the demographics of the company, the existence of bias, performance and compensation data; (b) create a business-focused vision and strategy for D&I that reflect the reality of today and the real potential of tomorrow; (c) engage leadership around an inspirational D&I strategy by articulating the business case and establishing supportive governance, policies and procedures; and (d) execute the D&I strategy across all elements of your business and talent ecosystem.

The trick is to ensure that the strategy is both aspirational and senior-management led, while also being very real and keeping the average employee in mind. A well-executed D&I agenda ensures that employees are comfortable in their own skin at work. This translates into the employees displaying better customer connect, greater community engagement and a sense of ease in their workplace. The ability of an organization to allow the individual to bring distinctive experiences and perceptions to the table both in groups and in work teams helps ensure a much higher level of problem-solving.

Thus, the agenda should have equal measures of ideas and programmes to create increased diversity at the workplace, which allows for a wider net to connect with a greater variety of people, while also focusing on inclusion to provide a much broader spectrum of different perspectives comfortably expressed.

HOW TO MEASURE D&I PROGRESS?

Interviewer: Ms Sultana, we are very happy that you have agreed to discuss your organization's key competitive edge—D&I! As the India Geography Head for Abhi Technology System's (ATS) operations, you are one of the most influential leaders in this country. You took over this position when the company was at a low ebb and now, you have brought it to success. Most interestingly, you credit the philosophy of D&I with having been the game changer. It would be great to have your views on how you made it work.

Ms Sultana: Thanks for your kind words! Yes, I deeply believe that it is indeed the twin principles of D&I that have made ATS the organization it is today.

Interviewer: Forgive my saying so, but are these not very 'airy' aspects that do not lend themselves to be tracked and managed very well?

Ms Sultana: You are right. D&I does have the imagery of being a very nebulous, imprecise science. People think that it cannot be brought to account the way other functions and initiatives can. But, that is not entirely true. It is fully possible to link and measure the effectiveness of D&I in achieving various goals, including people objectives as well as business objectives.

Interviewer: Could you give us an example of some of the goals that you set for the D&I process at ATS? That is, if it is not too confidential to share.

Ms Sultana: I am more than happy to share what we tracked. I would be glad if other organizations followed this, even our own competitors. First of all, I linked our D&I objectives to both customer satisfaction and employee satisfaction. This sent out a

powerful message that for me, both our internal audience and external community were equally important. Next, I looked at the employee retention rate. This we connected to the policies and programmes for better employee inclusion and monitored the cost of these. We then looked at the presence of innovation in business processes—the incremental number of ideas that each team produced, as a result of removal of blind spots and biases. Finally, we trained our attention on to the value add that customers experienced as a result of inclusion in teams. When diverse teams gelled well and approached the objective of creating a great experience for the customer, then that automatically added to our topline.

Interviewer: This is seriously amazing! You call it out as if it were the easiest thing to do. But I am sure that setting this whole idea in motion would have been very difficult. How did you do that?

Ms Sultana: I believe that the role of the leader is to consistently, relentlessly champion the benefits of D&I and personify the values. This is all that is required. The team will take care of everything else!

Most D&I implementers are very concerned about the tracking and measuring of D&I in their workplaces. Like most culture-building mechanisms, D&I too is easier said than done. In truth, D&I measurement begins with its alignment to your business goals. Every business is different and hence clearly aligning your business objectives with your D&I mission is paramount.

Subsequent to the creation of the D&I vision, mission and objectives, it is advisable to set specific performance targets for each section of the strategic intent. This could pan out as targets to be achieved in recruitment, retention, engagement, performance measures and eventually, business growth. The full power of D&I is unleashed when the organization creates a consequence-based assessment method, continually linking results to efforts. Many of these results could be long term and not immediately quantifiable, but the trick lies in allotting measurable outcomes by analysing aspects such as behaviour and culture and ascertaining the extent of change.

It is important to differentiate the goals separately for diversity efforts and inclusion efforts. Measuring diversity in talent acquisition and workforce creation is relatively less complicated. Many organizations may have multi-year diversity initiatives which include incremental change year on year. In such cases, targets broken down by defined periods of time, depending on business undulations, can be tracked and analysed. This analysis can help express the delta between aspirational goals and actual attainment.

When it comes to measuring and tracking the pace of change in inclusion, a continual improvement method is ideally placed to provide clarity in progress. By assessing each inclusion approach as a tool to remove barriers and create greater trust and respect in the workplace, the D&I team moves steadily towards the goal of a fully inclusive environment. When inclusion is associated with strategic objectives, the cause-and-effect relationship can be clearly predicted. Even for an esoteric goal such as inclusion, tangible outcomes can be linked to determine whether the plan is reaching its set aims or requires mid-path course correction.

I have observed that organizations make constant revisions to their D&I strategy in order to align their business priorities better with the policies or programmes being implemented. This is not a sign of weak planning, but a robust evidence of genuine intent. Such alterations will result in key metrics becoming further nuanced. This only proves the deep focus that the organization has on D&I.

D&I GAME: EXPERIENCING DIVERSITY AND INCLUSION

Organizations of varied sizes and forms are at different junctures of their D&I journeys. This self-assessment will help you understand where your organization is positioned along the aspirational curve of D&I. For every segment that follows, please tick the statements that are applicable to your organization.

SEGMENT 1

My organization:

- uses a formal, standardized definition for D&I that is communicated to the entire employee base.

- does not tolerate any form of discrimination or harassment.

- has a D&I council/committee that drives the D&I agenda.

- sees to it that workspaces have infrastructural inclusion.

- conducts at least one learning intervention on D&I, annually.

SEGMENT 2

In my organization:

- managers are accountable for diversity metrics.

- diversity hiring is a key recruitment focus.

- inclusion in organizational practices (from talent attraction to management to retention) is regularly audited.

- to be a leader, an inclusive mindset is a prerequisite.

- business plans factor in diversity goals.

SEGMENT 3

My organization:

- has sustained gender diversity ratios that are considerably higher than the industry averages, for the last five years.

- participates in nation-wide D&I benchmarking studies, consistently.

- has been recognized in national and international forums for diversity best practices.

- monitors and tracks data around organizational practices, slicing and dicing this data around D&I dimensions.

- follows a diversity strategy map, propelled by an inclusive work culture.

SCORING

- For every question you ticked in segment 1, give yourself a score of 1.

- For every question you ticked in segment 2, give yourself a score of 2.

- For every question you ticked in segment 3, give yourself a score of 3.

IF YOUR TOTAL SCORE IS BETWEEN:

- 25 and 30: Congratulations! Your organization has successfully embraced diversity and is an icon of inclusion.

- 20 and 24: Good! Your organization is fairly matured in the journey of D&I. Continue aligning your diversity goals to business imperatives.

- 15 and 19: Fair. Your D&I journey is compassed in the right direction. Strive to make your practices inclusive and leverage the benefits of diversity.

- 0 and 14: Your organizational journey on D&I has just begun. Continue on this path, improving workforce diversity and building your pace on the pillars of inclusion.

Dear Diary,

I almost put in my resignation letter today. After nearly 18 years at Striate Inc, it feels really horrible to even say this. This company has literally been my second home. I have grown with it, learnt so much and built so many relationships. And I think that the cause for this bitter feeling is something that I am deeply passionate about—D&I. Shocking, right?

Yes, you know that I had been elevated to the position of the Chief Diversity Officer (CDO) at Striate, after a long and interesting career that took me through various arenas such as quality, customer ops, programme management, HR and even a brief stint in selling! However, right through, I also felt very fervently about the need for inclusion and diversity at Striate.

So, when this position opened up, I was among the first to put up my hand and say that I was interested. The MD too thought that I was well suited to the role and so, a couple of months back, I was duly promoted and appointed. And then the problems began.

What was initially only the occasional watercooler chit-chat, became a regular flood of comments. First, the senior leadership team started asking what the objectives (that I was working towards) were. When

I gave them a document outlining what I planned to do, they came back with the remark that there was no cohesion in the plan. I reworked the entire thing, looking at it from the business perspective and presented it along with a manpower plan and budgets to the Executive Committee. The CFO who sits in the ExCom immediately replied stating that this is a nascent function whose relevance is unproven and we cannot allot people or money on this so early. This by itself was an unexpected blow.

Later, I blocked the calendar of the MD and sat with her to get perspective on what she felt the CDO should do. In fact, during that conversation itself, I felt that while the MD wanted someone in charge of the D&I function, she herself was not sure as to what she wanted me to do. Simultaneously, I began noticing that during senior-level meetings, my opinion would not be recognized or even heard. I started feeling that my role was more a decorative shelf-piece, something to mention to customers and investors proudly, yes, but one that did not really have any significance. But then, I understand the problem well. I know what is happening. Even I will not respect someone whose role is vague. If expectations from my function are unclear, then how can I prove that I am adding value to the organization? Frankly, I am not even aware of what are the competencies required for this role.

The last straw today happened when we were discussing the manpower plan for the forthcoming financial year. When I began voicing my opinion on the diversity of the candidates that we should target, the CHRO turned to me and said bluntly, 'We need to first discuss and get the important, hard business requirements out of the way. Later, over chai, we can

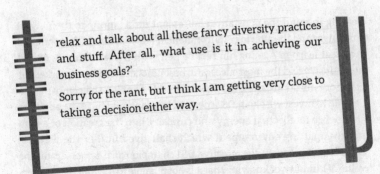

relax and talk about all these fancy diversity practices and stuff. After all, what use is it in achieving our business goals?'

Sorry for the rant, but I think I am getting very close to taking a decision either way.

When the D&I function is created without a clear business purpose, it often leads to disillusionment. The expectations and the resultant reality differ widely and this creates confusion around the entire initiative and the very reason for its existence. When the competencies and result areas of the D&I leader are not outlined unambiguously, the D&I discipline is itself often compromised.

The incredible pace of change in business has reiterated the necessity for the D&I function in order to develop new skills and knowledge to manage the frenetic transformation of the workplace. The role of the D&I leader, interchangeably referred to as the CDO or the D&I Champion, is a crucial role, one that helps the organization deal with the unchartered territories of global business and the consequential cultural mores that are needed to be demystified. The importance of the D&I function is that it cuts across all other functions and influences decision-making in every sphere of the organization.

The CDO is, therefore, as much a communicator, an interpreter and a behavioural practitioner. But more than all of this, for the function to be performed accurately, the CDO needs to be an influential leader whose opinions are valued. Organizations that have a successful D&I agenda in place, one that is working and yielding results, often have a dynamic, charismatic leader helming the D&I function. He/she must be a role model, one who lives the values and demonstrates the competency of inclusion. His own team should be a veritable example of D&I in action and his capacity to facilitate and enable others through their conflicts should be paramount.

Competencies of D&I Practitioners

175

Bearing in mind the constant requirement for adapting to the newest challenges and the altering environment, it is also essential that the CDO is a great learner. Arming himself/herself with the latest trends of his/her industry and the most successful best practices that have worked for other organizations, the CDO should be able to guide the company leadership to invest wisely in D&I spends. He/she should have the ability to channelize intellectual energy and curiosity into the creation of a constantly uplifting environment which shall give him/her the winning edge. Simultaneously, the effective D&I champion also demonstrates the value of humility, of knowing that it is not possible to have all the answers and that it requires courage to admit one's ignorance while making an all-out attempt to equip oneself. A great measure of expertise in the D&I practitioner is his/her acceptance of ambiguity and complexity in achieving the goal of inclusion and dealing with this with astute communication and decision-making.

DAY 67/99

WHO ARE YOUR D&I ROLE MODELS?

Carefully balancing the steaming cup of coffee and the thick sheaf of reports that she needed for the review meeting, Shradha walked down the gleaming passageway of AB Group's Mumbai facility. She was proud of her corner office—she was the CEO of AB Group's Homecare retail business! The media had gone to town about how Shradha was not just the youngest but also the smartest CEO to occupy that office. Though she was happy with the positive press, Shradha was not oblivious to the huge task she had on hand. As she settled into her chair, she doodled on the notepad while her thoughts raced on, prior to the review meeting with her D&I council. 'I need to ensure that we create a very diverse and inclusive culture at AB Homecare. How do I set D&I benchmarks? Would it be by comparing ourselves to the best in the industry or by looking at the best practices in my own industry?' There was a knock on her door and Sunil along with his four-member team trooped in. 'Before we begin the review, I have a fundamental question,' said Shradha. 'Do we even know whether we are aspiring for the right results? Can we view D&I plans the same way as business or HR agendas? Who are our D&I role models?'

The growing awareness of D&I as an organizational practice, as a cultural fulcrum to drive productivity, creativity and better problem-solving is calling for discussions among leaders on how D&I should be approached. More and more leaders are wondering how they should model their D&I journey. Who should they emulate? I have a simple answer. Choose an organization whose culture is aspirational to you. For companies in the FMCG space, Hindustan Unilever, Procter & Gamble and PepsiCo are role models. For IT organizations, IBM and TCS are vanguard leaders. For those in the consulting and operations business, Accenture, EY and Deloitte are amazing to follow. You can read about their inclusion journeys, their diversity practices, their workshops and programmes and decide what works for your organization.

An even simpler method would be to look at what your 'soft' objectives are with regard to your inclusion journey. Do you want to create integral change or do you want a 'visually' diverse workplace? Do you prefer that every team in your organization is diverse with a gender-balanced mix or do you wish to see your managers and leaders become more inclusive, more accepting? Identifying your D&I role models is about embarking upon a journey that has a decisive goal. Understanding your own industry's benchmarks is the first step. Setting inclusion targets that are far above your industry's average will lead to a pressure-filled recruitment focus, which could ultimately backfire. Instead, investing time and focus on identifying who your real role models are is the most astute path to progress.

'DIVERSITY FATIGUE' IS REAL

Vivek was ushered into Mr Reddy's beautiful large 17th-floor office by the latter's secretary with a request—'Mr Reddy is just wrapping up his previous meeting at the conference room. He requested you to wait. He will join you in about 10 minutes.' Vivek did not mind. The 35-year-old Plant Manager actually welcomed the opportunity to gather his thoughts and prepare himself once more for what he was planning to discuss with Mr Reddy, the highly respected HR Director of Yellow Snacks and Foods. The tastefully decorated room provided a gorgeous view of the silvery Santhome waters. Vivek rehearsed his opening lines—'Sir, I am not comfortable participating in the Womentoring programme. With this new POSH Act and also the many workshops that all of us attend about gender sensitization, etc., I am more and more concerned that even a simple gesture could be misconstrued. Plus, it is quite tiring to constantly walk on eggshells around my lady colleagues. Hope you can move me to a role where I do not have to manage diversity.' Satisfied with his flow, Vivek settled a bit more comfortably in his chair and noticed the beautiful plaque on Mr Reddy's table. It was a quote by Mahatma Gandhi: 'As human beings our greatness lies not so much as in being to remake the world—that is the myth of the atomic age—as in remaking ourselves.'

Of late, I hear many discussions centred around this topic—'diversity fatigue'. This essentially means two things: (a) the concept of D&I has not been fully thought through with regard to its acceptance by the said organization and (b) the communication of the D&I objective and its articulation by the right role models to the organizational audience has not hit the correct notes.

While companies in principle support the concept of D&I, to actually walk the talk by recruiting and nurturing diversity talent—whether it is persons with disability or returning women—requires consistent, committed effort. 'Diversity fatigue' is what managers refer to as the stress that they feel when KRAs pertaining to D&I also get added to their day-to-day business goals.

While ideologically varied opinions exist along the spectrum towards how exactly diversity must be approached, sometimes, it is also a resistance to things changing too fast, and too much. The discussion about D&I is today more prevalent in mainstream conversations with more and more organizations believing that in diversity lies the next big opportunity. However, articulation of diversity requires a well thought through strategy that anticipates friction and adopts a problem-solving approach.

Merely espousing a diversity policy or agenda will not serve the organization's larger purpose. Understanding the pain points of D&I implementation in your company or industry, assessing the best possible solution to create a lasting impact and approaching a coaching/mentoring approach to the actual execution is the best way. This is the approach that I have seen succeed.

DIVERSITY AUDITS AND BENCHMARKS

DAY 69/99

PD: Hey listen, Lux, got a moment?

LR: Rushing into a mtg. But do tell.

PD: Sry, this will take just 2 mins.

LR: Go on.

PD: Today, there's a D&I benchmarking session in a couple of mins that you have nominated me for. What do I expect?

LR: Oh, that's the meeting I am going to.

PD: Oh, shucks, wanted to catch you before you started. What's this D&I benchmarking all about?

LR: You are a social media marketing gal. What do you do in your mktg benchmarks?

PD: Well, the most recent thing I did was an IG (Instagram) benchmark of our products v/s competition.

LR: Awesome! So, what did you do?

PD: So, I got my team to do a full sweep of all IG stories of all our key competitors.

LR: And then?

PD: Dug up lots of data like formats, ideas, time periods, etc.

LR: And…?

PD: We figured out the metrics, so that we can do averages and medians and created benchmark cards for my boss to number-crunch.

LR: Brilliant! So what did it tell you?

PD: I guess it told us where we were as against competition, also product-wise, how we were performing, bottom-half or top-half. Gave us a bunch of insights on where we were going right or wrong.

LR: Fabulous! That's exactly what we do with our D&I benchmarking. Come on, let's get started!

D&I benchmarking is the process of studying industry or competitive practices in the functions of diversity and inclusion to find new ways to improve existing processes. Companies that are very specific about their D&I goals, use benchmarking to gauge their success and also pinpoint where they can do better. Increasingly, companies which invest significantly in the pursuit of D&I objectives use the method of benchmarking to identify problem areas in their own systems and select those competitors who are perceived to do better than them to assess the difference. Companies find that using D&I benchmarking allows them to study the success stories of competitors' initiatives and adapt them to their own environment. They subsequently make improvements to the policies and programmes to enhance effectiveness.

D&I benchmarking is a vital continuous improvement tool that enables an organization to up the game when it comes to operational excellence. Analysing interesting trends, a vigorous soul-searching and replicating useful best practices are the result of a well-conducted D&I benchmarking study. Benchmark reports also throw light on the D&I metrics which an organization must focus on in order to achieve success. An organization which shows a 20 per cent women's representation in the FMCG industry in India is said to be doing very well. However, if a benchmarking study against its key competitors reveals that industry averages are at around 25–30 per cent, then reality emerges. D&I benchmarks enable the company to create accountability for every goal in the D&I function and to drill down into performance gaps. The same holds true when a leader is ahead of industry norms and is at the forefront. It is imperative to determine the causes for such exceptional performance and how the same can be sustained.

D&I audits, on the other hand, are completely internal. They are conducted within the workplace, either by an internal resource or by a third-party consultant (just like a benchmarking study) and are intended to help the organization compare documented policies against actual performance. Aspects such as the relevance of programmes to the intended target audience, deficiencies in the implementation of policies and potential minefields which could create problems for the organization's culture and reputation are also flagged off. Audits also help to assess ways in which the company's D&I agenda can be optimized keeping in view the business objectives. From a compliance point of view also, a D&I audit enables the company to evaluate the strengths and weaknesses of the current system, whether all statutory requirements are met and if the redressal mechanism is in place. Audits, when conducted with rigorous single-mindedness, can enhance the company's credentials, increase employee awareness about D&I, ensure more effective compliance and will be regarded as a good-faith effort by the organization to genuinely improve its performance.

Diversity Audits and Benchmarks

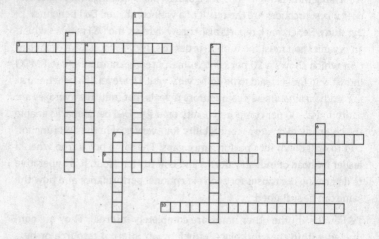

ACROSS

3 A work culture that acknowledges and promotes the acceptance and understanding of different cultures working in an organization. (16)

8 People engaged in or available for work, either in a country or area or in a particular organization or industry. (9)

9 The state of not being used enough or not being used to full potential. (16)

10 The ability to understand, appreciate and respond to the characteristics of co-workers from a diverse background that can ensure collaborative and cohesive working. (9,10)

DOWN

1 A measure of the degree of inclusivity in organizational practices. (11,5)

2 Widespread disparities that exist in the achievements between the majority and the minority groups. (11,3)

4 All individuals who are of legally employable age in a community and are employed or looking for work. (6,5)

5 An organization's capacity and preparedness to foster diverse viewpoints, support employees and partner organizations through inclusive and equitable practices and culture. (9,9)

6 The process of stepping down from a full-fledged, thriving career. (3-7)

7 A professional relationship in which a subject matter expert helps a junior professional in developing specific skills and knowledge that will enhance his/her professional and personal growth. The process is mostly one-to-one and is continual and evolving in nature. (9)

SECTION 8

BIASES AND HOW TO
FIND THEM

DIVERSITY AND INCLUSION LEXICON

S. No.	Words	Definition
1.	Bias	A preference for or tendency towards a particular viewpoint or outcome
2.	Gender parity	In an organizational context, this refers to the ideal organizational condition under which both genders have equal access to employment and development opportunities and are on equal pay scales
3.	Gender sensitization	Refers to the process of modification of individual behaviour by raising awareness on gender equality concerns
4.	Gender stereotypes	Simplistic generalizations (often over generalizations) about the characteristics, differences and roles of individuals belonging to a particular gender; stereotypes can be positive or negative, but they rarely communicate accurate information about others.
5.	Gender balance	In an organizational context, this refers to an ideal condition in which there is a 50:50 representation of men and women in an organization and they are equally enabled to reach their full potential.
6.	Gender bias	In an organizational context, this refers to unequal treatment in employment and growth opportunities within an organization (such as promotion, pay, benefits and privileges), and expectations due to attitudes based on the gender of an employee.

S. No.	Words	Definition
7.	Prejudice	A preconceived judgement or bias about an employee or a group of employees; a prejudice can be positive or negative.
8.	Sensitization programmes	Initiatives that focus on enhancing awareness and sensitivity of professionals on certain ideas, events, situations or phenomenon
9.	Unconscious bias	Natural people preferences whereby an individual routinely and rapidly sorts people into groups; this preference bypasses his/her normal, rational and logical thinking.

INTERLUDE: THE DANGER OF CARING TOO MUCH

DAY 72/99

'Are we all set?' asked Bharat as he pushed the sunglasses firmly back on his nose and adjusted the seat belt of the high-end SUV to make it more comfortable in preparation for the long drive. He quickly went through the series of checks that he usually did whenever he took over the car from their driver. Driving was a pleasure, albeit a rare one these days. Evita, her own seat belt strapped and ready, turned to look at the back seat where their two daughters Anga (9) and Sanga (4) were arranging what looked like an entire car load of toys, snacks, books, an iPad and other accessories required to fully enjoy the journey.

'I guess we are!' laughed Evita. These drives were very special to her too and she enjoyed riding next to Bharat. Since the days of their courtship, when they both had been young MTs at AcceLever, she had admired

Interlude

185

Bharat's driving skills. He used to drive a sky-blue Fiat Premier Padmini back then, she reminisced with a smile. Even that little car transformed magically under Bharat's expert driving without anything 'automatic' about it. They would play old Hindi songs and Ilayaraja's music on the boxy cassette player and time seemed to stand still as Bharat would manoeuvre the ghat roads with finesse. Those drives could put to shame any taken on the long line of fancy cars that followed, thought Evita wistfully.

And now, more than ever, Evita cherished the time that the long drive up the mountains to visit Bharat's dad gave them—to reflect, to debate, to speak about the hundreds of little things which the punishing routine of Bharat's everyday life could not allow. A couple of times a year, they would undertake this pilgrimage of sorts, driving up to the small hill-town where Bharat's dad lived. Dad had shifted there soon after Bharat had got married. In the 20-plus years, the senior Mr Manush had created a small community around his home. His garden teeming with perfect rose bushes was as much his pride as were the dozen odd children of the household help and from the village nearby whom he taught and supported with their education. A sprightly man, who looked younger than his 73 years, Dad was still fit and in good health.

It was a short 100-km trip that got done under 3 hours and yet it seemed to Evita that they would cover months of discussion in that time. Of course, that was if they did not require to intervene on the daughters' squabbles, chances of which to be fair to them, thought Evita, were rare. The sisters were very attached to each other. The 5-year age gap had ensured that there was no sibling rivalry; Anga considered herself a second mother to Sanga and their parents ensured that she was accorded the due respect of a responsible big sister.

As Bharat negotiated the car into the highway, his mind settled on the 99 Day Diversity Challenge. He had covered almost two-thirds of the manuscript. He enjoyed Paramita's storytelling method and realized how it was influencing his thinking. Just immersing yourself in a topic made you more aware, more mindful. It changed your behaviour. He was uncharacteristically quiet and reflective as they drove up the hill roads. The children had fallen asleep, the steady hum of the car's powerful engine acting as a lullaby. Even as Evita tried to engage him in a conversation, she realized soon enough that he was preoccupied. Settling on Kishore Kumar's hits of the 1970s, Evita allowed the music to fill the silence.

… … … … …

Dad's happiness at seeing his son, daughter-in-law and the kids was evident from the beaming glow that wreathed his face, as he pulled the children into a tight embrace while they squealed with delight. Yoda, Dad's 8-year-old golden retriever, went into paroxysms of joy as he jumped on both the girls, unable to decide who he loved more. The girls ran into the house with Yoda chasing them while Sundar, the gardener-cum-handyman, ran behind them to mitigate any accidental destruction to the properties of the house. Dad looked happily at the buzz of flurry that the children's arrival had created. It was a welcome change to the calm silence that usually enveloped the house at this time of the day.

Evita noticed that Anand, Dad's 60-year-old cook, was in the kitchen whipping up a big lunch complete with all the many items that Evita, Bharat and the kids enjoyed. 'Anand Bhaiyya, Namaste!' Evita greeted him with a warm smile. 'Namaste, Ma'am!' said Anand. While Bharat had always been 'Bharat Babu' to Anand, he maintained respectful distance with Evita since the time of her marriage. 'Any help required around here, Bhaiyya? You seem to be making so many dishes?' asked Evita. She inhaled the rich aroma of the cashew nut gravy that Anand was preparing to add to the curry. It was one of Dad's recipes. A great cook, Dad never shied away from the kitchen whenever he visited Evita and Bharat. He would throw on an apron and begin cooking for them. There had been days when a tired Bharat would come home from work to the welcoming fragrance of pasta with marinara sauce prepared as a surprise for him by Dad.

'Anand will manage all of that. Why don't you come and sit with me in the front porch?' Dad answered for Anand. 'I had asked him to make your favourite mint-chai with fresh mint from the garden.' Dad poured three cups of the steaming tea while Evita fetched a tray to place the cups in. They made their way to the old, worn-out, yet super comfortable sofas in the porch.

Bharat followed Anga and Sanga who disappeared into the backyard of the house with a hyper-excited Yoda in tow. The neat backyard led to the large garden that took up a lot of Dad's time. The lemon tree was the hero of the garden. It yielded fruit right round the year, except for a few spare months in between and occupied pride of place in the centre of the garden. It was Dad's much-loved favourite. He had planted it as a young sapling, brought from the home that he had shared with Bharat's mom. It had grown tall and began flowering within mere months, much to Dad's delight. Evergreen and seemingly immortal, it had withstood the anger and fury of storms in the past, bouncing back after even being uprooted entirely once. Thanks to the cast iron pillar that Dad had erected to support the tree, it now grew with cheerful abandon, greedily soaking up all the sun that the garden enjoyed. Not ungrateful, it brought forth enormous numbers of fruits the size of small tennis balls, which Anand and Sundar packed into bags and sent to every neighbour in the vicinity. A gnarled old gooseberry tree that had been part of the land when Dad bought it still claimed its rightful place in one corner, providing gooseberries in summer for Sundar's wife to make pickles while allowing a makeshift swing for his kids in its wizened yet strong branches. Yellow rose and bright pink oleander shrubs lined the garden alongside a vegetable patch where Sundar grew pumpkins, brinjals and greens.

As Bharat walked back to the porch and settled down in the sofa with his cup of tea, he could hear the children's gleeful laughter punctuated by Yoda's happy barks. They ran around exploring the new additions to the garden, stopping to smell a flower here and a fruit there, jumping over a tulsi plant and stopping to rub their fingers on the thick succulent leaves of the thyme that Dad grew in plenty. Bharat could hear Sundar's high-pitched voice calling out to them to ensure that the trio did not do too much damage to the plants in their excitement.

Bharat remembered his own childhood, largely alone but for the presence of a few concerned relatives who took up residence in his home after the passing of his mother. He was glad that Anga and Sanga had each other. The comfort of a sibling, the presence of a playmate, someone who travelled the journey with you when you needed a companion the most to make sense of this complex world was a gift unparalleled. In fact, it was largely his own experience of being a lonely, silent child, always surrounded by adults that had made Bharat cut short Evita's career after the birth of Anga. He had wanted a second child soon, but it was another 5 years before Sanga was born.

Dad's laughter in response to something Evita had said brought Bharat back to the present. 'I was asking her about this 99 Day Diversity Challenge that you are reading,' said Dad. 'It appears that Paramita has got you well and truly hooked to this concept!'

Bharat smiled a little sheepishly. 'I think it came into my life at the right moment,' he said, thoughtfully. 'It makes me reflect on a lot of things and I am seeing my work in a totally new light altogether,' he added.

'Speaking of work, I actually wanted to talk about Evita's work,' said Dad, 'or rather the lack of it.'

Evita appeared to be fascinated by a Mexican design on her tea mug while Bharat looked quizzically at Dad. 'I mean that it is time she got back to her career,' said Dad.

Bharat swallowed the familiar displeasure that arose in him whenever Dad brought up this subject. He rarely had any disagreements with Dad, having understood the care and concern that his father had for him, but this was a touchy topic. Evita had certainly been an ambitious, aspiring young professional when Bharat had met her for the very first time at the induction programme which AcceLever ran at the erstwhile Searock Sheraton in Bombay. In fact, it was that quality of Evita's— cheerful, competitive and focused—that had attracted Bharat. Even though they worked for different business units, he knew that she was one of the top performers at AcceLever whose boss had given her the charge of an entire department within months, seeing her dynamism and leadership skills.

But that was almost two decades ago. After a long courtship, when they had eventually married, they had had an understanding that her career would take a backseat to his. Evita had continued working at AcceLever for a few more years before Anga was born. Bharat felt that Evita herself had no complaints, although he would see her tracking the progress of her batchmates and mentioning occasionally to Bharat about how so-and-so had become the COO or VP of a big brand. It rankled Bharat that Dad always spoke about Evita's aborted career, with what appeared to be more concern than Bharat himself.

'Sanga is going to be 5 in another few months,' continued Dad. 'Don't you think it is time for Evita to get back to the workplace?'

'Well…' said Bharat with a sardonic smile, 'if she too wants to get into the rat race and catch those horrible early morning flights and stay in a different hotel each time and manage the pressures of performance and results, why not?'

'What if she wanted to experience all of that for herself??' asked Dad.

Sensing the tension in the air, Evita quickly chipped in, 'Actually, I had wanted to discuss about it during our drive, Bharat, but I felt you were a bit preoccupied and so did not want to disturb you.'

Bharat looked surprised and asked, 'Discuss what?'

'Well, there has been this offer from a boutique consulting firm. It's not an "offer"–offer but more like an invitation to a discussion. They are looking for senior professionals to lead their marketing practice and I was wondering if I should give it a shot…,' said Evita.

'I, for one, certainly think you should,' said Dad. 'Both the kids are old enough to understand that their mother needs time outside the home and I am sure our man Bharat too would realize that.'

'I have never been against Evita working,' replied Bharat defensively. 'I only feel that the children's upbringing should also be a priority for the mother. I missed the presence of a mother, Dad. You can't blame me if I don't want Anga and Sanga to go through the same.'

'Your life was different', said Dad shortly. 'I lost my wife to cancer and did not want to replace her. I tried my best to bring you up without you missing your mother but even then I realized that it is not possible for a father to take the place of a mother too. I know that you missed her and many of the decisions that you have taken have been a result of those experiences. But, that was then. This is now. Evita is a great mother and times have changed. She can ensure that she spends enough time with the children and you, while also pursuing something that excites and motivates her.'

'Well, I have seen that this dual-career challenge places enormous pressure on a couple,' came back Bharat, indicating that this was not something he hadn't thought about. 'Take the case of Aditi and Achal for instance. Aditi went through a nervous breakdown after a very hectic phase in her career, when their son was giving his 10th standard boards. What is the need to burn yourself out, when you can focus on other priorities?'

'That is just one instance, Bharat,' said Dad quietly. 'I know of several couples who have enjoyable lives with both partners doing what they wish to do.'

'I also keep reading about the pressures women face in the workplace. It is completely different from a man's experience,' added Bharat.

'Are you reading these articles because you come across them by chance or because you go seeking them out?' Dad's question was almost a challenge.

'I am merely quoting from the evidence that I have observed,' said Bharat.

'Sometimes, we only read what we wish to read. We only see what we wish to see,' Dad's cryptic statement was similar to another that Bharat had heard not long ago from someone much younger. 'Sir, one only sees what one knows. If you don't know, how can you see?'

'Dad, why don't we let Evita decide what she wants to do with her life?' said Bharat, a tad impatiently.

'I too have been reading a bit about inclusion,' said Dad, much to Bharat's surprise. He couldn't imagine the older man speaking about D&I. 'And I want to talk to you about filters.'

Dad got up from the sofa and indicated that Bharat too get up with him. Nodding at Evita to signal that he was having a private talk with his son, Dad placed his hand around Bharat's shoulder and gently walked with him into the driveway to the cottage. A true hill-station home, the driveway was lined with pine and eucalyptus trees. Bharat remembered how during a vacation not long ago, he and Dad had played cricket using the pine cones as balls in the winding road leading up to the cottage, with a little Anga cheering on. There was a picture somewhere of that, he recalled. She is growing up too fast … he thought to himself.

'Bharat, there is sometimes danger in caring too much,' began Dad as if reading his mind. 'As a father I wanted to protect you and hence would advise you all the time, giving you pieces of information that I believed were essential for you to be safe and secure in this world. As a father, a husband, why even as a gardener, one cares too much. Why did I put up the cast iron support for the lemon tree? It was a prop, a crutch. I had intended it to be short term, but today, the tree has enveloped the iron column and grown around it. Now, there is no way the pillar, whose purpose was merely temporary, can ever be separated from the lemon tree….'

Dad paused near a wild rose shrub that had grown almost into a small tree. He noticed a few dead flowers on the shrub and removed them. 'Parents or well-wishers wish to pass on information which we consider critical for our children or loved ones. And when the children grow up, they take decisions based on those bits of advice. Some of those pieces of information might not be relevant today, some might be downright ridiculous. But those fragments of advice, those bits of information get deeply embedded in our minds and become filters. Probably your attitude towards Evita's working is also the result of a filter.'

'But Dad, I am a grown man, a successful, responsible leader. How can I allow those filters to affect my decision-making?'

'That's the thing, son,' said Dad, giving Bharat's shoulder a squeeze with great fondness. 'The filters are not created overnight. And it's not conscious. Just think about who taught you right from wrong in your childhood. It would be me, a few of your teachers, some of your mentors, etc. As you grow older, you begin to choose whose values you align yourself with. Maybe one of your friends has a belief system not very different from your own. You then begin to believe that that particular friend's approaches are valid and intelligent, simply because it resembles your own. Then you begin seeking out media channels and reports that reinforce your system.'

They began walking towards the narrow pathway, covered on both sides with old trees.

'I have been observing my own biases and filters,' shared Dad, reflectively. 'I realize that I only watch those TV news channels whose ideologies I agree with. I read only the two newspapers which report the kind of news I like. I have been seeing that even the sites that I repeatedly browse on the internet are being seen by me again and again, because the algorithm has figured out that this is what I like!'

Bharat bent down to pick up a pine cone. He ran his fingers through its dried ridges, marvelling at its scales overlapping each other. He remembered a discussion with Dad, once, after they both had read Dan Brown's bestseller *The Da Vinci Code*, that the scales of a pine cone are arranged in Fibonacci number sequences. He realized how much he was influenced by Dad—by the older man's reading, his sense of humour, his value systems. Was it possible that Bharat had developed filters, unbeknownst to him which were making him less inclusive? Were they actually standing in the way of his allowing Evita to pursue a career of her choice? Was he trying to 'protect' her imagining that she too would go away like his mother did?

'It is important for us to learn new things to become truly inclusive. And equally important to unlearn. The world that your daughters would inhabit as adults will be a very different world. Are you ready to be a part of it? If you want to be included in their world, you might have to accept new "truths"! You would have to allow your concerns to take a back seat and permit new dimensions of thinking to challenge your present belief systems.' Dad smiled affectionately. 'Do you remember what it was like when I began cooking after your mother died? The horrible burnt curry, the bad tasting dal and yet today you love my cooking. One learns....'

'Bharat, it is time for you to assess your own biases and filters. And it is even more important for you to realize which pieces of advice have served their purpose and now it's time to dump them. Do you remember the story of the monkeys that got splashed with water each time one of them reached for a bunch of bananas? Over time, all the old monkeys were replaced with new ones, but none of the monkeys ever reached for the bananas because they had "learnt" that reaching for bananas meant getting dowsed in cold water. You no longer even remember the reason, but since the learning has been so deeply embedded in your psyche, you take decisions based on that "truth". Which truths do you have to junk in today's context, my son?'

Bharat suddenly turned to Dad and enveloped him in a tight hug. 'Thanks, Dad! For always being there, always saying the right things, always making me a better person.'

'Well, it's getting late,' said Dad gruffly, his voice laced with emotion. 'Evita and the kids would be waiting for lunch.'

DAY
73/99

UNDERSTANDING YOUR BIASES

Hi, I am Sheila, recently promoted as Assistant Manager— Institutional Sales. You think I am happy? Well, I am, a little bit. But I am equally unhappy because I know for a fact that I am not getting paid the same as the other AMs. Why, you ask? Let me tell you— it's not because I am a woman, it's because I am from a small town.

Just because I am from a Tier-III town, people assume that I am not as competent. Just because my spoken English is not as polished, they think I am not good enough for the job. Just because I wear slightly conservative clothes and not the sharp business suits like my other lady colleagues, they think I am not worth it.

But what they don't know is that numbers have no bias. My performance is out there for everyone to see and no amount of biases can hold up against the sheer power of hard data.

Today I am going to confront my manager. I am just hoping that it does not turn out to be dirty. This difference in pay, in spite of my having more experience, is not what I expected. I thought my organization would be larger hearted than that. And you know who told me about my getting paid less? One of those very same city-bred, sharp-dressing, hip AMs. And what really added insult to injury was when she said that for me to reach that same pay scale, I had to prove myself even better. Prove myself? Why should I? Did I not meet the numbers? Why should they make me feel uncomfortable just because I don't talk or dress like them?

Today I will challenge my manager to find a better performer than me. I will let my numbers do the talking. I will make it clear that if I am not accepted for who I am—the full package—then let them find another person to do my job.

The dictionary definition of 'bias' is a tendency, opinion, trend, feeling or inclination that is preconceived or unreasoned. A simpler meaning of bias is the phenomenon of interpreting or judging people or situations by standards inherent to one's own experience or learning. Pronouncing a judgement on someone either about the way they speak, dress or take decisions, keeping in mind a yardstick that is relevant to the judgement pronouncer and not the recipient of the verdict is the occurrence of bias.

In the world of business, there is a big premium placed on what people call 'instinct'. This instinct or intuition is relied upon in most scenarios as the magic factor enabling accurate decisions but without a solid rationale behind it. Today, there is another name for instinct—Daniel Kahneman in his book *Thinking, Fast and Slow* calls it System 1 thinking.

System 1 thinking is the reliance on automatic thoughts which stem from past associations that are embedded in your memory. Conservative dressers are low on ambition, people who speak English with a regional accent are not serious about their careers, persons from a particular community are not to be trusted—the world, not just the workplace—is full of such biases. When you arrive at a 'gut instinct' decision, most often it means that you have not consciously put your decision-making process to test and are going by a past experience. Speed of decision-making, which is a prized virtue, actually becomes the villain by compromising quality. Instead of looking at fresh evidence that is available at the present moment, System 1 goes back years, even decades, to retrace those neural pathways in your brain and fall back on a familiar route.

Biases exist for a reason. They were necessary for survival, since people remembered differences as a method of escaping from danger. Even today, System 1 thinking is what makes you leap out of the way of a raging bull, without going through a laborious process of fact-finding. Yet, the same mechanism of jumping to conclusions while assessing a candidate could lead you astray. Equally important is the process of decision-making. If we are always pushed to take decisions under stressful conditions with a paucity of time, System 1 thinking kicks in. Our mind rushes to take the path of least resistance—a familiar neural route—and ends up counting on the pre-existing bias.

Here is where conscious, mindful thinking, also known as System 2 thinking helps. By consciously disciplining the mind to take into account all data points and refusing to get drawn into an instinct-based analysis, it is entirely possible to stay in the present and avoid cognitive slips. And the truth is that nobody, not even the smartest entrepreneur or the most astute business leader or the completely empathetic colleague, is devoid of biases. Every human being carries a long list in their mind and unless we counter them with sentience, all of us could fall prey to the problem of bias. The antidote to biases is awareness. The simple act of being alert and cognizant of all facts before you arrive at a decision has the capacity to reduce biases almost entirely.

FILTERS OF PERCEPTION

Dear Diary,

Today was a terrible day at work. Once again, I had a huge clash with Meera. I am really completely at a loss as to why she behaves this way. It started off as a general conversation that we were all having around the coffee machine this evening. You know that Meera was previously miffed about the fact that I have been given in-charge of the new big data project. Now, she believes that everything that I do or say is to insult her and highlight her inability to land the project.

Today, I was speaking about the movie that has released where a brave lady collector fights all odds to save her region from open bore wells and the dangers of children falling into it. My team was standing around and I was recounting the story to them. Meera who walked by to the coffee machine heard me say, 'only some women are really able to get what they want, others try hard but never make it' (referring to the collector) and instantly assumed that it was about her. She hit me back with a venomous comment about how some women make it only because they steal the thunder of their colleagues. The argument became heated and Meera would just not let go. Finally, my manager had to step in and call a halt. I felt so embarrassed and angry. Why does she do this? Why does everything need to be about her??

A rather dangerous ailment that most of us suffer from is called the perception filter or perceptual filter. When our exposure is limited and we take little effort to include different experiences or points of view into our lives, we develop the perception filter, which misdirects us into perceiving information completely unrelated to us.

At the workplace, we often observe that when managers, who have very little or zero exposure to other cultures are given charge of a multicultural/diverse team, several problems arise due to the presence of these filters. Starting off from simple misunderstandings to a range of communication challenges, perception filters cause people to engage ineffectively and even go the extent of denying opportunities for advancement. The effect supplements or eliminates information from the original message, twisting it to perceive only what you wish to see. This extends also to receiving cognitive messages, ignoring visual stimuli, interpreting differently the meaning of spoken words and deciphering body language in a completely unrelated way.

Perceptual filters impact individuals, teams and organizations as a whole. There is no denying the fact that everything that you absorb is filtered through your mind in some way. However, if you are a victim of perception filters, then your assimilation of every communication is drastically altered to become only a fraction of its original intent. Perception filters have the effect of directing attentiveness away from the object or its bearer, virtually rendering them unnoticeable and dictating what we pay attention to. Filters distort reality and keep us from seeing things as they really are.

In today's world of information surfeit, it becomes imperative that an organization employs objective, universal methods to erase the effect of filters. Realizing that perception filters could block talent development and retention strategies and could result in very poor talent engagement, organizations have undertaken to train their managers on recognizing filters. Workshops and learning tools to educate people on the dangers of perceptual filters are leading to more awareness. At an individual level, filters can also be removed by a sincere effort to learn from someone who is different from you and becoming aware that there are always differing points of view.

D&I GAME: EXPERIENCING DIVERSITY AND INCLUSION

Do you think that biases are very uncharacteristic of you? That you will not let biases rule your decisions? That you are conscious of all 'bias' trigger buttons?

Given below are 15 statements related to situations that you might experience during the course of your work. Please tick the most appropriate answer for each statement given. Some statements may be characteristic or uncharacteristic of you. Nevertheless, try to relate each situation to your own experience and choose an answer that is most typical of you.

S. No.	Statements	Never	Rarely	Occasionally	Often	Always	Score
1.	I analyse the words and phrases I use with others to check if they are hurtful or disgraceful to others.						
2.	If someone has a background similar to mine, I am much more likely to look at that person with a positive mindset.						
3.	I take a keen interest in gaining in-depth understanding about the culture of different ethnic, religious and socio-economic groups and I am appreciative and accepting of the differences.						

S. No.	Statements	Never	Rarely	Occasionally	Often	Always	Score
4.	When I have to take a strong decision related to a difficult situation at work, I analyse the circumstances based on my own experiences and take instinctive decisions.						
5.	In my experience, men and women respond emotionally to situations but how those emotions manifest can be very different.						
6.	I prefer to hire people whose working styles, competencies and thought processes are similar to mine and I have seen them performing very well.						
7.	I spend time introspecting about my own mindsets and behaviours on how I am either mitigating or contributing towards biases in the society.						
8.	Women have a tendency to get emotional and this emotional weakness can be a major deterrent at the workplace.						
9.	I often reflect on how my upbringing, childhood experiences and the messages I have imbided as a child are influencing my decisions as an adult.						
10.	When I decide to allocate work that has high business impact, I assign it to people I am most comfortable working with.						

No.	Statement						
11.	I find that people from the same generation have similar values which are based on shared experiences.						
12.	In casual get-togethers, I find myself bonding easily with people whose backgrounds are similar to mine.						
13.	I deeply value the differences and strengths other people bring in to a team and I believe this creates synergy.						
14.	I feel that millennials, the tech-native generation, consider workplace benefits as prerogatives.						
15.	I feel that often preferences shown by parents and teachers regarding gender roles deeply influence children's perceptions of the world.						

SCORING

For odd number questions (1, 3, 5, 7, 9, 11, 13 and 15), please rate yourself using the following scale:

Never — 1   Often — 4

Rarely — 2   Always — 5

Occasionally — 3

For even number questions (2, 4, 6, 8, 10, 12 and 14), please rate yourself using the following scale:

Never — 5   Often — 2

Rarely — 4   Always — 1

Occasionally — 3

IF YOUR TOTAL SCORE IS BETWEEN:

- 60 and 75: Congratulations! You strive to methodically avert unconscious biases. Be at it, as you move ahead in your personal and professional journeys.

- 45 and 59: Good! You are conscious of your unconscious biases. Continue to watch out for biases, moving them from an unconscious to a conscious zone.

- 30 and 44: You are doing okay with your biases. While you are attempting to identify more biases, you may want to introspect on the stereotypes that might have created these biases.

- 15 and 29: Biases are deterring your journey to inclusion. Examine your psyche, critically and judgementally and identify situations where your biases have influenced your decisions. Write down on how you could have responded to these situations more inclusively.

DAY
76/99

SELF-AWARENESS
AND INCLUSION

Two years after they had rolled out diversity as an initiative, Ruma was worried as the employee feedback revealed that it was nothing more than a tick in the box. There was no conceivable change in culture. In her next brainstorming session with other members of the team, Ruma raised a question: 'How do we build inclusion? I want ideas for how we can think of all of us as a single team, even while appreciating diversity.' Mohan, a senior professional who had recently joined ThorpInc as VP—Marketing, leaned forward and said, 'Ruma, diversity maybe about policies and programmes, but I think inclusion is very personal. It is individual-oriented.'

Ruma was intrigued. 'Sir, could you explain that a bit more?' Mohan walked to the white board and began writing a series of words—gender, ability, generation, sexual orientation. In the next column, he wrote—accent, dress-sense, education, etiquette. And in the third column, he wrote—sense of humour, outlook towards life, value systems, energy. 'We are all different', said Mohan. 'In pre-historic times, anything that was different from ourselves was perceived as a threat. It was a matter of life and death. The thing is, even today, we do exactly that—we quickly and subconsciously look at all the ways in which someone is not "like us", and register that as a threat. Only when you become self-aware does inclusion actually begin. You have to realize that beneath all those differences, you are the same. That is inclusion!'

Contrary to popular assumption, inclusion does not begin with knowing about others; it actually begins with a greater understanding of yourself. In a land of spirituality like India, where many seers and saints have raised the question 'Who am I?' it is interesting that the same question should be one of the greatest mantras for inclusion at the workplace. Knowing yourself—what are your own stereotypes and prejudices, your triggers and barriers, what influences your thinking and decision-making—is the first step to inclusion. Self-awareness is the key ingredient to every inclusive workplace and is at the heart of strong leadership. Leaders passionate about D&I work constantly to improve this skill. When you begin focusing on self-awareness, you become aware of behaviour and actions that happen around you. You are keenly obser-vant of your own reaction to your team's behaviour. When you commit to greater self-awareness, you are more open to feedback. Your self-observation allows you to examine your own emotions and feelings which, in turn, allows you the benefit of greater understanding and empathy of people around you. Self-aware leaders are great at becoming inclusion champions, simply because they are more in tune with the diversity in their organizations and are able to pay greater attention to their employees' concerns.

So, how is it done? At what age/stage do you start becoming self-aware? The honest answer is right now. Commit yourself today to the life-long practice of self-understanding. Inclusion begins at that moment when you have identified that you are subconsciously gravitating towards people who are similar to you and exclude those who are different. Knowing yourself is the start of your inclusion journey to build bridges with those around you.

Once upon a time, King Akbar wished to test the intelligence of his minister, Birbal.

Calling Birbal aside after court one day, the king asked, 'Birbal, I have three candidates for the position of Chief of Food Distribution. You know that this is a critical role which requires ensuring that no one in my kingdom ever goes hungry. The person responsible for this role will have to oversee all my food kitchens and make sensible use of every grain of rice and wheat. I want you to assess all three candidates and let me know who you think is most suited to the post.'

Unknown to Birbal, the king had already selected one of the candidates. Yet, he wanted to understand how Birbal assessed the candidates and how they stood up to his decision-making process.

'Of course, your majesty. Please let me know who the three candidates are and I shall give you my decision by tomorrow morning,' said Birbal.

'Candidate Number 1 is a young warrior who has amazing energy. He is always enthusiastic about helping the poor and is a very brave young man who will protect my granaries faithfully.'

'Wonderful, my Lord! And the next?'

'Candidate Number 2 is a very wise and senior advisor who had a great track record of apportioning the daily rations in a perfect manner. He has been in this department before. As such, he is very well trained for this role.'

'That is very fortunate for us, your highness. And may I know who the third candidate is?'

'Candidate Number 3 is a middle-aged scholar, a phenomenal mind, one who is an expert in the mechanics of harvesting grains, saving them carefully and ensuring their appropriate distribution. He has a lot of academic credentials and is the kingdom's most illustrious expert on food production and distribution. Now, Birbal, who is your choice? Let me have your decision first thing tomorrow morning,' said the King.

'For sure, my Lord! I will be ready with the answers by sunrise tomorrow,' replied Birbal.

The next morning, King Akbar waited with anticipation. At the crack of dawn, Birbal appeared at the court, his face resolute.

'Good morning, dear Birbal! I see that you are nice and early. Do you have the decision I asked for?' The eagerness in King Akbar's voice revealed his expectation. 'A very good morning to you, Oh sovereign King! And yes, I do have the answer,' said Birbal with finality.

'Go ahead, illuminate me!'

'Oh King, the most important responsibility of this role is to ensure that nobody, not a single person in your highness's vast empire, goes hungry. In order to ensure this, what is required is not energy or academic credentials or prior experience.'

'Oh!' said King Akbar, disappointed. 'Then are you saying that none of my three candidates makes the cut as per your decision?'

'Not at all, my Lord. Thankfully, I found one person who had that specific characteristic that I was seeking. And with that yardstick, I pronounce your first candidate, the young enthusiastic warrior, as my choice!'

'And why is that, Birbal?'

'Your majesty, in order for this job to be done perfectly, it requires that the candidate know what it means to be *hungry*. Only then will he understand the pain that a starving person goes through. And this knowledge will help him most effectively discharge his duties.

I discovered that the brave young warrior suffered the ravages of poverty and hunger very acutely in his childhood and youth. That is the reason he is always keen on helping the needy. To him, this role will not merely be a function to perform. It will be personal,' replied Birbal.

'Bravo, Birbal!' exclaimed King Akbar. 'He is my choice too!'

The successful assimilation of inclusion into the culture of a workplace calls for a passion beyond the mundane. Organizations that have leveraged the values of D&I most effectively have not achieved this only through elaborate, high-cost communication extravaganzas. Often, it is the simple, personal and often unscripted message delivered directly by the leader that has had the greatest impact in instilling the value of inclusion.

The leadership skill most associated with creating a truly inclusive workplace is that of accountability. When the leader holds himself/herself personally accountable for driving inclusion and, in turn, also demonstrates confidence in his/her team to replicate value-based behaviour, the workplace reflects the culture of inclusion. When the occasion demands it, leaders make open statements about their personal commitment to drive change in their workplaces, be it at an external conference or an internal townhall. Since their personal values align with the value of inclusion, they do not look at diversity as a mere tick in the box. To them, the business case is not just about business, it is about leaving behind a legacy of a better, more inclusive world.

This accountability translates into treating team members with trust and respect, utilizing every opportunity to appreciate and acknowledge their contribution and cohere the team into one inclusive whole. The leader feels personally responsible for creating a work environment where every individual is comfortable being themselves. He/she demonstrates inclusive thinking by adapting his/her style to suit the different working styles of one's team members. Whether it be actively seeking contribution of the team members or acknowledging one's own limitations, the inclusive leader ensures that his/her organization treats inclusion not just as something to be practised at the workplace but as a skill to be learned for life.

'Ms Ethel, I am asking you why the books are missing, I am not blaming you for it,' said Professor Rao to the anxious librarian at the institute. It was an old and highly respected research institute, with an exhaustive library that was the pride of the entire town.

And Ms Ethel was among the most respected of all the staff at the library. She was a very friendly, warm person, always going out of the way to help a reader find a book, sometimes even procuring a book with great difficulty just because a young student from a poor family had expressed an interest to borrow that costly book which he could not afford to buy.

In the five years that she had taken charge as the Senior Librarian, Ms Ethel had gradually built a reputation as someone who did a lot to encourage reading among the students. During the annual book audits that were usually conducted by one of the senior faculty members, her systems and processes were appreciated, since she maintained a robust discipline of managing the issue and collection of the books. They had not yet got computerized, and even though the system was manual, there was very little error. After she had taken charge, there was a distinct increase in not just the number of books that each student read, but also in the number of people who frequented the large library with its high ceilings and vast rows of books. She had ensured that the library was accessible, inviting and helpful.

Which was why it came as a surprise to Professor Rao that several expensive and rare books that were the preserve of the library had gone missing. He felt a pang of sorrow looking at Ms Ethel's worried face, her fingers curling and twisting as she stood in his office, refusing to sit down. She was of the old school and the gross mistake of having lost a few very important and precious books was a mistake she took very, very seriously.

'Sir, Professor Rao, I don't know what to say. He had all the credentials. He said he knew you and that he was a student of this institute. He has regularly been visiting our library, borrowing books and returning them on time. But this time, I don't know where he is? I am so sorry, Sir. The only mistake I did was allowing him to borrow the books without checking his membership card. My sincere apologies, Sir.' Her voice broke and tears flooded her eyes.

'Ms Ethel, I fully understand your situation. We will do everything to ensure that we retrieve the books. Can you describe the borrower?'

'Well, he was tall, fair and middle-aged. He looked like a research scholar. He wore specs. He seemed so responsible, so erudite. He did not look like the kind of person who would steal books!'

'But he did not possess a library card, did he?'

'No Sir, he did not. But then, he was fair and wore glasses and I always thought that men who are fair and wear spectacles are good people and will not do something like this.'

Professor Rao smiled. Ms Ethel's blind spots showed glaringly.

A blind spot is a physiological phenomenon. It exists as a part of the visual field of each eye where there are no photoreceptors as such, resulting in zero image detection. However, quite interestingly, instead of appearing as a blacked out area which impairs vision, the blind spot does not really cause a serious problem. Those of us with working vision are able to clearly see without missing the part falling in the area of the blind spot. This is a scientific jugglery of the brain—which copies the gaps in the visual area, projects it on to the blind spot, giving us an impression that nothing is missing and ensuring that we get an illusion of a complete vision.

In psychological terms, blind spots are those gaps in a person's perception which are painted over by our conditioning seemingly to help us arrive at decisions better. Our brain fills the gaps with information sourced from past experiences and applies the same logic to complete the picture for us. While we may imagine that we have completed the blanks in spite of limited information, in truth, we have not. The information that is overlaid by our mind is incomplete, incorrect and prejudiced, often leading to erroneous decisions.

Blind spots are referred to as such, because they are actually invisible even to us. Our own blind spots, those areas of perception—both about ourselves and about others—that we are unaware of are often the reason for unconscious biases leading to errors. Paucity of time for decision-making, stressful situations and laziness in thinking cause the accentuation of blind spots. Very often, simple self-awareness and clarity, provided by a mentor or a coach, lead to elimination of blind spots.

In the sphere of self-development, the removal of blind spots leads to two major benefits: (a) one becomes more aware of one's own style of thinking, of decision-making and also of one's weaknesses and limitations, and (b) decision-making is never done in a haphazard 'assumptive' manner and is a robust process after gathering all required data. From an organizational point of view, programmes to create awareness about blind spots are critical to build inclusion. Many discerning leaders understand not only their own but also their organizational blind spots. They self-regulate to ensure the removal of bias from decision-making. They also insist on the following of processes and the elimination of shortcuts to arrive at fair and merit-based decisions.

Disciple: Master, may I disturb you for a minute?

Master: Ananta, the time for rhetoric is over. Ask away!

Disciple: I am having a minor disagreement with our sister from the mountain village. I request your kind intervention.

Master: Tell me, Ananta.

Disciple: Master, you always say that 'practice makes perfect' and this is what I too believe. However, our sister from the mountain village thinks that theoretical information is more important than practical learning.

Master: Ananta, you are speaking as if one can exist without the other. That is quite impossible. Theory and practice go hand in hand for excellence to be the outcome. Theoretical learning is the foundation, it is the basis of understanding the science. Practical application, on the other hand, is how that science is applied. Theoretical learning gives you an overview of the knowledge that you are trying to gain. Practical usage results in that knowledge getting internalized by you. In theory, you will learn about the experience of others, but when you apply it yourself, it becomes your own experience.

Disciple: But Master, what is the use of theoretical learning if it is not relevant practically? There is no point in gaining theory, if it is not utilized by practice. I can learn about swimming from a book, but unless I jump into a lake and actually make my way out, my book-learning is purposeless.

Master: Of course, Ananta! In the case of swimming, that is right. But take the case of the laws of chemistry, for example. Here, it is important that you know theory before you attempt to interact with different acids. In this case, your theoretical experience will have to come prior to your application.

Disciple: Ah, yes, kind Master; now I understand well.

Master: Learning happens at different levels, Ananta! When we learn a new skill, whether it's swimming or cooking or solving problems or a new language, we are actually changing how our brains are wired. With every new learning—both theoretical and practical—we are creating new neural synapses. At first, when we use the skill, the pathways are new and it might feel awkward and artificial. But over time, with practice, the skill gets natural and it flows effortlessly. Thus, it is indeed true that practice makes perfect, but it is also true that you can fake it till you make it!

Disciple: Master, thanks so much for the clarity! My problem with sister from the mountain village is now fully resolved!

Master: Yes, Ananta, that is because you are both right!

The relative importance of theory and practice in creating a diverse and inclusive workplace has been a topic of a lot of debate. Learning as defined in the D&I arena is a process rather than a mere collection of discrete data points. D&I-led learning is instrumental in creating a mindset change in the individual and these changes are relatively permanent. Apart from theoretical knowledge about what constitutes an inclusive workplace, it is critical to allow these skills to seep into real-life situations in order to create a workplace that reflects the values of D&I. Sitting in a classroom and discussing a certain topic varies widely from obtaining opportunities to converting the learning into application.

D&I professionals tasked with transforming a workplace often use a combination of classroom-based pedagogy blended with deliberate practice. The latter, defined as engaging in planned, focused activities, designed specifically to become impactful learning experiences, is today an important part of D&I training. This results in twin-fold benefits. Firstly, it aids in preparing the workplace for an eventual metamorphosis into a diverse one, while secondly, it reinforces the raison d'etre of inclusion.

Diversity Sensitization

211

Reframing an organization's D&I culture-building often involves a plethora of training methods. Broadly, it consists of (a) sensitivity training which helps in creating awareness among employees about cultural differences and identity filters and enables them to eliminate blind spots. Such training provides perspectives on what would be the right approach to solve conflicts and is the start of a culture of acceptance of diversity, (b) inclusion immersion which helps the organization set clear goals linking D&I to strategy, business goals and decision-making, and (c) specific training inputs to audiences such as men, women, persons with disabilities or millennials, providing them with valuable insights on what would be of special benefit to them in rising to the fullest of their potential.

The development of a truly inclusive workplace is a long process, in which theoretical, practical and metacognitive elements of knowledge are integrated creating the learning organization (LO) capable of adapting itself to all situations. The strongest business case for D&I training is the fact that to create an environment where trust and respect rule, it is important to set a framework in place which defines acceptable employee conduct. Training achieves this. Like the vision, mission and values of an organization, D&I training establishes the baseline and constructs the vision of the ideal workplace. However, there have also been instances of failure of training, when it has been used as a quick-fix to solve deeplying issues. In such circumstances, it is necessary for leadership to set the right tone, insist upon high adherence to D&I values and articulate out loud that exclusion is a no-no.

WORDFINDER

K	N	F	C	O	I	U	M	J	U	S	Z	G	A	U	I	O	P	Y	M	O
W	I	X	S	O	D	N	C	E	Z	E	G	P	Z	R	N	E	H	B	W	I
S	V	H	K	O	M	O	I	F	N	N	S	Z	P	P	I	C	D	A	Z	I
H	I	C	E	Y	Y	I	Y	O	S	S	V	W	M	R	C	A	P	T	I	O
S	S	Z	C	T	N	T	S	W	E	I	D	H	V	G	C	L	F	M	Z	D
A	A	F	I	I	N	A	X	N	P	T	E	W	Z	Y	E	P	B	A	L	T
I	I	R	D	L	S	Z	O	B	Y	I	E	Q	J	X	D	K	V	X	D	E
B	B	P	U	A	R	I	N	V	T	Z	H	I	X	F	C	R	N	B	G	K
S	R	R	J	N	C	T	H	J	O	A	M	L	T	C	P	O	O	G	E	R
U	T	Q	E	O	U	I	S	X	E	T	S	O	P	M	P	W	F	W	N	A
O	G	H	R	I	T	S	C	H	R	I	G	I	G	H	Y	E	Q	S	D	M
I	H	Z	P	T	B	N	H	N	E	O	Z	S	K	D	I	V	S	N	E	R
C	X	S	O	C	P	E	H	F	T	N	V	G	Q	B	H	I	L	C	R	U
S	D	C	F	E	N	S	P	H	S	P	B	D	C	T	P	S	V	J	P	O
N	L	O	E	S	I	R	Z	G	R	R	K	X	S	A	O	U	U	U	A	B
O	N	C	M	R	R	E	A	E	E	O	U	N	O	D	F	L	A	D	R	A
C	U	Z	H	E	F	D	T	W	D	G	K	J	U	E	O	C	M	G	I	L
N	Y	Z	N	T	S	N	V	T	N	R	X	G	A	Y	V	N	S	K	T	U
U	A	T	G	N	H	E	T	N	E	A	C	Z	A	W	J	I	I	T	Y	R
C	J	U	M	I	M	G	U	Q	G	M	R	D	K	V	A	E	T	L	J	B
T	S	F	M	V	W	U	M	X	V	S	D	M	K	G	E	X	J	C	F	X

WORDS

Bias	Prejudice
Gender parity	Gender sensitization
Gender stereotypes	Sensitization programmes
Unconscious bias	Labour market
Intersectionality	Inclusive workplace

SECTION 9

CREATING EQUITY IN
THE WORKPLACE

DIVERSITY AND INCLUSION LEXICON

S. No.	Words	Definition
1.	Cultural competence	Set of academic and interpersonal skills that allow individuals to increase their understanding, sensitivity, appreciation and responsiveness to cultural differences and the interactions resulting from them
2.	Customer diversity	Differences amongst individuals in an organization's customer base in terms of age, gender, cultural background, physical abilities, race, religion, sexual orientation, education, experience, etc., amongst others
3.	CSR	Refer to projects or programmes undertaken by companies for social and/or environmental welfare and improvement
4.	Equity	Refers to the process of creating equivalent outcomes for members of historically underrepresented and oppressed individuals and groups
5.	Employee engagement	A measurable degree of an employee's positive or negative emotional attachment to his/her job, colleagues and organization that profoundly influences his/her willingness to learn and perform at work
6.	Differently abled	A physical, mental or cognitive impairment or condition that characterizes an individual
7.	Gender inclusivity	In an organizational context, this refers to the practice of ensuring complete inclusion of all genders without any biases, in recruitment, training and development, promotions and other organizational initiatives

S. No.	Words	Definition
8.	Gender bilingualism	In an organizational context, this refers to an approach that when ingrained in the organizational culture can ensure that all employees, both male and female, are able to 'speak the language' and understand the behaviours of both genders, rather than just those of their genders
9.	Gender equality	An ideal organizational (and social) condition in which professionals of all genders are entitled to equal and fair treatment
10.	Socio-economic diversity	In the organizational context, this refers to representation of individuals with different social and economic profiles.
11.	Supplier diversity	A proactive business programme which encourages the use of minority-owned, women-owned, veteran-owned, LGBT-owned, disabled-owned or any other historically underutilized business vendors as suppliers
12.	Talent pipeline	A pool of candidates qualified to assume open positions that have been created or vacated through a retirement or a promotion
13.	Talent pool	A database of candidate profiles who are eligible for working in an organization; they could be limited to a specific area of expertise or focused on a broad grouping of individuals who are capable of performing a variety of job tasks.

INTERLUDE: BONSAI
TREES AND APPLE BOXES

It was a balmy day, cloudy and humid, and the light streamed into the corner office as Saahitya Daya, Director HR for AcceLever, stood next to Mrs Abel's cubicle, laughing at something that the (otherwise serious) Executive Secretary to MD had just said. It seemed that the general mood in the office was lighter, happier.

Mrs Abel adjusted the tray containing an ornamental bonsai peepal tree on her desk to receive the sunlight better. To Saahitya, the tree looked strangely anthropomorphic. Its twin trunks seemed like two stout legs and the small crown of leaves gave it the appearance of a gnome's head. Saahitya's own cabin too had a bonsai gulmohar gifted by Bharat to all his direct reports, but to her great relief, it did not look spookily human.

She wondered what Bharat's fascination with bonsai was. She suddenly realized that she was deeply uncomfortable about the whole bonsai cultivation practice. There was something unnatural about it, as if one were restricting the natural growth of a tree and reducing it to a dwarf. She pondered whether it was her human resource background that made her feel uneasy about stunting the evolution of something. Her 20-plus years of work across companies had taught her that Human Resource was not a function—it was a calling, a deep commitment to people. With such an approach, she had had quite a few disagreements with her previous bosses.

But Bharat was different. In her 2 years of leading the HR function for AcceLever and reporting to him, Saahitya had found Bharat to be very reasonable, very sorted. No doubt he was an astute business head whose priorities were clear to the board and his shareholders, but that did not make him ruthless. He found time to meet with not just his immediate team but also as much of a cross-section of AcceLeverites as he could. Scrupulously impartial, he would be very particular about appraisals being conducted in the fairest manner and was generous with his recommendations. He was invested in the personal growth of his team and believed that every individual had untapped potential.

Which was why Saahitya found his interest for bonsai to be an anomaly. She remembered that she would have the same feeling of disquiet with the bonsai banyan tree that Bharat had in his own room. It was an entire tree, complete with its tiny leathery leaves, small, perfectly widespread branches and eerily pint-sized adventitious prop roots. 'I must ask Bharat about this someday,' she thought to herself.

They had just finished a good performance year and she had got a sizeable budget for HR. There was lots of work to do, more specifically with policies and programmes around diversity. And Saahitya had a point of view that seemed in conflict with what AcceLever had done for decades. She wondered how she would convince Bharat about it. He had developed a sudden interest in the subject of D&I and was constantly asking her for data about various metrics relating to different demographic groups within AcceLever. But what she was about to tell him could not necessarily go down well.

'Ok, so tell me, Mrs Abel,' asked Saahitya, 'am I going to be able to meet Boss today? Will I be able to have a conversation? Will he be able to spend some time with me?!' Both of them laughed again at that really weak pun on Mrs Abel's name.

'I cannot speak for your ability Ms Daya, but I can speak for mine. I will tell you his programme and you decide,' said Mrs Abel in her characteristic blunt manner that showed that no one, not even the head of HR who controlled her PF and gratuity, could subdue her authority.

'He has an external ad shoot scheduled post lunch and a journalist is meeting him at 11:00. Do you want to join him for a working lunch? 1:00 to 1:30. I can check with him,' said Mrs Abel.

'Done! I will bring my lunch box and be present here. Do block my calendar,' said Saahitya as she sped away, her mission accomplished.

... ...

'Hello, hello!' Bharat looked up from his laptop, slim reading glasses perched on his nose and waved to Saahitya to come in. He was looking forward to the discussion with Saahitya, whom he trusted a great deal. She was thoroughly competent, wonderfully articulate and a true-blue human resource professional. In the last two years that he had come to work with her, he found her candour refreshing and polished, her ability to manage the sudden undulations of business a valuable strength. Yes, she could get carried away sometimes with a cause and become an evangelist, but he felt it was needed in a HR leader. The fact that she always had a robust business case to substantiate her stand made her a teammate that Bharat relied on totally.

Her arms full with her lunch box, a couple of files and a sheaf of papers, Saahitya had a brief moment of confusion wondering what to put where. Bharat quickly moved around to a glass table at the corner of his suite and gently lifted the bonsai banyan, placing it on a small teepoy. Gesturing to Saahitya to bring her lunch to the table, Bharat made sure that the bonsai was secure before he brought his own lunch bag.

'That bonsai is clearly special to you. Or are all bonsais special?' As they opened their respective lunches, Saahitya decided to get this doubt out of the way.

'I quite like the idea of bonsai cultivation in general, but this one is definitely very special. It was gifted to me by Paramita, who I consider my guru,' replied Bharat with a warm smile.

'I kind of guessed that this had some exceptional significance,' said Saahitya and plunged right in with her next question, 'but Bharat, don't you think that bonsais are in a way representative of stifled potential?'

'Like dwarfing?' asked Bharat.

'Exactly!' said Saahitya.

Bharat smiled and shook his head in response. He got up and stood beside the bonsai, like a curator next to artistic exhibit at a museum. 'I am no expert on bonsais or dwarf varieties, but let me share what I know. Bonsais are very different from dwarf trees. A dwarf tree is a genetically modified specimen where you continuously mate a normal specimen till you get a small tree of a specified shape. It is a kind of genetic engineering. But a bonsai is a piece of art. It could possibly be a small part or branch of a tree which is pruned and cultivated till it looks like a complete smaller version of the original tree.'

'So, a bonsai only gives the illusion of a full real tree, while actually being just a part of it…?'

'Yes! The bonsai metaphor is almost like that of the entire ocean contained in a single drop. Just like you would have a painting or a photograph of a flower or a countryside to bring back memories, I have this bonsai banyan to tell me that ethics and justice is very important in business. This bonsai was created by a very talented Indian artist, a student of the Japanese bonsai grandmaster Kyuzo Murata.'

'Wow. So, like a piece of art, the purpose of a bonsai is to inspire,' said Saahitya reflectively.

'Absolutely!' said Bharat. Gesticulating with energy to demonstrate the composition of the bonsai, he continued, 'A bonsai will have a front and back. The portrait it creates encompasses the tree and the tray. This tray for instance is a Good Earth handmade ceramic tray. Look at the whole picture! It will have line, proportion and balance. To me, a bonsai is a constant reminder that it is possible, with consistent effort, careful nurturing and attention to detail, to create something seemingly impossible like a miniature banyan tree!'

Lifting the heavy tray with its precious banyan carefully to shoulder height and gazing upon it with what seemed like deep adoration, Bharat said, 'When I look at this banyan, I am reminded of the way ancient Indian merchants would sit below its branches.' Turning the bonsai gently around to illustrate his point further, Bharat's voice seemed to go back in time. 'All merchants would sit under the shade of this sacred tree. It was said that you could not lie when under its branches. The tree was the ultimate authority. It stood for integrity, impartiality and dispassionate judgement. You could transact business only in the fairest, most just way possible. Here, everyone was equal. Everyone was governed by the same law. The tree did not discriminate. Everyone gets the same treatment. There is no high or low, no prejudice or partiality. To me, this banyan tree is symbolic of the fact that to a leader everyone is equal!'

'But what if everyone is not equal, Boss?' Saahitya's question, after a quiet pause, seemed to jolt Bharat back into the present.

'What if "fairness" is more than just simply equal treatment?' continued Saahitya.

'Bear with me Boss, while I try and explain this.' She closed her uneaten lunch box of sprouts and lentil salad and stood up to face Bharat. 'One of my points of discussion today with you was about policies for our women employees. See this.' She picked up a report and opened a page filled with graphs. 'The gender audit that we just completed states that in spite of the policies that we offer, we are steadily losing women. Why? Because these policies just don't do the job! They don't address the basic problem of women—that they are different from men. I believe we have to have some positive discrimination here. We have to treat men and women differently, simply because men and women are not equal in the workplace!'

Bharat's forehead creased into a furrow as he spoke in a flat tone. 'Saahitya, let me understand this. What you are saying is that we have to have different policies for men and women, different ways of appraisals, different performance measures. Is that right? Is it even fair?'

'Bharat, treating everyone exactly the same is not actually being fair. Sometimes, equal treatment ends up not taking into account the reality of the different contexts that we each come from.'

'What is the objective of business?' asked Bharat. 'Is it to look at achieving social justice or deliver profits?'

'The two need not be at cross-purposes with each other, Boss!' said Saahitya. 'You know that we have lost several key women of AcceLever to competition. Even if it is not to competition, we have had to let go of some of our prominent leaders—Paramita Acharya herself being a case to point. Some women have stated that they have left just because it is unsustainable to work at AcceLever. We need more women at managerial positions. We need to look at what policies and programmes will get them there.'

'But if only different policies will work for women, then is it fair to the men?'

'Boss, let me give you an example from my own life,' said Saahitya with a wan smile. 'My older one, Sarvesh, is dyslexic. We had put him in a normal school where there were different types of learners. Some kids were auditory learners while others were visual. Sarvesh is neither. He is tactile. But being in a class full of kids who were auditory or visual, he would find it very difficult to cope. He was at a tremendous disadvantage, while his classmates were at an advantage because their teacher would lecture all the time using power point slides or the blackboard to illustrate. Every day, Sarvesh would come back frustrated because he would not be able to comprehend what took place in class. Thankfully, we changed his school to a more enabling one, and it's magical. They customize teaching styles according to the learning ability of each child. They use more of lab sessions and practical classes with 3D science models and it's amazing. Sarvesh is on fire! You should see him! He understands all the concepts perfectly, simply because it has been taught in a way that he is capable of appreciating! To me, this is equality, Bharat, because it takes into account the differences in children.'

'I get it,' Bharat settled in his chair, his lunch too forgotten. 'But is it possible to extend the same principle to the workplace, Saahitya? Are you suggesting that just like Sarvesh's new school, every manager should be able to customize policies for men and women differently?'

'It may be difficult at first, Bharat,' agreed Saahitya. 'But I think over time, we would establish a way of prioritizing gender equity over equality. Gender equality assumes that everyone requires the same help. But equity gives different people different support systems and thus levels the playing field. This is what happens at Sarvesh's new school. They prioritize equity over equality.'

'To me, equity appears to be a tad unfair,' Bharat countered animatedly. 'Because it inherently doesn't treat everyone equal. Are we not an equal opportunity employer?? Do we then redefine the term "equal opportunity"? Doesn't it become very complicated? What might be fair to you might not be fair to me.'

'Boss, not everyone starts at the same place,' Saahitya's voice had become quiet, even introspective. 'Not everyone has the same needs. You are concerned with equal opportunities, but I am talking about equal outcomes. The village in which my mother was born had a practice of not educating girls because they would find it difficult to manage their periods in a school which did not have separate women's toilets. Today, the same school has more girls' toilets than boys', simply because the need is more. And the outcome of that is we now have equal numbers of girls and boys completing their secondary education. This is not equality, but equity. Let me take an example closer home—our own maternity leave. What is it but a case of gender equity? We provide our women employees 6 months maternity leave accompanied with salary but no man ever gets anything like this, simply because as males they do not get pregnant. Is that not equity?'

Bharat looked at his watch. He had another 10 minutes before starting for the ad shoot. He wanted to close this conversation. 'I feel we are getting too caught up with this concept of equity and equality. Maybe we should look at what will be effective and realistic.'

Saahitya noticed Bharat's impatience and spoke quickly. 'Boss, I have one more point to make. I don't say that we should forever focus on equity. We should do it just so long as it takes to actually have equal numbers of men and women in our workplace. Once that is achieved, then we can revert to equality.'

'Don't you think that a completely gender-balanced workplace is quite impossible?'

'Bharat, like you said, as in the case of your bonsai, with consistent effort, careful nurturing and attention, won't it be possible to create something that is seemingly impossible?'

Bharat smiled at the smart comparison. This was why he respected Saahitya. 'I do believe that impossible is just delayed possibility. But I am not convinced about this differential support that you speak of.'

'I know it's getting late for your next appointment. All I would like to say, Bharat, is that gender equality is the goal, but to get there we need gender equity. You can think of equity as a kind of temporary support, a short-term prop.'

'I can't imagine how we can justify a short-term prop to the board,' said Bharat, sounding a little piqued. 'And in any case, it won't be really short term, will it?'

'For us to have a well-balanced workforce, we have to have differentiated enablers. Right now, we need more women managers at our Band 6. We have less than 10 per cent women at that level. We need to see what can be done to get more women to Band 6.'

'Okay.' Bharat got up from the chair and reached for his satchel. 'Let's say for argument's sake, that we are looking to promote someone internally to the new managerial position that has opened up in our AI business. And I have, again hypothetically, three likely candidates—Vimal, Ashok and Liza—all equally qualified. Ideally, and that is what we do right now at AcceLever, we should evaluate each of these candidates for their ability—their work ethic, attitude, competencies, the different business skills they each possess and rate each one of them independently. And then, the best person should get the job. I think this is gender equality. But your theory says that I should reject meritocracy and simply promote Liza, just because we don't have enough women managers. And empower her with temporary props. Do you think we can get our board to accept this?'

… … … … …

The location where the AcceLever ad shoot was to be held was a buzzing hive of activity. It was the 14th floor of a prominent studio and there was a sense of coordinated mess that seemed to manifest itself. Other than the central area which was lit with what looked like halogen bulbs and contained the neat set where the shoot would happen, everything around was chaos. The two TV artists who were acting in the film sat with their respective spot boys, correcting their make-up. The lead cinematographer stood on a box issuing directions to control where the light was falling. A property master ran around, his arms full with various props, distributing them like sweets to various people. The assistant director (AD) seemed the most hassled person on the sets, with sweat pouring down his face and his hair looking like a couple of birds had chosen to nest in it.

It seemed unbelievable to Bharat that to create an ad which would run for a total of 30 seconds on primetime TV, a team of not less than 25 people, not to mention a humungous budget, was required. The crew were completely involved in their work and no one noticed Bharat push out a large empty box and sit on it, waiting for Krishna to come.

Krishna was Bharat's friend and the Director of today's shoot. A highly successful film director, Krishna was away at another location, filming with some of Bollywood's top stars for a movie. While most of his films were box office hits, there were a few duds too and Evita and Bharat would make it a point to rag Krishna about those films over dinner. Laughing about the typical eccentricities of stars and the illusions that movies created, it was always fun to spend time with Krishna and his smart, down-to-earth, non-Bollywood wife, Divya. It was Divya who managed the home efficiently and ensured that their two children were cared for. Krishna's career had taken off brilliantly in the past few years and the feverish pace at which he travelled the world for both shootings as well as receiving awards did not seemed to have changed his warm, friendly personality. Evita and Divya got along famously and the men were often at the receiving end of their jokes.

Bharat wondered how it was possible for Krishna to manage such a frenetic pace of living, with days and nights blurring into each other. Picking up his phone to find out how much longer Krishna would take, Bharat was greeted by a friendly punch on the shoulder as Krishna walked around the box and sat next to Bharat.

'Hey, hotshot, I was just going to call you! What happened? Your 100-crore star giving you trouble?' teased Bharat.

The 99 Day Diversity Challenge

226

'Why? Were you getting a few minutes delayed to make your next billion dollars??!' shot back Krishna and the two laughed.

Krishna shouted to the AD to bring two cups of chai and got up to turn a nearby pedestal fan to face them.

'Aren't you feeling hot?' asked Krishna as he pulled the collar of his shirt down at the back to get in more air. 'These HMIs radiate a lot of heat.'

'What is an HMI?' asked Bharat, looking around.

'Those lamps. They are hydrargyrum medium-arc iodides, otherwise known as HMIs. They are an amazing light source—a favourite of mine,' said Krishna as his sharp eyes took in the work being done by the electric and production design crews. They were a step ahead of the cinematographer and the sound engineer and were already preparing for the next set. With a satisfied smile, Krishna called out to the AD with a few clipped instructions which had the AD scurrying to implement them.

'I thought they were halogen,' said Bharat.

'Well, you see, halogens are not as expensive as HMIs and I need to make a living!' laughed Krishna and then proceeded to explain, 'HMIs are used by cinematographers to create a perfect daylight illusion. They are the best alternative to shooting in the outdoors.'

'But how will you ensure that the different angles of light falling, which happens in the real outdoors, is replicated here?' asked Bharat, looking at the set which now seemed to have changed drastically with both the actors wearing different costumes.

'Well, that's what apple boxes are for!' laughed Krishna and continued, 'I see you have chosen the most comfortable apple box for us to sit on!'

'Apple box? I didn't know that these are boxes used to pack apples,' said Bharat innocently, looking at the sturdy wooden box which had a grip on the side.

Krishna laughed louder. 'An apple box is a technical name for this prop,' he explained. 'This is one of the most useful pieces of equipment on a film set. I have seen our prop master fight bloody battles over a mini-apple box. We use apple boxes for a variety of things. Whenever anything needs to be propped up temporarily or supported, we use apple boxes. We prop up furniture or light stands on it. When we need different levels of lighting, we place the light sources on apple boxes of differing heights.'

The steaming glasses of chai arrived on a chipped tray and Bharat thought about the tray back at his office which held the bonsai. Different strokes for different folks, he thought with a sense of something unfolding in his mind.

Krishna picked a glass up and offered it to Bharat. 'Careful, it's really hot,' he said, before turning to the handyman who had brought the tea. 'Thanks Rajendran!' he said. 'Give a glass to Naren,' he added, referring to the AD who looked as if a typhoon had hit him. 'He would not have had lunch.'

'Yes Sir!' said Rajendran as he chased after Naren who was rushing at a breakneck speed to say something to the cinematographer who had stepped off his apple box and was peering at the set through his camera.

'Sometimes you have a heroine who is taller than the hero, but the audience desperately wants to see them together. You can't ask that actor to go home and come back after he has become taller! Guess what comes to his rescue? Yes, the apple box. And then, there are occasions when we need to make an actor appear taller, not because they are short, but to fit the composition of that particular shot. Yes, again, it's the apple box which does the trick!'

Krishna stopped as he saw Bharat's expression change. 'You suddenly remembered something?' he asked.

'Yes!' said Bharat, a great smile enveloping his face. 'I just realized how I can pitch apple boxes to my Board!'

EQUITY AND EQUALITY

The animal court was in session. Singa the Lion King sat in his great throne, ready to hear the case. His council of ministers was seated in their ornamental chairs flanking him on both sides. The Minister for Strategy, Mayil, Commander Snake of the Imperial Army, Treasurer Cerf and other ministers under the guidance of Chief Minister Gaja were in attendance.

The Chief Justice of the kingdom Jamba, the bear, rose to describe the case.

'Your Majesty, we have the case of these two friends, the Fox and the Crane, who have now turned bitter rivals. When enquired, both complain that they are in the right and the other is wrong. No amount of counselling is able to sort out the conflict between them. Their enmity is turning very acrimonious and it appears that the peace of the lower valley, where their groups reside will be compromised. Hence, we have summoned both of them to court to mediate and deliver justice by your honourable self.'

'Let us hear each side,' said Singa.

'The Crane may first rise to present his facts,' announced Jamba.

The Crane walked gracefully to the centre of the court, his long legs and longer neck accentuating his poise. 'Your majesty, I belong to the crane family, having settled in the lower valley for several generations. We are not migratory and do not leave under any circumstance. Unlike our cousins the herons, we fly with our necks outstretched, not pulled back. Anyone who has interacted with us, knows how much we value our necks.'

'Is there a point relevant to this case that you are making, Crane?' questioned Singa, his royal impatience evident.

'Yes, Sire. I was invited a few weeks back for dinner to the house of Mr Fox. We have been friends for a very long time and have always been speaking about catching up for a meal. So, with great anticipation, I went to his home. Even as I entered, I could sniff the fragrance of fish soup, spiced with berries. It was a nice evening and Mr Fox is a good conversationalist, albeit opinionated, and soon it was time for dinner. I was quite hungry and was waiting for the food to arrive. Then I saw the plates. Plates, your majesty! The soup was served on a flat plate! It appears my Lord that all along, it was the malicious intent of Mr Fox to insult me, mock my long neck and make a fool of me by presenting the soup in a plate. While he happily slurped away at the soup, I stood there, ashamed and insulted, more angry than hungry. When I confronted him, he simply said that he was fair and equal. Is this equality, my Lord?'

'Indeed it is, Crane. This is equality. But I completely understand your point. While Fox was trying to play the equality card, he did not realize that you could do it too. Which, from the facts of the case, I gather you did. You served a meal the next day in a long jar, which of course Fox could not reach.'

'I am ashamed of it, My Lord, but there was no other way I could teach him a lesson. Even I was being equal. And since then we have been hostile foes to each other,' said Crane, his voice low.

'In this game for equality, both of you have forgotten the value of "equity" and it is time to remind you of what that means,' said Singa in an even tone.

We often hear the terms gender equity and gender equality used interchangeably as if they mean the same thing. This is a common misconception. Equity and equality maybe similar but they mean completely different things when it comes to effective execution of D&I policies. For D&I practitioners, it is crucial to understand the difference and also appreciate the values of each of these terms.

To illustrate the point, let us look at these questions: Should the policies for men and women be exactly the same? This is a question of equality. However, if we reframe the question to ask, should the objective of the

D&I programme result in the overall development of all employees by providing more support to those in need of it, in order to ensure that they can catch up? This becomes a question of equity. While it is certainly important to make sure that all employees have equal access to the policies and programmes of the organization, the truth is that some employee segments, such as certain categories of women, persons with disabilities, first-generation professionals and senior citizens, might need more support, even to reach the promise of equality.

This is the premise of equity. The gaps that exist among various employee cohorts starting from pay gaps to motivation gaps to achievement gaps to even the sheer number-based metric of workforce participation are ample reason for customized programmes. The principle of equity states that while every employee must be given equal access to resources, what is more important is the 'means' to utilize these resources differently, in order to reach the same destination. Equity, therefore, operates with the value of 'fairness'. It takes into account the differing life experiences of certain segments of the employee base and provides differentiated support to each. When there are sufficiently large numbers in the employee population who come under a particular category, compensation is made to everyone in the group for historical disadvantages.

Equity can therefore be defined as the leveller of the playing field. It is the pathway to the achievement of equality. In fact, it can even be stated that once equity-led measures are truly effective, they become redundant and result in equality, which does not require segregated measures for development.

EMPLOYEE RESOURCE GROUPS

Hi, I am Jasma, an LGBT ally and proud of it! I have a problem. There is talk in my organization that employee resource groups (ERGs) meant for the LGBT population are going to be dismantled and in their place councils are going to be formed to drive policies and programmes more effectively. I don't agree with this at all. At our organization, Sticwal Inc, we originally started off an informal community of lesbian and gay 'out' folks. It was just a handful, even in the large population of over 14,000 workers here at Sticwal, but they wanted a safe space and this got created with the support of a few understanding leaders.

Then, it got formalized as an ERG and grew to cover not only lesbians and gays, but also bisexuals and transgenders. As someone who has a lesbian sister, I understood the challenges that the community faced and hence volunteered my time and support as an ally. As you know, allies are members of the majority community, in this case, straight, heterosexual folks, who work to support those who are oppressed. We began having frequent, regular meetings, which focused on how the workplace can be more empathetic to the needs of the LGBT community and what we allies can do for the same.

Now, I hear that the ERGs, not only for LGBTs but also for persons with disability, women, senior citizens, etc., are going to be disbanded. The perception is that it is getting more exclusive rather than inclusive. I do not agree at all. Communities which have a history of facing discrimination and oppression require a separate platform to be themselves, to express their views. Even with a whole bunch of sensitivity training, sometimes it is not possible to make that bigoted employee obtain an unbiased view towards a lesbian. Am I right or not?

The purpose of ERGs or employee networks is to provide a voice to a minority which otherwise does not have the confidence to speak up about its needs and requirements. ERGs can exist in many formats—formal or informal and driven by business or HR. In today's connected world, ERGs are virtual too, taking life in Facebook and WhatsApp groups and equally effective as a platform for expression.

ERGs started off when people who were different from the majority wanted a sense of belonging in order to create relationships at the workplace with people of similar backgrounds. In countries where racial discrimination was rampant, ERGs were a method to create 'safe spaces' in order to work towards unifying a collective voice. Over time, ERGs became a priority for all employees who were concerned about the growth of the organization, via the growth of its people. Thus, the concept of 'allyship' got created, with people who were 'on the outside', who did not belong to the core group, becoming part of it in order to communicate their support. Male allies, multicultural allies, LGBT allies and PWD allies are trained specifically to contribute meaningfully to the discussion. ERGs are often the first step in the creation of a D&I strategy and probably one of the most effective methods of demonstrating the value of diversity.

Increasingly, it is becoming critical to identify and clarify the purpose of existence of ERGs. In organizations where the overarching culture is not sufficiently powerful and inclusive, ERGs tend to become a closeted community that has lesser focus on enabling people and a greater intention of providing a 'cribbing corner'. Organizations which seek to blend the ERGs purpose with a larger business outcome often discover that unless the ERG is structured like yet another department/function, the results are not encouraging. It is, therefore, imperative to refine the core purpose of the existence of ERGs as an effort to provide support, information, resources and ultimately be accountable for the success of the diverse people in the workplace.

Employee Resource Groups

D&I GAME: EXPERIENCING DIVERSITY AND INCLUSION

Please read the values given below carefully and think about the examples for each value that you have seen and/or experienced both within your team and within organization.

Values	Example(s) Relating to Gender Equality in Your Team and/or Organization
Dedication	
Integrity	
Value creation	
Excellence	
Respect	
Sensitivity	
Inquisitiveness	
Trust	
Youthful energy	

Values	Example(s) Relating to Gender Equality in Your Team and/or Organization
Innovation	
Nurturing	
Creativity	
Learnability	
Uniqueness	
Safety and security	
Individuality	
Open-mindedness	
Natural/nobility/non-bureaucratic \	

LANGUAGE AS A DIVERSITY FACTOR

I was once invited to deliver a series of webinars for a leading IT organization on the topic of inclusion. In order to make use of their state-of-the-art teleconferencing facility, I had to travel to their premises to deliver the sessions. Over the months, I became friendly with Chitra, the IT helpdesk person who helped me with the smooth conduct of the programme by ensuring that the technical aspects were taken care of. I once happened to ask her about her background and we discovered to our pleasant surprise that we both shared the same hometown. This created a bonding and Chitra began opening up to me as regards her career aspirations.

She revealed that she had actually applied for a client-facing business analyst role. But because of the poor quality of her spoken English, with a heavy mother tongue influence, she was not considered for that position. However, her extremely sound technical knowledge ensured that she got a job, but in a back-end function, where her English language was not a barrier. As I tried to understand if this was a disappointment to Chitra, she further revealed that the role per se was not a problem. She enjoyed the work she did as part of the technical team, but what bothered her was the clear discrimination that she faced due to her poor English skills.

In a workplace that had two dominant languages, she was conversant in neither. This created a lot of gaps since her manager was not particularly concerned about including Chitra in all decisions. The manager felt that the onus was on Chitra to work on her English and ensure that she did not miss out on important messages. However, Chitra felt that there was an automatic bias in the minds of her colleagues about her, which could not be cleared just by speaking good English. 'I will always have this mother-tongue

235

influence, Ma'am. It will never go away. And I know that the minute I open my mouth to say something, people are judging me. I am just not able to manage this. Maybe I just have to search for another job where there will be more people like me whose English is not all that great and who will not discriminate against me for this,' she confided one day.

Language is one of the strongest creators of a shared culture. It is the foundation on which identity emerges and is used to distinguish speakers as parts of unique groups. With the advent of globalization, it became imperative to identify one language that would be used extensively and bond employees to a singular vision. For this reason, language diversity in the workplace is often not encouraged. Like in systems of education, there is a primary language of business and then there are secondary languages that large groups use.

The emergence of English as the universal language of the workplace has created a need for it to be learnt and used well for effective communication. In much the same way that literacy has become a basic requirement to participate fully in civic society, the knowledge of English too is now a hygiene factor. Over decades, English has moved away from being a language that defined the elite and those in power, to one that is an essential requirement for communication in the workplace. It is the language of instruction and communication and as such those employees whose fluency in English is very high, find themselves in a position of advantage.

The usage of English also has different dimensions according to the industry. Employees in the call centre industry are trained to use a neutral English accent in order to serve different markets and customers around the world. For the same reason, those enterprises in the verticals of consumer-facing businesses such as FMCG or retail required a knowledge of the vernacular in order to communicate easily in the medium that the end customer understands. However, even in such industries, the corporate office still favours English, while regional centres might use other languages.

Often language diversity in the workplace is an inconvenience which generates problems around articulation, interpretation and reach. Language, therefore, has a very significant role as a gatekeeper and a pathway—automatically creating cohorts whose understanding and empathy is increased simply by sharing the same medium of communication. Hence, in today's diverse workplace, the role of language actually moves beyond simple communication and becomes a reference point for inclusion. The D&I practitioner is required to understand these dynamics and create solutions which engender an inclusive and trust-filled workplace, where language is not a barrier.

INCLUSION AND CSR

DAY 87/99

RK: Hey Tams, are you coming today for the walkathon?

TS: No da. Some last minute work has come up. I am planning to excuse myself.

RK: But this is something you really like! It is about education of young girls to ensure that they break out of poverty.

TS: Yes, I have been reading a lot about it. It is about taking the D&I function outside the office and making it relevant to the community we serve.

RK: You know so much about it. Then, why don't you come with us?

TS: I have a small difference of opinion, actually.

RK: What is it?

TS: I feel that D&I and CSR are two entirely different fields. CSR should not be a business imperative. Whereas, D&I has a clear business purpose.

RK: But so what if they are different? What is important is that good stuff is being done that helps people.

TS: But if the definition is not clearly laid out, I have a problem. I don't want to do something that I don't feel passionately about.

In the early days of D&I, it was often mistaken for an extension of CSR. In fact, several organizations find it easier to club the two functions under one leader. However, the two have very different purposes. CSR as a function is all about the organization's need to give back to society. It spells out the company's alignment with the social, economic and environmental ecosystems that it is part of and is often a reflection of the vision of its key stakeholders. It usually takes the form of an initiative or engagement focused on the community or aligned with a specific charity. Organizations, especially large conglomerates, frequently fund their own non-governmental extension/foundation which is involved in a long-term project with a high-impact factor that is of interest or relevance to the company.

D&I, on the other hand, is a very internal-focused function that looks at culture-building via recruitment, retention and development of a diverse workforce. The D&I function concentrates on equality, equity and inclusion. It works to ensure that there is no tokenism and that true inclusion—ensuring that the contributions and opinions of the diverse population are valued and acted upon—is the end result. It also focuses on the future sustainability of the business, by analysing demographic trends to predict where the best talent for the organization will emerge from and how the company can engage with such talent. It also improves business processes and decision-making style of the organization by creating a culture of inclusive problem-solving.

The intersection of these two functions happens in their common objective of good governance and reputation management. Both CSR and D&I emphasize the requirement of organizations to behave responsibly and ethically, creating a positive, energizing workplace while also giving back to the community. As such, these two functions sometimes meet in the middle and there could be overlaps in the deliverables. In the end, the goal of both these functions is to ensure that the firm is valued by clients, the productivity and creativity of its employees are enhanced and its profitability guaranteed and put to good use.

INCLUSION AND RESPECT

88/99

Interviewer: Hearty Congratulations, Mr Gupta! Tell us how you feel about being recognized as the HR Leader of the Year 2018! What made you win this coveted award? In a country where over a million HR professionals exist, it is amazing to be recognized as the foremost of them all. What would you state as the single-most important reason as to why you have emerged the winner?

Sushant Gupta: Thanks very much for your wishes, Ms Banerjee. It is indeed an exhilarating moment! In fact, it is a long-term dream come true! And if you ask me, what is the single most important reason for my winning this award, the answer is very simple—it is my team. I owe it to my team for having enabled me to win this award—both the team that reports into me and with whom I work, as also the Board of Directors who I report into.

Interviewer: The citation states that you have won this award for having created a highly diverse and yet at the same time inclusive team. Could you explain this in detail? Does your team have equal numbers of men and women? Does it have a good balance of different generations?

Sushant Gupta: Actually, my answer might surprise you! My team has the greatest diversity of all—thought diversity! The key to effectiveness of my team is that we believe that there is more than one right answer. Each member of my team brings very different perspectives. Each of us negotiates this world and interprets it on the basis of our past experiences, our cultural filters and, therefore, our identity. When you have greater diversity in your team, it automatically means greater variation in perspectives and approaches. The success of an inclusive team is how you leverage all these

off

239

different thought processes and harness them to arrive at the best possible decision.

Interviewer: That's fascinating! But a question that just jumps up is, how do you manage all the conflicts? When you have people in a team who each think differently, doesn't it mean that you will take a long time arriving at a decision?

Sushant Gupta: Great point, Ms Banerjee! Diversity of thought is among the greatest innovation boosters that a team can possess. It is critical to understand your team really well, before you harness their diversity. Some of my teammates are analytical thinkers, some others are creative while others are great at process-mapping. One of my teammates is an astute planner while another is spontaneous in ideation. This diversity helps us guard against 'groupthink'—a rather dangerous tendency in groups to prioritize mainly on consensus, which is often at the expense of making the right decision. (After a pause) However, the answer to your question lies elsewhere. It lies in building respect within the team. We each are different, but we also respect our differences.

The phrase 'workplace diversity' originally meant the primary strands of diversity such as gender, ability, generations, race and ethnicity. However, over a period of time, diversity enthusiasts realized that diversity could also mean varying work values, differences in information processing, work styles and changes in perspectives due to differences in hierarchical levels. An employee whose primary career anchor is to create impact will have a very different approach to work when compared to another employee whose anchor is strictly economic. However, the organization has to ensure that both employees are treated with fairness and respect and both are motivated equally to deliver to their fullest potential.

Research on the topic of employee engagement and discretionary effort states that respect is the key attribute which ensures that people feel included, irrespective of their role, status or position.

The importance of respect in creating a diverse workplace that promotes mutual alignment of professional goals, in spite of personal differences, cannot be understated. Recognizing employees' varied talents and contributions while not being biased or prejudiced by their gender, age, culture or race is the hallmark of a respectful workplace. Researchers have found that a high-respect work climate provides a strong underlying mechanism whereby D&I are able to transmit their fullest positive impact on productivity and engagement.

One of the core aspects of diversity training is the embedding of respect in the workplace processes and systems. Whether through formal classroom training or via blended learning, such as webinars combined with instructor-led training, it is important for a workplace to inculcate respect among all its employees. A workplace that is low on respect or devoid of it entirely will have a high incidence of conflict. Such conflict has a deep negative impact on productivity, morale and job satisfaction. Workplace respect occupies pride of place as one among the top five engagement drivers of all employees, the other four being stability, compensation, health benefits and work-life integration.

In today's environment, especially, which has a majority of millennials, respect is a non-negotiable factor. Gone are the days when older generations would keep their head down and allow their work to speak for themselves. Recognition, which is closely allied to respect is very high on the list of workplace requirements. Employees who respect their teammates are likely to also respect and recognize their colleagues' level of expertise and breadth of knowledge. Simply put, when diversity practices enhanced with a respect-filled culture coexist in an organization, it increases employee engagement.

IS YOUR HIRING INCLUSIVE?

It was 4:30 PM and the press conference was set to begin on time. All the panellists had taken their seats at the head table facing the long rows of chairs on which the journalists sat. The MD, a distinguished old gentleman in his 60s, his silver mane and golden frame adding to the picture of sombreness, sat in the centre, his President (Sales & Marketing) and Vice President (Finance) flanking him on either side. The Corp Comm head sat in one corner while the MD's daughter, his understudy, occupied the other.

The meet was being held at the Chennai headquarters of the conglomerate in a large colonial room with its high ceiling, pastel blue on its walls and paintings by Raja Ravi Verma adding to the feeling of ancient beauty. Tables containing dainty vegetable and cheese sandwiches and fragrant coffee in a steel dispenser lined a wall, while an adjoining table contained glasses of water. The MD was very vocal about the environment and hence all public meetings shunned the use of plastic.

He noticed that his nemesis, Audrey Clair, a young journalist who had been writing scathing pieces against the company's untrammelled and supposedly unethical growth, was sitting alert in the audience, notepad and pen in hand. He nodded at her and Audrey returned the greeting with two fingers to her forehead, a brief captain's salute. To the MD, it felt more like a gun to his head.

He left tired. 'I hope this gets done soon,' he thought to himself. The Corp Comm head whispered something in his ear and the MD straightened up in his chair. He took a sip of the warm water from the glass near him.

'Good afternoon, dear friends!' he began.

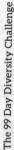

'We are delighted to share the results of the first quarter of this financial year with you. We have outdone our performance targets by 40 per cent and hence are announcing a dividend of 28 per cent!'

The room broke into thundering applause. 'I would particularly like to emphasize the way we have achieved this success. I am proud to state that we have broken the long-held belief that focusing on the environment and society is at odds with making a profit. We have looked at inclusive growth, which by definition, looks at sectors in which the poor work, takes place in areas where the less fortunate live and reduces the prices of those items which the underprivileged consume.' The MD caught the eye of another senior journalist who had just walked in and smiled broadly.

'In other words, what we have achieved is not just profits but also inclusive economic growth through which we have reached the most vulnerable people of our society.'

Even before the MD could complete his sentence, Audrey's voice was heard clear and loud. 'But Sir, while you are speaking about inclusive growth, which frankly to me, looks like you are making a huge fortune from the bottom of the pyramid, I don't see any inclusivity in your hiring. For instance, your annual report states that you have only one woman member on your board who happens to be your daughter. 90 per cent of all your new hires are MTs from some of the most pedigreed B-schools of India. More than 75 per cent of your middle managers are people from 2 or 3 distinct communities of South India.

Where is the inclusivity in your hiring and talent acquisition, Sir?'

Diversity hiring is quite a tricky terrain since the debate of diversity versus meritocracy crops up almost instantly. As such, the talent acquisition team is often the first point of change management when hiring for diversity. Recruiting based on merit, while also ensuring that biases that arise from set prejudices relating to a candidate's gender, age, religion, race or sexual orientation do not derail the process of choosing the best candidate.

Is Your Hiring Inclusive?

243

The essence of effective diversity hiring is to safeguard against stereotyping that will cause a candidate to be rejected, or selected, based on decisions entirely unrelated to competence or job performance. Prejudices can creep in from any aspect of the candidate's identity and sometimes could even take the guise of a proven business call. The complete buy-in of the necessity for diversity, by not just the talent acquisition team but also the hiring managers (who are internal customers to the TA team), is required to adopt diversity hiring practices. In order to recruit talented and creative employees, it is important to completely cleanse the system of any pre-existing biases which could lead to either the consistent hiring or rejection of a set of candidates.

A prejudiced company, most often suffering from unconscious bias, will find itself getting the raw end of the deal, not just from a people perspective but also economically. Prejudiced hiring leads to the rejection of people for no rational reason and this means that the company has lost out on a great candidate, simply because there is an irrational objective causing the rejection. Business gets hit when people who are not the most suited for the job from a skills point of view get eventually selected. Consistent hiring of candidates for a specific level (like MTs) from a particular cohort leads to demoralizing of staff who see a prejudiced pattern in this.

Preparing data points which actually point out the cost of a mis-hire and also the benefit of a competent hire serves to drive home the virtues of diversity hiring for business folks. It is also important to create a good diversity hiring team from cross-functional groups by deciphering who is really good at conducting interviews and choosing the right candidate with the best fit. Educating the business as well as hiring managers on what we exactly mean by 'diversity' is also crucial. For businesses to serve their own diverse customer base in the most effective manner possible, it is important to get the most suitable combination of the different strands of diversity.

CROSSWORD

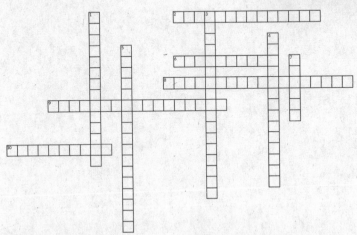

ACROSS

2 An ideal organizational (and social) condition in which professionals of all genders are entitled to equal and fair treatment. (6,8)

6 A database of candidate profiles eligible for working in an organization. They could be limited to a specific area of expertise or focused on a broad grouping of individuals who are capable of performing a variety of job tasks. (6,4)

8 This refers to an approach that when ingrained in the organizational culture it can ensure that all employees, both male and female, are able to 'speak the language' and understand the behaviours of both genders, rather than just those of their genders. (6,12)

9 Differences amongst individuals in an organization's customer base in terms of age, gender, cultural background, physical abilities, race, religion, sexual orientation, education, experience, etc., amongst others. (8,9)

10 Refers to the period of an individual's successful profession. (6,4)

DOWN

1 The difference (expressed in units of time) between the amount of housework done by women and men. (6,5,3)

3 A physical, mental or cognitive impairment or condition that characterizes an individual. (11,5)

4 The term that has a plumbing connotation and refers to a pool of candidates qualified to assume open positions that have been created or vacated through a retirement or a promotion. (6,8)

5 In an organizational context, this refers to the practice of ensuring complete inclusion of all genders without any biases, in recruitment, training and development, promotions and other organizational initiatives. (6,11)

7 Refers to the process of creating equivalent outcomes for members of historically underrepresented and oppressed individuals and groups. (6)

DIVERSITY AND
INCLUSION LEXICON

SECTION 10

INFUSING THE SPIRIT
OF INCLUSION IN YOUR
WORKPLACE

DIVERSITY AND INCLUSION LEXICON

S. No.	Words	Definition
1.	Career and home orientation	A 'career orientation' in which the concerned individual has an abiding interest in pursuing a career but treats it as equal and sometimes secondary to family responsibilities
2.	Career aspirations	The tangible/intangible outcomes an individual aspires to achieve by pursuing a career; some common aspirations include career advancement, job security, gaining professional expertise and/or achieving work-life balance.
3.	Career break	A period of time during which a professional chooses not to be gainfully employed, typically to cater to familial responsibilities or pursue other interests
4.	Career breaker	Any factor (professional or personal) that results in a career break for a professional
5.	Career comeback	The process of resuming one's career after a sabbatical
6.	Career continuity	The extent to which a professional's career is interruption/break-free
7.	Career counselling	Guidance a professional receives from an external agent (boss/mentor/colleague/family/friends or others) that enables him/her make informed career choices and develop a career plan
8.	Career de-railers	Factors that pull a professional away from a progressive career, very often domestic commitments

S. No.	Words	Definition
9.	Career driver	A factor that drives a professional towards pursuing a career, such as being the breadwinner of the family, to meet the financial goal for the family or self-career achievement
10.	Career enablers	Support systems that a professional avails of that in turn help him/her manage professional and domestic responsibilities efficiently without conflict, thereby enabling his/her career aspirations; there are essentially three types of career enablers: (a) self-initiated (b) organization based (c) family/society based.
11.	Career focus	The extent of focus and dedication a professional places on his career which forms the basis of his/her career plan
12.	Career goals	The tangible/intangible goals a professional aims to reach through active involvement in his/her career
13.	Career growth	The extent to which a professional has successfully climbed the corporate ladder
14.	Career identity	The distinction given to an individual by a third party that defines the nature of the value that he/she brings to the workplace; for example, project manager, receptionist, customer service representative and curriculum designer.
15.	Career influencer	The support network that influences and shapes a professional's career path that includes (but is not limited to) his/her family, colleagues, boss, mentor, friends, etc. Career intentionality gap: The gap in career intentionality between two genders
16.	Executive coaching	Defined as working with a coaching professional to reach specific professional development goals—particularly those that are required or expected in high-level corporate positions

S. No.	Words	Definition
17.	**Flex quotient**	A measure of the effectiveness of policies of an organization to ensure greater work flexibility
18.	**Flexi worker**	An employee who avails of any flexible working arrangement in his/her organization
19.	**Flexible working arrangements (FWAs)**	A term used to refer to work arrangements that are unconventional and in which the employee has autonomy over the time during which he/she works and the place from where he/she works
20.	**Home-based family member caregiver**	A family member(s) of a professional who has the will, reliability and health to carry out domestic commitments (household duties and childcare/eldercare) while the professional is away at work
21.	**Home-based non-family member caregiver**	A caregiver who is a non-family member hired by a professional to take care of household and is in charge of the professional's caring duties while he/she is away at work
22.	**Job sharing**	An alternate, flexible work arrangement in which one job is shared between two people, who might work alternate days, half weeks or alternate weeks, or one person working in the morning and one in the afternoon
23.	**Job rotation**	A situation in which employees are moved among two or more jobs in a planned manner, with the objective to cross-train employees, exposing them to different experiences and a wider variety of skills to enhance job satisfaction and advancement
24.	**Male ally**	Men who actively champion the cause of gender inclusion and work with an open mind work alongside women for a better organizational culture and a better society
25.	**Part-time work**	Requires employees to work a lower number of hours than would be considered full time by their employer

S. No.	Words	Definition
26.	Partial work, partial pay	Working for a certain 'percentage' of hours every day and getting that 'percentage' of full-time pay for the designated role
27.	Remote work	Defined as working offsite (often at home) on a full-time basis
28.	Right to flexible working	Refers to the right of every employee of an organization to request for flexible working to his/her employer under fair circumstances that warranty it
29.	Staggered hours contract	A flexible work arrangement under which an employee can start and finish work at different timelines
30.	Telecommuting	A flexible work arrangement in which employees work offsite (often at home) as per circumstances
31.	Term-time work	A flexible work arrangement whereby an employee is contracted to work particular number of weeks per year on either a full or part-time basis; his/her non-working time is scheduled at regular, planned periods which are accounted for by a combination of annual leave and unpaid leave. Designated working weeks will normally coincide with school terms.
32.	Uberization of workforce	Refers to a transition to an economic system where corporates exchange underutilized capacity of existing human resources while incurring low transaction costs
33.	Work time diversity	In the organizational context, this refers to the representation of individuals who follow different work time patterns (including flexible work arrangements)
34.	Work-life integration	Seamless integration of an employee's work and life outside of work that can be achieved through smart prioritizations of demands at work and those at home

Diversity and Inclusion Lexicon

INCLUSION AND FLEXIBILITY

The dappled light in the forest fell on the beautiful cottage in which the bear family lived. They were getting ready to go someplace. Papa Bear finished clearing up the breakfast table, while Mama Bear put away the dishes in the kitchen. Baby Bear knew that they were going for a walk and so got up, toddled to his chair and wore his little shoes.

'Remember to keep the porridge out so that we can have it when we come back,' said Papa Bear. Mama Bear replied, 'Yes, that's what I am getting ready,' and began pouring the porridge into three bowls.

The largest bowl with the hottest porridge was for Papa Bear. He needed a lot of calories, since he was working out with his friends and was constantly measuring his weight. So Mama Bear added a couple of eggs, some almond and banana slices into his oatmeal. She herself was on a diet and so her own bowl contained diluted low-fat porridge with strawberries (that she had picked herself) and grapes (which Baby Bear had helped her pick). Also, she believed that hot food added more weight (she was not entirely sure of this, but Papa Bear always said this) and so her porridge was at room temperature. As for Baby Bear, she prepared a separate bowl with the porridge sweetened more than usual, because Baby Bear liked it that way. She added chocolate chips and small pieces of apple, smiling to herself when she thought of how Baby Bear would discover the apple right at the bottom of the bowl and throw a fit.

Papa Bear saw the individual bowls that Mama Bear had prepared and kept at the kitchen counter and took them to the table. He noted the different ingredients of each of the bowls and felt happy.

He was particular about these things. He arranged the chairs properly and placed pretty place mats under each bowl.

'Shall we leave?' asked Papa Bear.

Just as they were stepping out, a little girl dashed into the clearing, breathless, panting with the effort. It appeared that she had run a long way. She had gorgeous golden tresses and wore a pink frock with lots of lace. She looked so young and sweet and seemed so frightened that Mama Bear and Papa Bear immediately let her in. Mama Bear quickly went to the kitchen and brought a tall glass of lemonade for the young girl.

Goldilocks, for that was the girl's name, caught her breath and took a few sips of the lemonade. She noticed the table with one large chair, one middle-sized chair and one small chair. And yes, she also noticed the three bowls of porridge, with three different spoons—a large wooden spoon, a slim ceramic spoon and a cute baby spoon.

Even though she was hungry and wanted to eat the porridge (especially the one which contained the chocolate chips), Goldilocks was very intrigued by the endearing little cottage. Forgetting that she was in the presence of three bears, one of which looked particularly large and menacing, Goldilocks walked further into the house. There she found three beds—a large bed, a mid-sized one and a Baby Bear's tiny crib-bed.

'How wonderful!' exclaimed Goldilocks. 'This is most interesting! You are the most amazing bear family I have seen! Different strokes for different folks! Personalized chairs, customized bowls of porridge and separate beds! How inclusive!'

Flexibility, by definition, is a tool meant to ensure that all employees are able to perform at their best while managing life situations that are inevitable. However, the success or otherwise of a flexibility initiative lies in the creation of an inclusive environment. When organizations are committed to creating a workplace that allows every employee to participate fully and be as productive as possible, the secret lies not just in setting up a flexible work system, it lies in making sure that the unspoken culture allows its usage equitably. And here is where inclusion steps in.

Work flexibility is successful only when senior management and business leaders encourage employees to work in ways that prioritize output rather than manner of input. When inclusion is the spirit that drives the cultural mooring of a company, then flexibility becomes a norm, not an accommodation. Creating a flexible culture is not always easy, and even today, in an environment surfeit with technological advancement, deciphering what works and what does not is a tricky thing. However, an inclusive culture that emphasizes trust and respect is able to lead the way to successful implementation of flexibility. Thus, in order of priority, an organization should first focus on instilling the value of inclusion, before embarking upon a flexi-working system.

Flexibility, especially with the advent of millennials, is a sure-fire component of the futuristic workplace. Inflexibility or, in other words, a very structured environment fixated on 'presenteeism' is perceived as a conservative, old-school method which places the interests of the organization over and above those of the employee. It assumes that the organization and the employee take adversarial positions when it comes to usage of time. Thus, flexibility is demonstrative of inclusion and inflexibility relates to exclusion. When it is an accepted norm that the business world is perennially changing, it is not wise to approach flexibility with a 'one-size-fits-all' view that essentially goes against inclusion. When the discourse of flexibility is placed within the value of inclusion, it leads to an effective implementation of the people agenda.

WORK–LIFE BALANCE AND WORK–LIFE INTEGRATION

Nischaya looked up hurriedly from her laptop and braced herself to accept the time that the clock on the wall directly before her pronounced. It was 2:00 PM and her heart sank. She needed to go for her 11-year-old son Aswath's parent-teacher meeting and unless she started this very minute, she would not make it on time. And that meant another bout of lose–lose arguments with Kishore, her husband. She recalled the morning's debate.

'Kishore, today is Aswath's PTA meeting. We discussed this last time. Have you spoken to your boss? Would you be able to go?'

'You tell me now? In the morning? For a meeting that is at 3:00 PM, today??' Kishore's agitated reply meant that there was a very slim chance of him going to Aswath's school.

'But I thought you would have remembered, Kishore. I even sent you a calendar invite months ago.'

'Unless the calendar invite gets accepted, it does not mean the other person is going to do it,' said Kishore, dryly.

'So, you did not accept my calendar invite on purpose?' Nischaya regretted asking that rhetorical question the minute it slipped from her. And the rest of the morning disappeared in a haze of defensive arguments.

As Nischaya packed up her laptop, feeling a sense of inordinate guilt at every decision that she was taking—leaving early, not being a good mom to Aswath, not being a more efficient professional—Sudha popped her head into the cubicle and said cheerily, 'I am stepping out for a massage, girls! Be back in 30 minutes!'

Sudha was her super boss, the manager of Ashok, Nischaya's supervisor. A leader who everyone looked up to, Sudha seemed to lead a charmed life. Her two sons went to a top school, her husband worked for another successful company and it was said that she hosted amazing dinner parties for her friends. If she was not so likeable, Nischaya would have hated her, envied her. But then, Sudha was Sudha, a role model that Nischaya looked up to, perpetually energetic, enthusiastic and ready to give a hand. As she joined Sudha in the elevator, Nischaya decided to ask her the million-dollar question.

'How do you do it, Sudha? How do you manage it all? I just don't seem to be able to do even 10 per cent of what you do. This work-life balance just beats me.' As she punched the button for the ground floor, Nischaya's voice reflected both defeat and longing.

'Simple, Nischaya,' said Sudha, adjusting her sling bag's strap on her shoulder and looking deep into Nischaya's eyes. 'I don't attempt to balance at all.'

'But, but, if you don't balance, how does everything then magically fall into place?' asked Nischaya.

'I did not say I don't prioritize, I merely don't balance,' said Sudha cryptically.

'But if you do prioritize, how do you get to do all these many different things? Like spearheading the latest growth project, managing your home so beautifully, taking a massage now and then....' In spite of her dull mood, Nischaya smiled.

'That's called work-life integration, Nischaya, not work-life balance!' laughed Sudha. 'Block some time on my calendar tomorrow and I will tell you all about it,' she said as she waved goodbye.

The decades of 1980/90 began looking at the issue of balancing time between 'work' aspects and 'life' aspects. Work-life balance was a hot keyword. But therein lay a keen problem. Work and life are not two conflicting parts meant to be balanced. They are intertwined with each other. The problem, therefore, is with the word 'balance'.

If we look at the literal definition, the word 'balance', in the context of work-life balance, infers that there is a kind of equilibrium or apportioning of time between what are essentially two opposing activities. Imagine a physical balance. And now imagine putting 'work' on one scale and 'life' on another. There you have it—work-life balance, therefore, implies that when one aspect goes up, the other goes down. When work and life are juxtaposed as two opposite sides, then it boils down to choosing one at the expense of the other.

Work-life balance, therefore, means that the two are hostile to each other—one's rise lies in the fall of the other. Even more importantly, the pursuit of balance is to bring the needle to dead centre. So, your two plates must be filled with exact equal time, down to the second—if you want the needle to reflect a true balance. The analogy fits perfectly to the concept itself—'balancing' of work and life brings it down to creating an environment where the two are at odds with each other.

Social researchers began to see that apart from instilling a false sense of pressure in attempting to balance these two apparently confrontational sides, isolation of work from the general flow of your life means a shift of energy every time. If work becomes taboo at home and if anything relating to your personal life is off-bounds at work, then it comes down to creating two parts of your identity—the work identity and the home identity. Each time, you are caught in the hurry to remove your work hat and wear your non-work hat.

Some men and women seem to have got the secret sauce very easily. They seem to be accomplishing more with the same amount of time. While there are many reasons for this, the key difference is in what they call it—it is no longer work-life balance. It is work-life integration. As they say in neurolinguistic programming, words become thought and thoughts convert into action. By not calling it balance, the pressure to divvy up time is removed.

Work-life integration is the skill of allowing parts of your work to flow into your non-work time and vice versa. It is the ability of scheduling your time most effectively without laying boundaries on what are work zones and non-work zones. Most effective 'integrators' select the calendar as a weapon of choice in eliminating conflicts. They use the calendar as a tool to manage both professional and personal priorities. This calendar is then shared with folks whose work and life are connected with yours, so that confusions are removed.

The second most important aspect is to create allies both at work and at home. If you are in pursuit of excellence, then everyone important to you—both at work and at home—ought to know about it. These quasi-colleagues at home and quasi-family at work help you to remove that sharp wedge which separates the different parts of your life. This, in turn, allows a certain level of freedom in managing all the different parts of your life which ultimately mesh into one whole.

DAY
94/99

MEN AS ALLIES

Hi, I am Shilpi. I am an Area Sales Manager at Duhig Food Products and have been with them for almost 5 years, ever since I left B-school. I am dreading the forthcoming sales conference that I am going to be a part of. It's not because my performance is poor or anything. On the contrary, my performance has been great. I have met my targets and my performance score should ideally be an A minus, which would translate into possibly a promotion in the next performance cycle.

It's the one-on-one discussion with Boss that I am dreading. Why? Because he just does not get it.

The questions that he asks me are sometimes ridiculous, bordering on insensitive.

'Shilpi, leaving at 5:30 PM? Is it half-a-day for you today? You never told me.'

'Why should I know about your personal problems? We are all here to work, not give sob stories.'

'I just don't understand why we have to do all this D&I business. It's a distraction and a waste of time.'

'If only you did not take off so often for these personal reasons, Shilpi, your performance would be so much better.'

'Here at Duhig, we don't believe in working by the clock. Unless you pull long hours, how can you be the best?'

'I am not comfortable with this working from home. I think it should be called 'working "for" home'. You just finish your house chores and don't do any office work at all.'

'If women are keen on working, then they should be prepared to do everything that a man does. Not crib and complain.'

'Managing your home is your headache. Why should the company be bothered about it?'

You are asking me, why am I here at Duhig in spite of this?? Well, the money is good and my colleagues are decent. If I complete another year here, then I can leave for some fancy multinational which will treat me better.

I just hope I can get through the sales conference without too much heartache.

The critical importance of a diverse workplace in creating a profitable, creative work environment has been proven beyond doubt in the past decades. And this brought in a spate of programmes on improving the leadership skills, networking skills and ambition of women. For a long time, all initiatives relating to crafting a diverse workplace focused on the woman. Needless to mention, the mentoring and training of women is indeed a critical component in the D&I mix. But those companies which stopped with only that found themselves back to square one. After much soul-searching, they deciphered that in order to accelerate the extent of change, gender diversity must obtain the same attention as any other business imperative. And that means that men, who form the majority of workers, majority of leaders, majority of decision-makers, must actively engage to drive results.

The true success of diversity initiatives, especially gender diversity, lies in how inclusion gets assimilated into the culture. And like in the case of every cultural approach, unless it gets accepted and internalized by the majority, the plan fails. In most workplaces around the world, men form the majority and it is evident that without the full support of men, D&I plans will not succeed. Most far-sighted organizations have embarked upon the strategy of making men full partners and leaders with skin in the game when it comes to gender diversity and inclusion of women in the workplace. To drive real culture change, the transformation has to begin at the very top and then cascade into every function seamlessly.

Fully engaging male leaders in the D&I effort is shown to make greater progress than when just women speak about including other women. Apart from becoming a robust business focus, a gender diversity plan that is driven and sold internally by men has a much more powerful connect with the organization. Research shows that when men become involved in the D&I council by chairing it or by being recognized as a champion for change, the project is perceived as something important. While the inclusion of women and their move towards an equal representation in leadership calls for greater intentionality on the part of the women, the role played by men cannot be underestimated. When men get involved in creating the cultural shift and accept the several unconscious biases that permeate the workplace, there is a palpable difference. With the presence of male allies, the workplace transforms into one where the majority work fully with the minority to bring about positive change.

THE SUPERWOMAN SYNDROME

Interviewer: Ms Gupta, as the first woman CEO of Goldsmith Consulting, what has been your experience? How does it feel to be a woman leader? Could you share it with our viewers?

Ms Asha Gupta (AG): First of all, let me say that there is no such thing as a woman leader or a male leader. A leader is a leader. A CEO is a CEO. Period.

Interviewer: But then, are there not greater obstacles that are faced by women in the rise to leadership than men?

Ms AG: Compared to men, women are recent entrants into the workplace. For them to figure out the working of corporates, to understand what are the most effective workplace behaviours and also the ability to work well in a team is a competency that has to be learnt. Many women are also first-generation professionals. They don't have role models from whom to imbibe behaviours. But then, impediments are in the way of everyone. There is no leader who has not travelled a journey without hardships.

Interviewer: Let me rephrase this. Are there particular challenges that you faced as a woman leader during your rise to the top spot?

Ms AG: Frankly, when it comes to women in leadership, I think Goldsmith is more evolved than many other corporates. I have spent 30 years here and in this entire time, I have not had to make a case for any kind of special treatment just because I am a woman. For that matter, nobody has to fight for any special privileges. Your manager is fully empowered to help you—man, woman, senior, junior, first-generation, second-generation—with whatever you need to be successful. For a woman, oftentimes it would be enablers such as flexible work timings or work-from-home options. For a man with family responsibilities, it could be a soft-loan or some time off. For a person with disability, it could be a special ramp or a computer equipped to help them function better.

Interviewer: That's very interesting! So, you feel that if the workplace provides whatever support systems are required by the employee, then there are no specific gender-based requirements.

Ms AG: As an organization, Goldsmith is a very fair and a just workplace, where everyone gets great opportunities to make the most of your time. When it comes to women, I guess today, everyone has progressed a lot more. At discerning organizations like Goldsmith—and there are several like that—biases are recognized, stumbling blocks are challenged and it is understood that a woman's career trajectory would be vastly different. In the 30 years that I have been in the workplace, things have changed substantially.

Interviewer: Yes, I agree that the whole perspective towards women leaders has changed hugely over the past 30 years. Ms Gupta, is there anything you wish to share with our readers by way of advice?

Ms AG: Yes, certainly! I find the conversations so different today from when I first entered the workplace. I find women becoming so much more open about their aspirations, their career goals. They are aware that personal choices impact professional decisions and are much more accepting of the changes that personal milestones such as marriage, maternity or motherhood bring. But, I also find many women suffering from the superwoman syndrome. They have a million things to do and don't seem to have time to do those. They are very hard on themselves and are increasingly disappointed if they don't finish all their tasks. They have a high probability of developing mental health issues.

Women in leadership positions are still like the legendary unicorn. They are rare, awe-inspiring and almost mythical. Over the past decades, while the absolute percentages of women in leadership roles have increased, the challenges they face have only compounded. While early generations of women faced patriarchy, today's women leaders face a gamut of problems such as the superwoman syndrome, the imposter syndrome and the manifestation of guilt.

The term 'superwoman syndrome' came into usage after author Marjorie Hansen Shaevitz wrote the eponymous book in 1984. The notion of women suffering from a syndrome such as this was a product of the second wave feminist movement. Many women leaders admit to have gone through this phase before they discovered coping tactics. The archetypal superwoman pushes herself to excel and if she succeeds in one sphere, she is not satisfied until she experiences the same adrenaline rush in another arena. When this becomes a challenge, the woman experiences low self-worth and develops severe stress-related symptoms. Women who suffer from the superwoman syndrome have a feeling of constantly needing to please everyone, are overwhelmed often and experience mood swings, irritability and emotional outbursts.

Senior women leaders advise that in order to quell this syndrome, women professionals must have a planned and realistic approach to achieving their aspirations. Obtaining the support of a network of people or mentors who support and motivate is very important. It is also essential to indulge oneself once in a way and take things lightly. The more evolved woman professional accepts a setback at certain points of time and looks forward to a better tomorrow.

INCLUSION AND THE SALSA CULTURE

I was once part of a virtual focus group run by a leading, well-respected journalist on the benefits of a strong culture. The discussion was specific to the presence of a unifying culture in the context of mergers and acquisitions. One set of participants were of the opinion that a strong homogeneous culture was an inevitable must-have to ensure better productivity, less complex decision-making, increased motivation and higher employee engagement. Another set were of the opinion that it was only in decision-making that a homogeneous culture required to manifest itself, in all other aspects of the organization's systems and processes, diversity of thought and opinion was a greater enabler.

Speaker 1: I believe that homogeneity of culture or the presence of a strong core culture tends to improve the efficiency of an organization. In companies where a strong homogeneous culture is present, there is better delegation, less monitoring, faster coordination, better communication and less influence activities.

Speaker 2: Let us first define culture. As an expert on mergers and acquisitions, I feel that while members of a merged firm might disagree on the best approach to doing things, the extent to which they come together during decision-making defines culture.

Speaker 3: I agree. Having observed many different organizations, I would prefer to define culture as the degree to which members have similar beliefs about the best way of doing things.

Speaker 4: What then is the benefit of experimentation? Is it not crucial for an organization, especially in this world of disruptive innovation to allow experimentation and trying different things? Should not the culture allow diversity of beliefs and thought processes to enable the company to try different routes and also learn about the pay-offs of each set of actions?

Speaker 5: That is where we must get into the discussion of the cost-benefits of a unifying homogeneous culture, versus the lack of it. One of the most intriguing things that I have observed about a strong homogeneous corporate culture is that firms with a strong culture have an easier time arriving at decisions.

Speaker 6: However, a strong homogeneous culture automatically means that all voices will not be heard. That inherently defeats the purpose of D&I focus.

It is said that even organizations that do not consciously cultivate a culture end up having one. Every organization has a culture, even if it is acknowledged or not. The beliefs, value systems, decision-making styles, behaviour during crises, all of these amalgamate to create the culture of the organization. The stand taken by a leader consistently when managing people issues, the language of the workplace, the way rewards and recognition are determined, the 'tribal knowledge' carried by the stories told by employees are the ways culture manifests itself. Today, even the tweets by the CEO are part of organizational culture.

D&I is a value that sits within the cultural manifestation of an organization. How a company reacts to inclusion and diversity is the result of the kind of culture practised. The response of an organization to both internal and external stimuli is defined by the deep-rooted cultural practices, which usually have been set in place either by the founder or by the leadership. An inclusive culture emphasizes the importance of each employee in the workplace. Consistent practice of the freedom to voice opinions, the ability to provide honest feedback and correction, transparency in processes, all tie into the value of inclusion.

However, a common misconception is that the practice of inclusion, where every employee's voice and opinion is equally heard, works at cross-purposes to the creation of a unifying culture. Scholars state that an organization's culture serves two important functions, (a) that of creating a sense of unifying purpose and cohesion among employees and (b) constructing a set of behavioural patterns that enable the organization to face the external macroeconomic environment within which the company exists.

Until the prevalence of the 'D&I' thought, there was a pressure on individuals to blend in with the mainstream culture. The thinking was that the culture was meant to be a 'melting pot' where everyone had to either lose or disguise their identity in order to fully 'fit in'. This can be likened to the 'soup' culture. In this culture, everyone blends in and differences are not really encouraged. However, upon the pervasiveness of inclusion as a philosophy, the 'soup' concept has been replaced by the 'salsa' concept. Here, rather than assimilation, the accent is on integrating into the culture, while still retaining one's identity.

DAY 97/99

THE IMPOSTER SYNDROME

Disciple: Master, I have been noticing that you are more silent than usual. We have not had the benefit of your wise sayings during the past couple of weeks. I also see that you seem very withdrawn. May I ask you why, Oh kind Master? Apologies in advance if I have offended you in any way.

Master: Ananta, why are you and the others so dependent on me? What is it that is so special about my teaching?

Disciple: Master, everything that you have taught us is valuable, precious. All of us here at the retreat have utilized your teachings for betterment of our lives. Is this a rhetorical question, Oh Master?

Master: Not at all, Ananta. Of late, I feel that all that I am doing is just pure chance. This retreat, these inmates, the books that I have authored, I feel all of it is a fluke. I often wonder how I got here.

Did I trick people into believing me? What will happen if they realize that I am actually floundering about without knowing anything?

Disciple: Master, but you are among the greatest instructors that the world has seen! Your wisdom is unparalleled. With your permission, may I say something? Kindly pardon me if you think it is offensive to you.

Master: Go on Ananta. I am ready to listen. After all, I have a lot to learn.

Disciple: Master, you seem to be suffering from a malady called 'the imposter syndrome'. This affects a lot of very accomplished, successful individuals and makes them feel that they are not deserving of their achievements. They develop an irrational fear of being exposed as a 'fraud'. They feel that any recognition they enjoy is just a result of luck and not due to any skills or intelligence that they possess.

Master: Ananta, today, the disciple is veritably the master!

While organizations do a lot to root out the presence of biases, a significant impediment to progress is the 'self-bias' that the individual carries within himself. This is the voice of the inner critic who tells you that you are not good enough and hence it is futile to even try. This is called the imposter syndrome and both men and women suffer from it, though women, as relatively recent entrants into the workplace, go through it a lot more.

The imposter syndrome is defined as a collection of feelings of self-doubt, inadequacy and low self-esteem, which persist in the individual despite glaring evidence to the contrary. Especially in high-pressure, high-performance environments, it is quite common to see very successful people who frequently get paralyzed by this inner sceptic which can prevent them from rising to the fullest of their potential. This inner voice repeats that you are a fraud, your success is a fluke and you will be caught out anytime. Even though the individual does know that the thought is irrational, it does not prevent him/her from being crippled by it.

When an organization is in the journey of creating an open, positive and inclusive work environment, it is important to have spaces and options for people to be vulnerable, authentic and share their feelings. Messages or conditioning received from parents or other significant influences during impressionable years can contribute to the prevalence of this syndrome. Race, gender and religion can also lead to the development of this syndrome, especially when family values or societal expectations are in conflict with the individual's own needs. Often, children who grow up in families that impose unrealistic goals, that are very critical and have a lot of repressed anger also suffer from this syndrome.

The inclusive manager understands the challenge of the imposter syndrome and helps his teammates manage the feeling of anxiety by pointing out that nobody knows all the answers. Encouraging people to be appreciative of others and enabling a process of feedback whereby people remember their worth are great ways to manage this. When the individual gains perspective and realizes that this is an irrational defence mechanism created by the mind, he/she learns to balance periods of being stretched and under stress to occasions of relaxation and self-awareness.

DAY
98/99

ARTIFICIAL INTELLIGENCE AND INCLUSION

[Scene: An AI workathon (a blend of a company retreat and a hackathon) is in progress at a beautiful mountainside resort. Friends and colleagues Raj, Chander and Prabha are busy with their programming while Mona and Jay are standing by chatting. Dua Lipa is belting out new rules from Chander's computer.]

Chander: I only wish Alan Turing were here to see what I am doing!

Raj: Now why are you dragging the Father of Artificial Intelligence into your miserable lines of code?

Chander: No, seriously, this is some deep stuff, man!

Prabha: What have you been smoking, Chander? Stop hallucinating! We are all working on parts of the same code and we will know if it's cool only when we see the result.

Chander (with bluster): Well, when my bot starts telling you that she likes me better than Raj, then you will see....

Mona (walks to the workstation from the window where she was admiring the hillside view): Chand-man, I have a question.

Chander (continuing the swagger): Go on, shoot away. You are talking to the boss of AI. Ask anything, girl!

Mona: You and I know that AI systems are powered by pattern recognition and classification. Right?

Chander: Of course, milady! Even as we speak, my program will be sifting through millions of faces and identifying sentiments.

Mona: Ok. Here's my question. I know that you are biased.

Chander: What? No! I am not biased.

Mona: Ok, so if I arrange for you to go on that long pending date with my pretty friend Lara, will you or will you not?

Chander: Wow! Course, I will. Lara is gooood!

Mona: So, yeah, that shows you are biased towards pretty faces or, clarifying that further, faces that align with your definition of prettiness.

Chander: Come on! That's not a bias, that's preference.

Mona: Po-ta-to, Poh-tah-to.

Chander: Ok, what you got to say?

Mona: Let me continue. I know you are biased. As a result, I feel that your data selection for creating the training set for machine learning will also be biased. I feel that your selection will only reflect these hard-core biases that you carry. Because of this, AI, which is supposed to be free of human prejudices, actually becomes exclusionary itself. So, our ideal of creating an AI-based selection tool that will rank and score people, irrespective of their gender or ethnicity, is itself flawed. For, who does the machine learn from? From you who is biased! Simple. OK, answer this. Why should digital assistants be called Alexa and Siri?? Don't you see a clear bias there??

Chander: Aw, snap!

It would be one of the biggest clichés of this century to say that AI is here to stay. AI and its related technologies are shaping global economy in ways that are profoundly impactful, which we may not even be able to conceive of presently. Every industry, every sector is witness to the influence of AI with the uptake of AI-based solutions on a rapid high. The promise of AI-based technologies is mesmerizing and the resultant benefits appear to lead to unprecedented changes in life, not only in the workplace but much beyond it. The consumer can benefit from wise choices, the shop floor can benefit from efficiencies and the average layman can see positive difference in quality of life.

The flip side to the dawn of AI is rather worrying. The uncertainty of careers, the centring of power in the hands of machines, the forever yawning digital divide and the ambiguous governance models that might emerge are causes of deep concern. Equally burdensome is the idea that technology which until now has been a great leveller could actually become prejudiced under the ambit of AI. This factor has had behavioural professionals pivoting the attention of data scientists in enabling the collection of varied data sets that allow the machine to learn from a wide assortment of cases. Thus, the notion of social inclusion in the age of AI is a complex one, which is rooted in the type of data that is fed to the machine, resulting in the advent of a certain type of machine intelligence.

Conceptualizing inclusion in the context of AI-based decision systems is a difficult task. Very often, decisions made by AI developers are based on a very specific or personal concept of the 'average case' and the 'reasonable accommodation' of a particular sample into the case set. However, this notion could itself be heavily prejudiced and filled with contextual noise. The challenge for AI professionals is to ensure that the same biases

The 99 Day Diversity Challenge

which afflict human decision-making should not creep into machine learning and in a round-robin way, return to deliver a double whammy to the user.

For organizations that either already use AI or are about to integrate AI into their systems and processes, the key question to be answered is how they can build conscious inclusion into the base level programming. When elimination of biases are focused on during the input stage itself for an AI creation, the benefits are not just huge, they are exponential. The result is not just better decisions, but a way of creating a self-perpetuating bias-free society.

THE INCLUSIVE LEARNING ORGANIZATION

DAY 99/99

Krishna and Arjuna were seated in the grand courtyard of the Pandava palace, enjoying a cool drink of fresh Aamras. It was a bright summer morning and a long day stretched ahead of them. As advisor to the King Yudhishtra, Arjuna was pondering over a decision, which he decided to ask Krishna who had ridden over from the riverside village where he lived.

'Krishna, are knowledge and wisdom one and the same?' asked Arjuna.

Krishna looked up from the goblet containing the sweet mango juice and smiled. 'That depends on the context my dear Arjuna. In some aspects, the mere possession of a particular knowledge is itself a sign of wisdom. However, there are also cases where knowledge is just a stepping stone to the larger pursuit of wisdom.'

'In our court, we have so many learned scholars from such different backgrounds. We have truly enshrined the value of inclusion and diversity. Yet, many of the decisions that we take don't seem very wise. What is the reason, Oh Krishna?'

'Arjuna, let me ask you a counter question,' said Krishna, a divine smile playing on his face. 'About 100 yojanas north of this city are a set of 10 villages that do not have a river or lake or any other large water body. They are only dependent on the monsoons for their water supply. However, I find that some villages are prosperous with a flourishing farming community, while a few others do not have anything growing. Why is that?'

'Krishna, I gather you are talking about the villages which practised a regular rainwater harvesting system, while the others did not. The ones that did were not dependent on one source, but ensured that each house and dwelling was able to become self-sufficient,' replied Arjuna, carefully choosing his words.

'Yes, Arjuna, absolutely!' Krishna slapped his thigh in delight at his mentee's intelligence. 'So what did the villages which invested in rainwater harvesting actually achieve?'

'They were able to utilize the source of water equitably across the entire village.'

'Correct, Arjuna! Likewise, it is only when an organization ensures the passage and cultivation of learning all across its entire system that it benefits from the D&I that it has achieved. It is not sufficient that your environment boasts of D&I as a philosophy. It can be translated into action only when the organization becomes a self-sufficient learning enterprise. The next stage to the attainment of a diverse and inclusive workplace is to ensure that it has embedded these values that you speak of, in every part of their structure,' said Krishna and finishing the drink in the goblet in one large swallow, added, 'This Aamras is incredibly sweet!'

'Not as sweet as your advice, Oh Krishna!' said Arjuna happily.

'The learning organization' was first discussed by Peter Senge in his book *The Fifth Discipline*, which defines an organization as a learning-based one when it actively facilitates the learning of its members, thereby transforming itself continuously to remain competitive. The additional focus on becoming an inclusive LO is all the more relevant when one considers the diversity of today's workplace. The inclusive LO not only creates a diversity programme, but also goes the full measure by embedding the culture of inclusion in every aspect of the talent strategy.

In a marketplace that is reflective of the archetypal 'red ocean', the LO that also embodies the philosophy of inclusion builds its learning systems to facilitate different styles of knowledge gathering and absorption. Technology is leveraged not only to enable different styles of learning but also to provide easier access to information. In an LO, employees are constantly encouraged to think differently, and diverse perspectives are routed back into the learning mechanism to be of use to everyone.

In an era that is getting increasingly machine-dependant, it is important for the LO to clearly demarcate where data end and insights begin. Thus, it is important for the LO to conscientiously focus on ploughing back human perceptions and wisdom by building inter-generational KT capabilities. Erasing any unexpected bias that might creep into the learning processes, the LO also understands that the mere procurement of information does not really count as learning. Thus, the LO creates a system whereby people learn to blend their different perspectives to create a robust organization that delivers superior outcomes. It is the goal of an inclusive LO to eventually create an effective culture that transforms with time and allows the collective experience and knowledge of the group to become a vigorous aid to near-flawless decision-making.

The **99 Day Diversity** Challenge

ENDS

EPILOGUE: THE RED CARPET

The chandeliers appeared bigger and brighter to Anga, as she held her mom's hand while walking down the red carpet. It was a beautiful hotel and 10-year-old Anga had never been there before. She looked at the bright red curtains that covered entire walls in the large auditorium and wondered how they would be to touch. They looked like velvet, so they would probably be soft. She wished that her best friend Latha had been here. Latha was so funny. Together they could have stared at the gorgeous outlandish clothes worn by the women that evening and also giggled at the other kids. True, they both got into a lot of trouble with Mrs Jones, their class teacher, on account of the uncontrollable laughter, but it was still worth it. Latha was so much fun and her jokes always had Anga in splits.

Today, she and Sanga were dressed in identical peach-coloured frocks that had specially been made for them by Mumma's favourite dress-maker. It was a special evening, their Dad was receiving a big award and everyone had come to celebrate. Suddenly, Anga was thankful that Latha was not there. It would have been embarrassing to be seen wearing the same dress as Sanga the baby.

Evita thanked the usher who helped her, the girls and Dad get seated in the first row. It was a large crowd, numbering over a thousand. It appeared that every business heavyweight was there. She looked around and smiled at several familiar faces. Mrs Gurnani from a couple of seats away waved to Evita and gestured that she looked beautiful. Robin Caver, the young serial entrepreneur creating waves in AI, was there with his girlfriend, a beautiful young actress. Audrey, the hotshot business journalist, quickly walked across and bent to whisper in Evita's ear that she looked gorgeous. Evita smiled and made a mental note to send some flowers to Abhi, her dressmaker. The embroidered linen boat-necked blouse and floral silk sari in pastel tones were just perfect for the evening.

She had been at this event before with Bharat, a couple of years back. They were just spectators then and she had realized Bharat's disappointment when he came to know that he would not be winning one of those awards. Today, it was his day. Her eyes sought Bharat and she found him standing a little distance away, speaking to some of the organizers. Dapper in a light green *bandhgala* (a high-collar jacket made popular by Indian royalty) and a cream suit, his grey crown did become him, she admitted to herself.

Evita felt a deep sense of peace and happiness. She quickly chanted a prayer as was her habit whenever she felt grateful. After the last visit to Dad's place, she and Bharat had decided to check out the consulting job offer that Evita had received. The interview went exceedingly well and now Evita had begun working for the boutique marketing consultancy. She was involved in a couple of projects in online marketing and digital strategy and found herself enjoying the time that she spent at office with her impossibly young colleagues. She had never had any dearth of spending money, but when her salary got credited into her account, she felt a thrill like none other. She took the kids and Bharat out to breakfast at a fancy new restaurant that served a hundred varieties of canapes and gifted Dad a handy Kindle. The conversations at home had changed, she realized. They laughed more often at the dinner table, both she and Bharat, recounting their respective experiences from work to Anga and Sanga. Bharat's thinking had significantly changed over the past few months since he had begun the 99 Day Diversity Challenge, and Evita thanked Paramita. She looked around to see if Paramita and Shekar had arrived.

Paramita and Shekar were seated a few rows further and were sharing a laugh. Shekar had noticed one of their erstwhile acquaintances at the event and it had brought back some funny memories. Quite a while since she and Shekar had attended one of these dos, she thought to herself. Back at the farm, their days went by watching and delighting in the growth of the newly planted trees and flowering bushes, both at the garden and at the NGO where Paramita worked. At her office, she planted ideas and watched them bloom. She felt grateful that she had taken the decision to present the 99 Day Diversity Challenge to Bharat.

But she also realized that the book was a mere catalyst. It had no meaning unless it was experienced, unless its philosophy was tried and tested in the toughest of laboratories—the workplace. If it had remained just concepts, it would not have brought about the change that Paramita had wanted. Only when a certain degree of personal commitment, passion and involvement were into play, did theory come alive. And it also required a mindset that lent itself to inclusion. Only then does the leader get drawn towards this focus, feels an affinity towards his/her teammates, senses that everyone is living out their own story and does not require judgement, only understanding.

And Bharat had done just that. He had absorbed more than the essence of what the book wanted to convey, even if Paramita had not articulated all of it. The book had become a window through which he had begun to observe his team, his workplace, the policies and programmes that AcceLever ran. She realized that he had been ready for this. 'When the Disciple is ready, the Master appears, goes a proverb, but in my case, when the writer was ready, the reader appeared!' she thought. Bharat was already half-way into the inclusion thought when the book happened. Was it his early-life experiences? Was it the unquestioning acceptance that Evita gave him? Or was it the role modelling of Mr Manush Sr, who lived a life of unselfish giving?

Dad laughed at something that Sanga pointed to him and settled more comfortably in his seat. He was preoccupied with thoughts about his latest baby—an orange rose bush that had suddenly developed mildew. He and Anand had tried some home-made preparations to cure it, but realized that time was running out and he needed to go to the horticultural society and get the medicines. It almost felt like the worry he would experience when Bharat was a little boy and fell sick. Mr Manush thought of the times when his wife would try giving medicines to Bharat, tricking him into thinking that it was grape juice. 'Bitter medicine has to be camouflaged by sweet taste,' he thought to himself and pondered over how much easier it was bringing up children than flowering shrubs. At least the former told you if they were feeling better.

Saahitya and Advaita sat a few rows behind, discussing the forthcoming inclusion day that was being celebrated at AcceLever. Advaita was delighted not only at this invitation to what was clearly an amazing evening but also at the chance to have her HR Director all to herself. She wanted to quickly bounce off a few ideas with her HR Director. Having recently become part of the D&I team of AcceLever, Advaita was working directly with cross-functional leaders to assimilate inclusion into every aspect of the organization. It was the team's responsibility to integrate inclusion within AcceLever's culture—within its beliefs, behaviours and values. It seemed easy enough to articulate, but when you got down to action, you realized how challenging it was and what all it entailed. Advaita was glad that Saahitya and the management team were strongly behind this change. 'Diversity is the art of thinking independently together'—Malcolm Forbes's quote flashed in her mind as Advaita recalled her first meeting several months ago with Bharat and the start of the 99 Day Diversity Challenge. So much had changed since then, she realized.

'Congrats, Saahitya! Heard that you have been inducted into the Board of AcceLever!' said Audrey the journalist from LifeStreet, as she scooted into a vacant seat next to Saahitya. 'Thanks Audrey!' said Saahitya, her voice cautiously cordial. Audrey was a tough one, always looking for headlines.

'I can see that you and Bharat have changed the definition of diversity at AcceLever! Most companies are hiring diversity candidates, but then they get them to adhere to uniform codes of conduct and behaviour and end up killing the diversity for which they were hired in the first place. You guys are incorporating diversity into all aspects of the company. Great!' said Audrey.

'Yes, Audrey, we are trying to ensure that the diverse experiences and perspectives of our employees are included into the way the company does business.'

'I heard that at AcceLever, flexibility is offered more to employees in their mid-40s and mid-50s than the typical millennial, who is usually thought as desirous of work-from-home and telecommuting. Am I right?'

'Yes, you are right, Audrey! Your sources are reliable,' smiled Saahitya while Audrey laughed uproariously at the shrewd comment.

'Why do you offer differential flexibility?' Audrey pursued the question.

'Our demographic research shows that we have a large proportion of employees who in their 40s and 50s are responsible for the welfare and care of their extended families, especially from Tier-II towns, coming from conservative backgrounds. A lot of them were facing burnout since they were managing multiple responsibilities. So, we have devised a way of providing them work from home and other flavours of flexible working, in order to help them integrate work and life better.'

'Oh, great!' said Audrey, her mobile on record mode. 'I am given to understand that your incentive plans are also different for different employees?'

'Yes. We looked at both financial and non-financial rewards at AcceLever. Sometimes, financial rewards are apt only for certain cohorts of employees, while non-financial rewards may be more relevant for certain other groups. Hence, we have tried to change our motivational systems to suit people's individual requirements.'

'I find your job advertisements have also changed significantly. Is it true that even your performance appraisals are customized? I heard that you call it the Apple box Programme? What is this?' Audrey inched closer, her interest evident in her eyes.

'Bharat is an inspiring, far-thinking leader. His ideas have been hugely successful in the marketplace. I am sure his ideas will also be very successful within the company that he leads!' said Saahitya carefully. She decided that she had spoken enough.

'I want a quick couple of sound bytes from Bharat before he gets whisked away backstage. Nice catching up with you, Saahitya!' said Audrey smartly realizing that she would not get any more inputs from Saahitya.

Even as Audrey left to meet Bharat at the front row, a young event management coordinator invited Bharat to get 'wired up'. Audrey clucked her disappointment and got back to her seat at the press enclave.

Bharat had mixed feelings about receiving the Business Leader of the Year award from the prestigious Business-Life media group—one of the world's largest composite media conglomerates whose growth in the recent few years had taken the offline and online media universe by storm. While on the one hand he was thrilled with this acknowledgement from his own peers, he was also anxious that he should communicate everything he wanted to. Bharat's acceptance speech was supposed to be for exactly 3 minutes. Bharat had practised his speech a few times to ensure that he covered all points. He had been asked to make his address 'tweet-friendly' so that the media group could amplify it across all its various formats.

The energy of the evening was palpable. Every single one of India's top business leaders was there. This was the largest event that India Inc saw and it was the Prime Minister of the country who was going to deliver the keynote address.

From his place at the backstage where the assistant was pulling the collar mike in and around his *bandhgala*, Bharat saw his family and his invitees. Evita, the kids, Dad, Paramita and Shekar, Saahitya and Advaita—each of them had a role to play in his journey and he felt grateful that they were here to share his special moment. Were their interactions and discussions with him the cause of his journey from intolerance to diversity and from dogmatism to inclusion?

Soon enough, the Prime Minister's address ended and before he knew it, the anchor announced, 'And please help me welcome to the stage, Bharat Manush, our winner of The Most Successful Business Leader award 2018!' A great applause ensued and Bharat received the award from the hands of the PM who congratulated him with an affectionate pat of the shoulder. A burst of multiple flashlights and the moment was captured for posterity. Bharat could see several members of the audience rise to give him a standing ovation and he felt immensely grateful.

The anchor invited Bharat to the podium and the audience intensified their applause which lasted a full minute. Saying a small prayer, Bharat began his address.

'Good evening, honourable Prime Minister of India, dignitaries on the dais and my dear friends. It is an unforgettable moment as I stand here and I am immensely thankful to the jury and the management of Business-Life for having chosen me for this very significant recognition.

I know this is not part of the protocol and certainly not part of my prepared speech, but with your permission may I call out to the following people to rise so that I might acknowledge their incredible contribution to the journey that has led me here?' Bharat addressed his question to the anchor, who after a second's hesitation, nodded vigorously. She had just noticed the Prime Minister smiling and she took that as an approval.

A sudden hush fell over the audience and people looked around with anticipation.

'For having taught me that wisdom can come from unexpected sources, I thank my young colleague, Advaita!

'For having taught me that the tallest lighthouses cast the longest shadows, I submit my sincere thanks to my mentor Paramita!

'For having always held my hand from the moment I was born till now and for having taught me that there is danger in caring too much, Dad, I humbly bow my head in gratitude!

'For having made me realize that there is an apple box for everyone, I thank you, Saahitya!'

The audience broke into applause as the four stood up to receive Bharat's thanks.

Clearing his throat and fighting emotion, Bharat continued, 'Ladies and gentlemen, I know this might sound very puzzling to you—lighthouses and caring too much and bonsais and apple boxes, but to understand this, I urge you to read the 99 Day Diversity Challenge, written by good friend and industry expert, Paramita Acharya.

'For the past 99 days, I have immersed myself in stories which taught what diversity and inclusion really mean. And guess what I discovered? I realized that D&I is closer to life than to the world of business. It is the stuff that our relationships are made of; it is what creates magic in our worlds.

'And yet, the purpose of the 99 Day Diversity Challenge is not to tell stories. It is to hide that kernel of practical wisdom which will otherwise be dry and unpalatable. When I was a kid, my mom would give me orange- and strawberry-flavoured medicine. The idea is not to taste the fruit, it is to get better by absorbing the medicine hidden within.

'And that is what the 99 Day Diversity Challenge is. It was a challenge for me to devote less than 10 minutes each day to reading one chapter and reflecting on how that aspect of D&I is going to influence my life, not just as a CEO but also as a son, husband, father, leader, colleague and friend. The 99 Day challenge is all about committing to a change, a change so beautiful and so mind-boggling, it leaves you amazed. And when it translates into clear unbiased decisions taken at the workplace, your organization becomes exemplary too.

'At the end of the 99 days, dear friends, I have moved from I to D and D to I—meaning, from intolerance to diversity and from dogmatism to inclusion. I am enjoying diversity. I come alive with inclusion.

'To everyone in this hall, to everyone who is watching this event, to everyone who knows me, I tell you this—diversity is life. Diversity is you and me. Diversity is all the many gorgeous variances that make you "you" and me "me".

'But inclusion! Ah! Inclusion is the essence of life. Inclusion is what binds us together. Inclusion is what makes us realize that actually you are me and I am you. It is what tells us that underneath those layers of identity that define and separate us, we are "one" and the same.

'To that beauty of diversity, let me shout hurray! To that common thread that runs through you and me, let me raise a salute! And to that universal spirit of inclusion which binds us all together, let me bow my head in respect! Thank you, everyone!'

The crowd stood up as one. The applause lasted for a very long time. The 99 Day Diversity Challenge was won.

AFTERWORD

Dear Reader,

Hope you enjoyed the story of how Bharat Manush discovered D&I.

I must also share with you my own story of discovering D&I!

I am an average small-town girl of the 1990s. My school, college and university were all within the same 25 km radius! I landed a great job on MBA campus which took me to a large super-metro. But after 3 very exciting, memorable years, I took the proverbial break, forsaking my career on the altar of marriage and motherhood. A few years later, I got back on a part-time role, teaching management at a college in Chennai.

The years 1996–2000 were deeply significant in my life as they served me well to understand both as a researcher and as a woman what ailed the Indian woman professional—why she was perennially underrepresented in the workplace. Was it the high career expectations caused by her equally high educational attainments, her inability to manage work and home having been raised by a stay-at-home mother (who set impossible standards) or the poor preparedness of the average corporate in dealing with someone caught between conventional societal demands and a complex workplace norm? You might think this has generous shades of the autobiographical, but let me assure you that many hundreds of thousands of Indian women (and I daresay women around the world) grapple with these problems.

It was 2000 when I decided that I just had to do something about this. I turned entrepreneur and AVTAR was born as a recruitment firm that focused on both traditional and non-conventional talent pools. And no prizes for guessing which segment we focused immediately on—women with breaks in their career! This segment fascinated me. Not only was it incredibly close to me, personally, but also it represented a seriously untapped repository of talent that could actually be the most engaged employee cohort ever.

The AVTAR I-WIN network was launched in 2005 as a destination for women with breaks in their career. Within weeks, we had over a 1,000 women registered on the site and we began the arduous task of understanding our audience. We called every single woman who registered on the site. We had a list of profiling questions that were quite different from what a typical interviewer would ask. Our style of profiling too was more like a behavioural consultant's—friendly, interactive and inclusive. Once we had a good set of profiled women candidates whose breaks we clearly understood, we began knocking on company doors. It was a hard sell. We pitched the candidate's talent while trying to downplay her breaks. We were quite successful too. More than 95% of our candidates got shortlisted. We prepped them for the final interview and almost 8 out of every 10 'second-career women'—a term which we actually introduced to Corporate India in 2005—landed a job!

An HR leader whom I met in 2006 (and who I shall not name!) was extremely passionate about the work we did. When I asked why, he delved into detail about how differences—whether on account of ability or gender or work styles or life choices—were key to making the workplace culture a really robust and energetic one. He was particularly thrilled about our work in bringing back returning women into the workplace. He told us that we would soon become an inextricable part of the 'D&I' initiatives of organizations!

That was when I first heard the term 'diversity and inclusion' in the context of an organizational endeavour. It intrigued me. Is it really true that all these differences can actually lead us to become more productive, more efficient and, possibly, happier?

A few years after that, when I received my doctorate in women's workforce participation, it dawned on me that D&I was not just something that organizations needed to 'do'. It is what every individual requires to 'be'. Managing and leveraging differences is the equivalent of a brain gym—it helps your mind work through the truth of multiple truths—the harmony of multiplicity.

Over the past couple of decades, ever since we began working with women to help them build sustainable careers and with organizations to enable them to become positive magnets of talent by employing an inclusive mindset, I have learnt that inclusion is a very personal thing. No 'organization' can become inclusive—only individuals can. It is only when the 'inclusion thought' permeates the organization from top to bottom, across levels, across functions and allows barriers to be broken that diversity gets a chance. And that is why the software of D&I—training programmes, workshops, audits, immersion sessions and dialogues—are so crucial.

Not a day passes without my recalling the almost prophetic words of my friend, the HR leader. Today, AVTAR is the preferred consultant of choice of almost 350 companies, shaping their D&I journey. This book is a collection of real-time experiences that people working with D&I have gone through—the many thoughts, conflicts, questions and even simple doubts that can emerge when you begin questioning stereotypes and long-held beliefs.

In their own way, thousands of individuals have contributed to this book, giving me a ring-side view of deciphering how D&I came to be one of the biggest movements in India! My thanks to each of those unnamed individuals who after every workshop or keynote would walk up to me and tentatively ask their question. It is in trying to answer your queries that I have found answers to mine.

Dr Saundarya Rajesh
(Email: sr@avtarcc.com)

ANSWERS TO CROSSWORDS

SECTION 1 CROSSWORD PUZZLE SOLUTION

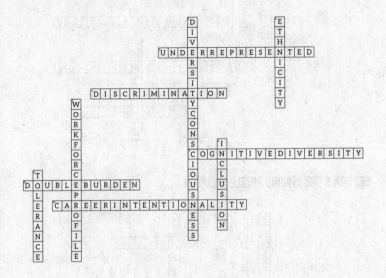

SECTION 3 CROSSWORD PUZZLE SOLUTION

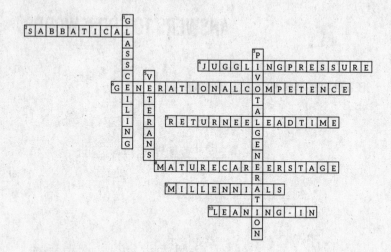

SECTION 5 CROSSWORD PUZZLE SOLUTION

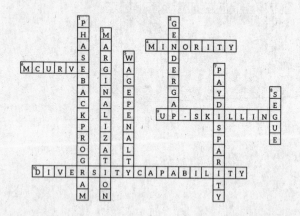

SECTION 7 CROSSWORD PUZZLE SOLUTION

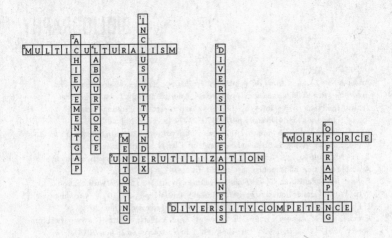

SECTION 9 CROSSWORD PUZZLE SOLUTION

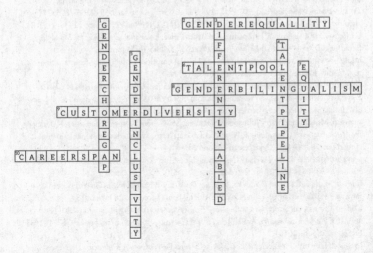

BIBLIOGRAPHY

Anderson, Redia, and Lenora Billings-Harris. *Trailblazers: How Top Business Leaders are Accelerating Results through Inclusion and Diversity*. Available at: https://www.wiley.com /en-us/Trailblazers%3A+How+Top+Business+Leaders+are+Accelerating+Results+ through+Inclusion+and+Diversity-p-9780470593479 (accessed 28 June 2018).

Annis, Barbara, and Keith Merron. 2014. *Gender Intelligence: Breakthrough Strategies for Increasing Diversity and Improving Your Bottom Line*. New York City, NY: HarperBusiness.

Banaji, Mahzarin R., and Anthony G. Greenwald. *Blindspot: Hidden Biases of Good People*. Available at: http://blindspot.fas.harvard.edu/ (accessed 28 June 2018).

Bohnet, Iris. *What Works: Gender Equality by Design*. Available at: https://www.amazon.co.uk/ What-Works-Gender-Equality-Design/dp/0674089030/ref=pd_sim_14_2?_encoding= UTF8&psc=1&refRID=602KAW5X6XEPGGJ48MWE (accessed 28 June 2018).

Cross, Elsie Y. *Managing Diversity—the Courage to Lead*. Available at: https://www.questia.com/ library/3561733/managing-diversity-the-courage-to-lead (accessed 28 June 2018).

Estlund, Cynthia. *Working Together: How Workplace Bonds Strengthen a Diverse Democracy*. Available at: https://www.questia.com/library/102657976/working-together-how-workplace- bonds-strengthen-a (accessed 28 June 2018).

Frost, Stephen. *The Inclusion Imperative: How Real Inclusion Creates Better Business and Builds Better Societies*. Available at: https://www.amazon.co.uk/Inclusion-Imperative- Creates-Business-Societies/dp/0749471298/ref=pd_sim_14_6/258-5717766-7878827?_ encoding=UTF8&psc=1&refRID=5EBGQDSX8QMVQJ1E90KW (accessed 28 June 2018).

Gardenswartz, Lee, Jorge Cherbosque, and Anita Rowe. *Emotional Intelligence for Managing Results in a Diverse World: The Hard Truth about Soft Skills in the Workplace*. Available at: https://www.goodreads.com/book/show/4212910-emotional-intelligence-for-managing- results-in-a-diverse-world (accessed 28 June 2018).

Gregory, Raymond F. *Women and Workplace Discrimination: Overcoming Barriers to Gender Equality*. Available at: https://www.questia.com/library/103160598/women-and-workplace- discrimination-overcoming-barriers (accessed 28 June 2018).

Johnson, Meagan, and Larry Johnson. *Generations, Inc.—From Boomers to Linksters—Managing the Friction between Generations at Work*. Available at: http://www.amacombooks.org/book. cfm?isbn=9780814415733 (accessed 28 June 2018).

Johnson, Michelle T. *The Diversity Code*. Available at: http://www.amacombooks.org/book. cfm?isbn=9780814416327 (accessed 28 June 2018).

Kaplan, Mark, and Mason Donovan. *Inclusion Dividend: Why Investing in Diversity & Inclusion Pays off*. Available at: http://theinclusiondividend.com/ (accessed 28 June 2018).

Kollen, Thomas, ed. *Sexual Orientation and Transgender Issues in Organizations Global Perspectives on LGBT Workforce Diversity*. Available at: https://www.springer.com/in/book/9783319296210 (accessed 28 June 2018).

Liswood, Laura A. *The Loudest Duck: Moving Beyond Diversity while Embracing Differences to Achieve Success at Work*. Available at: https://www.wiley.com/en-us/The+Loudest+Duck% 3A+Moving+Beyond+Diversity+while+Embracing+Differences+to+Achieve+Success+at+ Work+-p-9780470485842 (accessed 28 June 2018).

The 99 Day Diversity Challenge